Praise for *Business the NHL Way*

"By telling insightful stories inspired by the world of hockey, Norm O'Reilly and Rick Burton teach us valuable lessons about achieving successful outcomes in business, leadership, management, and sports. They show us how the NHL has thrived in the face of the health disruptions of the COVID-19 pandemic that threaten business sustainability in every sector. *Business the NHL Way* is essential reading."

Scott Smith, President and Chief Operating Officer, Hockey Canada

"In *Business the NHL Way*, Norm O'Reilly and Rick Burton use hockey as the vehicle to teach us about building successful businesses. The authors take us into rinks, locker rooms, and front offices to illustrate the shared strategy of hockey and business, which is, as the great Wayne Gretzky said, 'always knowing, always skating, to where the puck is going, not to where it has been.'"

Joan Ryan, Author of *Intangibles: Unlocking the Science and Soul of Team Chemistry*

"*Business the NHL Way* is a lively and engrossing romp through hockey history told by a pair of insiders who are not afraid to shake off the gloves. But it's also a sharp-eyed take on a question that bedevils every successful legacy business: How do we adapt and evolve without abandoning our essential character?"

Sam Walker, *Wall Street Journal* Leadership Columnist, and Author of *The Captain Class*

"*Business the NHL Way* is a fascinating read. Hardcore and casual hockey fans and those interested in the business of sport will enjoy the behind-the-curtains insights that Norm O'Reilly and Rick Burton provide. As someone who grew up playing and loving the game of hockey, I never expected I would be able to spend the bulk of my working career engaged in the business of hockey. Readers will learn about the inner workings of the NHL and better understand what drives decision-making at the club and league level. You will be impressed at the data and details provided. I know I was!"

Cyril Leeder, Former CEO, President and Alternate Governor, Ottawa Senators

BUSINESS
THE
NHL WAY

LESSONS FROM THE FASTEST GAME ON ICE

NORM O'REILLY and RICK BURTON

FOREWORD BY
GARY BETTMAN

AFTERWORD BY
HAYLEY WICKENHEISER

ÆVO UTP

Aevo UTP
An imprint of University of Toronto Press
Toronto Buffalo London
utorontopress.com
© University of Toronto Press 2022

Library and Archives Canada Cataloguing in Publication

Title: Business the NHL way : lessons from the fastest game on ice / Norm
   O'Reilly and Rick Burton.
Names: O'Reilly, Norm, 1973– author. | Burton, Rick, author.
Description: Includes index.
Identifiers: Canadiana (print) 20220242526 | Canadiana (ebook) 20220242593 |
   ISBN 9781487508760 (hardcover) | ISBN 9781487538910 (EPUB) |
   ISBN 9781487538903 (PDF)
Subjects: LCSH: Success in business. | LCSH: National Hockey League.
Classification: LCC HF5386.O72 2022 | DDC 650.1 – dc23

ISBN 978-1-4875-0876-0 (cloth)
ISBN 978-1-4875-3891-0 (EPUB)
ISBN 978-1-4875-3890-3 (PDF)

Printed in Canada

We wish to acknowledge the land on which the University of Toronto Press operates. This land is the traditional territory of the Wendat, the Anishnaabeg, the Haudenosaunee, the Métis, and the Mississaugas of the Credit First Nation.

University of Toronto Press acknowledges the financial support of the Government of Canada, the Canada Council for the Arts, and the Ontario Arts Council, an agency of the Government of Ontario, for its publishing activities.

Canada Council
for the Arts

Conseil des Arts
du Canada

ONTARIO ARTS COUNCIL
CONSEIL DES ARTS DE L'ONTARIO
an Ontario government agency
un organisme du gouvernement de l'Ontario

Funded by the
Government
of Canada

Financé par le
gouvernement
du Canada

Canadä

"Great moments are born from great opportunities."

— Herb Brooks

"The day I stop giving is the day I stop receiving. The day I stop learning is the day I stop growing. You miss 100% of the shots you don't take."

— Wayne Gretzky

Contents

CHANGING THE LINES

THIRD PERIOD

Foreword

When Norm and Rick first asked me to write the foreword for a business playbook – one that coined the concept "from the ice to the office" – I had to smile. After all, when this book is published in 2022, I will have been commissioner of the National Hockey League for 30 years and the longest-serving active commissioner of any pro sports league. Having spent nearly three decades in the NHL's offices, I suppose I may be suited to reflect on just how the game has traveled since 1992.

As a college student at Cornell University, I knew hockey was huge. Big Red huge. Cornell's 1970 team, coached by the great Ned Harkness, had gone 29–0–0 en route to winning the National Collegiate Athletic Association (NCAA) championship. No college team has ever run the table like that in Division I hockey. It was Cornell's second national crown in four years (following the Ken Dryden–led championship of 1967).

Harkness was so good he made the jump from college to the Detroit Red Wings. That was a feat no college coach had ever accomplished. What was wilder was knowing his replacement, Dick Bertrand, had not even graduated from Cornell yet.

During my years on that beautiful Ithaca campus in upstate New York, we went to the Frozen Four in 1972 and 1973, missing winning the NCAA championship in 1972 to a great Boston University team. So, it should come as no surprise that hockey was a dominant topic of discussion at Cornell.

Later, following law school at NYU, I would end up beginning my sports career at the National Basketball Association (NBA). But when the opportunity came to make the switch to the NHL, I was ecstatic. Our game, the fastest sport of America's big leagues, features many dynamics that can be smoothly translated into the contemporary workplace.

I know that because I've had the good fortune to watch some of the greatest athletes in any sport ever and to subsequently play a role in preserving legacies built by players like Maurice Richard, Gordie Howe, Bobby Hull, Bobby Orr, Mario Lemieux, Brendan Shanahan, Grant Fuhr, Martin Brodeur, Patrick Roy, Wayne Gretzky, Manon Rhéaume, and Dominik Hašek to name but a few. These legends all featured resilience, elite performance, the ability to crash glass ceilings, commitment, and a rare team-centric focus in times of increasing individualism.

As many NHL fans will tell anyone who will listen, the game is much more than an entertainment option. It is difference-maker. It informs opinions, strategies, decisions, even in some cases marriages.

Hockey and business are a marriage and I believe the exemplary traits our players, coaches, officials, owners, and administrators bring to their work reflect systems and strategies that can be translated into business success.

If you are reading this foreword, I imagine you are thinking about thumbing through the book, stopping at the table of contents to see if the topics can help you solve a problem at your organization. Perhaps it can. This book is written by two authors and friends who love the game and believe the best of the NHL and ice hockey can inform your non-hockey challenges.

On numerous occasions I have welcomed Norm, Rick, and their students to our headquarters (or have met with them via Zoom). Their approach to teaching has always seemed so inclusive. Norm and Rick write fully of inclusion and diversity, of overcoming obstacles like COVID-19 (when the NHL needed to play in a "bubble"). And from challenges that required courage, commitment, and love.

I hope you'll like this book. I certainly did and appreciated the personal way in which two long-time observers of our game have made their work so approachable.

Enjoy.

Gary Bettman
Commissioner, National Hockey League
Hockey Hall of Fame 2018

Preface: A Word from the Authors

As the COVID-19 pandemic lurched into existence in late 2019, and then raced around the globe during the 2020–1 and 2021–2 National Hockey League (NHL) seasons, coupled with the 2020 Black Lives Matter movement, many businesses and traditional activities were completely disrupted. Loved ones died. Family providers lost jobs. Live events stopped. Inflation skyrocketed. Schools were closed, with classes postponed or offered online. Industries went digital. Supply chains stalled. Restaurants shut down, air travel ground virtually to a halt, and regional economies flattened.

Around us, professional sports leagues delayed the end of seasons, canceled games, and postponed opening days. More than one league was forced to play in a sterile bubble. Suddenly, saving lives was far more important than staging games and sincere condolences were of far greater significance than goals scored or wins.

Somehow, though, the NHL persevered and, given our respective corporate experiences and love of the League, we tracked the NHL's crisis management of 2020 and found ourselves truly impressed with the NHL's efforts in concluding the 2019–20 season.

Our admiration only increased when the League started the 2021 season that January with an innovative geography-based, 56-game format. And while it was warm outside, the Cup was once again held aloft in July by Tampa Bay for the second year in a row. It was impressive. To boot, the 2021–2 season started as scheduled in October 2021.

In closely following the NHL's crisis management and successful awarding of two Stanley Cups in distinctly unconventional formats (while the rest of the ice hockey world and many live events slowed or stopped), the NHL created an overwhelming impetus to examine how sport can benefit any kind of business.

Indeed, with the sole exception of Hockey Canada hosting the World Men's Junior Championships in a fan-less bubble in Edmonton in December 2020/January 2021, almost every major hockey competition (e.g., Kontinental Hockey League [KHL], Canadian Hockey League [CHL], American Hockey League [AHL], Swedish Hockey League (SHL), Senior Men's World Championships, Senior Women's World Championships) was canceled from 2020 up to the last-minute postponement of the 2022 World Men's Junior Championships in Alberta on December 29, 2021.

Yet, here was the NHL, getting it done. It made us ask what someone could learn from these achievements and whether the League, in dealing with an ongoing crisis, could be dissected so others benefitted.

Could we reveal the business principles of a great League in an easy-to-enjoy fashion? Could the joy of playing in or watching the NHL be translated into a book? Could the NHL's responses to the pandemic from 2020 to 2022 facilitate holistic learning for organizations of all sizes and time-starved professionals?

The answer to each question was a resounding YES! The NHL is a meaningful business and studying it could deliver benefits to employees and business operators everywhere.

CEOs, managers, professionals, and hourly workers alike could take something from NHL stories and use them locally to leverage the learning toward getting promoted, advancing a career, or staying employed.

That premise was intriguing. Business the NHL Way. We could provide stories from the fastest game on ice. From men and women at the top of their trade. Best of all, this was our arena or backyard rink. In-game, this was our power play.

Our confidence came from knowing we are globally experienced business professionals who have been validated as experts in the business of sport. We consult, teach, write, analyze, research, sit on boards, manage projects, and frequently influence corporate decisions.

From a credential standpoint, Rick previously served as the commissioner of the National Basketball League in Australia and as chief marketing officer of the United States Olympic Committee. Norm worked significantly with the Canadian Olympic and Paralympic Committees and is a long-time partner with one of Canada's leading sports marketing agencies. Both of us have testified in major legal cases, including one involving the US Government and another with the Government of Canada.

Combined, we have worked or consulted for brands like the Canadian Hockey League (CHL), Canadian Tire, Exxon, Federal Express, Gatorade, Hockey Canada, Miller Brewing, the National Football League (NFL), Nike, PepsiCo, Scotiabank, Ultimate Fighting Championship (UFC), Visa, and many more. It has allowed us to frequently use our knowledge in publishing research and in teaching award-winning sport management classes at great universities in two hockey-loving countries. We've also co-authored a dozen books as well as regular sport industry journalism pieces. What it should suggest is a capacity to make this material fun and easy to read, informative, and best of all, grounded in hockey.

We want readers to understand the lessons hockey teaches. Former NHL stars Eric Lindros and Gordie Howe famously, and respectively, spoke of the importance of work ethic: "It's not necessarily the amount of time you spend at practice that counts; it's what you put into the practice" and "You find that you have peace of mind and can enjoy yourself, get more sleep, and rest when you know that it was a one hundred percent effort that you gave – win or lose."

Legendary NHL goalie Jacques Plante discussed the pressures of playing in the NHL by asking, "How would you like a job where, every time you make a mistake, a big red light goes on and 18,000 people boo?" That quote alone reveals some of the unique context we want to cover.

For starters, we needed an inspirational quote to post in the locker room. What we picked was something that currently hangs on a lot of bedroom walls. It comes from Pittsburgh Penguins great Sidney Crosby who offered: "Dreams are so important. You need to have big goals and expect a lot of yourself, but you have to enjoy the ride too."

For fans of the NHL, the League's players are a source of admiration for their work ethic and for having achieved their dreams in such a fast-paced, aggressive game. Not all of us are cut out to become elite athletes. But all of us want to make the most of our lives. Each of us knows winning tastes better than losing. That underestimating anyone is to risk defeat. That desiring to win should make us want to "get better."

But we need to savor the journey as well. We know firsthand (and firmly believe) hard work, pressure, and aggressive game strategies build winners. The structure of the book has been written in four parts that provide consistent actionable "lessons," as follows:

- **Dropping the Puck** sets the context for how learning about the business of hockey can yield important leadership lessons and other lessons for business.
- **Winning the Draw** focuses on specific business subjects, such as innovation.
- **Changing Lines** focuses on diversity and inclusion issues and efforts in the NHL and other game-changing initiatives and developments.
- **Third Period** offers concluding chapters widening out from the hockey lens.

That's the goal for our book. To make it fun, quick, and easy. To give you big-picture stories quickly with first-hand evidence (Winning the Draw) but also to provide case studies (Changing the Lines) topped off with a summary (Third Period).

As two guys still wanting to lace 'em up and hold onto beer league glory days, we'd suggest hockey only matters to us when the NHL is in season, or when the Olympic Women's Ice Hockey Tournament (won in February 2022 by Canada over the US in a close game, 3–2), World Juniors, Frozen Fours, or Memorial Cups are underway. When the Olympics or Paralympics (sledge hockey) are on. When we're thinking about the NHL draft or great Stanley Cup finals. Or NHL expansion (yes, for the record, we believe in Quebec City!).

In other words, we think about hockey all the time. Along the way, this singular game shaped us and the life choices we've made. Somewhere in our past, hockey made life clearer. Drilled into us the value of a passing to your teammates versus trying to deke the other team alone. Taught us you can balance integrity and class with aggressive competition. Explained that comments like "keeping your head up," "playing your position," "digging in the corner," and "skating it off" were life lessons.

That a hard-working, competitive, team-first approach means hockey is much more than a game to us. Just as the NHL is so much more than a league.

We believe a book about the NHL and its wide-ranging business initiatives can help anyone learn how to build their business acumen and professionalism.

Let's see if we can help you build your career or company using a hockey-centric lens with dozens of hockey-related stories to assist your personal goals.

So, let's forecheck, backcheck, and block that screened slap shot from the point, because unconsciously we know where the puck will suddenly appear. Maybe that analogy, a line borrowed from the Great One, Wayne Gretzky, is always knowing, always skating, to where the puck is going, not to where it is. That sentiment is key.

Gretzky's approach made him the greatest scorer in NHL history. A mere 2,857 total points (nearly 1,000 ahead of the second best), including 894 goals. If readers (that's you) start thinking about what will happen next, if you project how to solve a problem before the issue arrives, if you make the right decisions at the right time, then this concept will have worked. You will have influenced your own personal success.

We'll build chapters and stories around a simple 165-gram piece of rounded vulcanized rubber with an intention to help readers emerge from the financial disruption of the COVID-19 pandemic by putting you in a better position to build business sustainability. To counterattack, manage risk, and prevent losses.

We'll take you with us as we come around our own net, grab the puck, and rush up ice, stickhandling our way through the distractions. We'll take you from the ice to the office in an age where a lot of fast-skating defenders want to knock you, your department, or your business flying. Things like virus-related distractions or racial and discriminatory aftershocks. Tough topics like systemic racism, bias, and sexism that still appear every game, every shift.

Our "cases" will reveal how brands, institutions, associations, teams, and individuals associated with the NHL have consistently survived a variety of challenges. We'll analyze the NHL and, acknowledging its 105-year history, show how it has weathered a Great Depression, wars, lockouts, the retirement of star players, social movements, re-located franchises, two major pandemics, and even dealt with corruption.

We'll also use the NHL to explore specific business-related scenarios and link each lesson back to strategic leadership outcomes. To inform business leaders on best-practice ways to achieve strategic outcomes and perhaps a few personal ones.

We also want to share some of our own experiences and open up about our journeys within sport, hockey, and the NHL. We'll do this by sprinkling in a set of *Norm's Nostalgia* and *Rick's Recall* stories providing first-hand experiences that illustrate big concepts. We're hoping that by sharing these life experiences, readers take even more away from this hockey journey.

Selfishly, we hope readers will take value from the purposeful marriage (as Commissioner Bettman mentioned in his foreword) of hockey and business. We also encourage learning how to translate hockey skills into professional achievements, as highlighted in Hayley Wickenheiser's afterword.

So, enough chatter. Let's go to work. Everybody lace 'em up tight and hit the ice. Game on!

DROPPING THE PUCK

1

It Starts at the Top

As we started writing this book, we recalled a time in late 2019 when we were crafting one of our monthly columns for *Street and Smith's Sport Business Journal* (SBJ), a prominent US sports business magazine. We thought hard about the NHL's business savvy and the crazed notion the NHL was capable of surpassing Major League Baseball (MLB), a league as American as Chevrolets and apple pie in market share, visibility, and popular prominence.

It was a bold prediction, but in compiling what it would take for the NHL to emerge as North America's number three sports league, we liked our supporting evidence. Suddenly, the NHL accolades we were flinging around seemed formidable. Our analysis started here:

- The season-long lockout in 2004–5 (that deeply bothered fans) ultimately gave the NHL cost containment, fiscal security, and a cost-efficient, sustainable business model. While the lockout was horrific to fans (and the media enjoyed a field day bashing the League), the resulting agreements between the NHL and its players emerged as a brilliant piece of counter-intuitive planning. It was a strategic pivot most sports leagues would never make, and one that has led to unprecedented League revenues and players' salaries ever since.

- In 2016, the NHL boldly placed an expansion team in Las Vegas when the giants of sport (the NFL and NBA) refused to go there. With good fortune smiling, in their inaugural season of 2017–18, the Golden Knights took a rag-tag team of castoffs (players essentially selected from the second line of their previous teams) and beat all the odds by reaching the Stanley Cup finals in their first year, with every home game sold out and merchandise flying off the shelves. Suddenly, Las Vegas was an NHL town.

- In 2021, the Seattle Kraken became the 32nd franchise.

- Willingly sending NHL players to the Olympics in 1998, 2002, 2006, 2010 and 2014 Games (held in hockey-friendly markets like Salt Lake City, Vancouver, and Sochi, Russia) but issuing a fat "no-go' for the less appealing 2018 PyeongChang Games in South Korea. That seemed bold. But then, after missing out on 2018's Olympic coverage, the NHL and its players reversed direction and announced they would participate in the 2022 (Beijing) and 2026 (Milan-Cortina) Games. Unfortunately, due to the ongoing health and safety concerns of COVID-19, the NHL pulled out of the Beijing Games just weeks before their opening.

- Coming out of the lost 2004–5 season, the NHL made sweeping rule changes to ensure a faster game with more scoring. Those adjustments might not have been transformational, but they certainly contributed to the NHL's growth. Additionally, changes to the revenue structure of the League (i.e., salary caps, revenue sharing) coming out of the 2004–5 lockout, drove the League's impressive revenue growth from 2006–19, with a decline reported in 2019–20 largely due to COVID-19.

FIGURE 1.1 *NHL: Total Annual League Revenues, 1994–5 to 2025–6*

Data source: Forbes Business of Hockey Lists (https://www.forbes.com/nhl-valuations /list/)
* League sources indicate the NHL achieved record revenues of at least $5.2 billion in 2021–22, an all-time record (https://www.sportsbusinessjournal.com/Daily/Morning -Buzz/2022/06/16/Bettman-revenue.aspx)

Figure 1.1, compiled by the authors based on reports by *Forbes* magazine's annual valuations of NHL clubs, outlines the growth and projected future growth in League revenues since the 1994–5 lockout to the 2025–6 season.

- Aggressively promoting young players ready to join the Crosbys and Ovechkins. New stars become newly minted celebrities in local markets, growing the game's appeal – names like Leon Draisaitl (Edmonton), Miro Heiskanen (Dallas), Jonathan Huberdeau (Florida), Nathan MacKinnon (Colorado), Cale Makar (Colorado), Auston Matthews (Toronto), Connor McDavid (Edmonton), Elias Pettersson (Vancouver), David Pastrnak (Boston), and Brayden Point (Tampa Bay), and who were all their 20s and captivating fans globally. In turn, these celebrities would drive ratings, sponsor support, attendance, merchandise, and social media.

- Attempting to "conquer" Europe faster than the NBA or NFL because the hockey footholds in Sweden, Norway, Slovakia, Czech Republic, Russia, Ukraine, Switzerland, Germany, and Finland already deliver standout players to the NHL. The marketing and revenue potential for the NHL is endless if fan engagement, merchandising, and sponsorship can penetrate these markets, with the dream of an NHL Euro-Asia division (or two) not as far off as some might think.

Of course, that story featured only enough content for the aforementioned trade journal. Now we knew there was a bigger story about lessons for business from hockey. But where to start? That's when we pulled out an old quote from Commissioner Bettman that had been simmering on our back burner for more than 15 years. It went like this:

> Our economics are not baseball's economics. Our game is not baseball's game. Our owners are not baseball's owners, with one or two exceptions. Our union is not baseball's union. What we do has to be crafted and suited to address hockey, to address the NHL, to address our 30 teams and our 700-plus players.
>
> Gary Bettman, NHL Commissioner, February 15, 2004[1]

That was it. The NHL was different. Sure, it is headquartered in New York City (since 1989), just like MLB, the NFL, NBA, and Major League Soccer (MLS), but only because the traditional broadcast networks and national ad agencies are all based there. To stand as a big-time sport business, you must be there. But the NHL has something else going for it.

It is the world's premier ice hockey competition and one of the 10 highest revenue-generating professional leagues in the world. In fact, as shown in figure 1.1, *Forbes* reports that the League hit the US$5 billion revenue mark for the 2018–19 season, staying at that level (US$4.9 billion) for 2019–20. That was more than a billion dollars higher than the $3.98 billion the League generated in 2014–15 just a few years earlier. Revenues dipped, according to *Forbes* (see figure 1.1) to US$2.9 billion in 2020–1 in the COVID bubble season, then bounced back to US$4.8 billion for the 2021–2 season, and were forecasted to hit US$5 billion again in 2022–3 and US$6 billion by 2025–6.

Additionally, Commissioner Bettman has directed the League since 1993. He is currently the longest-serving active league CEO in the world and has served as the top decision maker at the NHL for three decades. That tenure has included more than a quarter century of Stanley Cup finals, six new expansion teams, six Winter Olympics (dominated by NHL players), four team relocations, three work stoppages, two divisional re-alignments, and the brief League ownership/sale of one team (the Phoenix Coyotes). As any smart business professional knows, stability in leadership is a key success factor for many organizations.

For this reason, we started at the very top. We knew intuitively if readers were hockey fans, then they already understood the commissioner was frequently blamed for a range of unpopular decisions. Teams placed in the American South instead of the Canadian North. Divisional rivalries played in distinctly different time zones. Three player lockouts that shortened two seasons and completely canceled a third. In other words, Saturday rain, sunshine on Mondays.

We knew no injustice (as determined by the NHL's fans) was too small. Despite those "incidents," we felt Commissioner Bettman is

misunderstood, just as many business CEOs and company founders are vilified.

Fans in many places, on both sides of the border, routinely boo
the commissioner. But many of those "fans" fail to fully grasp difficult concepts such as finance, national and international economics, revenue sustainability, investment strategies, legal liabilities,
franchise governance, and health risks. We accept that diehards,
even with extensive business skills, often don't care about "facts."
Their loyalty comes first. Balance sheets are for day jobs.

In our curiosity, we asked what if we could figuratively lift the
lid off the commissioner's head and peer inside. Could we use
his success and strategic acumen to help businesses all over the
world? Could we illustrate that big decisions made in the League
offices can be replicated in a small tool-and-die shop in Manitoba?
Speaking of Manitoba, the Winnipeg Jets, who returned to the
League in 2011 after the previous version left town in 1996, are a
great case study of business success (in a very small market) that is
discussed in chapter 12.

First, though, we needed to frame certain historic realities.
Running a sports league is a highly visible, highly volatile undertaking that regularly generates strong emotions. Those challenges
don't exist for a small-town plumber or electrician simply trying
to stay in business. And, on that note, what are the challenges for
a Winnipeg club trying to compete on the same level as one based
in New York, Toronto, Chicago, or Montreal?

Admittedly, pleasing fans, spectators, and the daily media is not
Commissioner Bettman's primary job. Yes, he is the chief steward
of the game. But including Seattle, the NHL's newest club, the
commissioner has 32 masters to serve. The NHL's owners. In that
very practical sense, he has 32 very demanding bosses.

This is not unlike a corporate CEO having to satisfy a board of
directors or the founder of a start-up having to deliver acceptable

results to multiple investors. For a small business operator, it may be akin to keeping a bookkeeper (often a spouse at home), a bank, and suppliers or vendors satisfied. In other words, as the musician Bob Dylan once sang, "You're gonna have to serve somebody."

The NHL's 32 owners (which make up the board of governors) employ Bettman, evaluate him, tie their considerable financial fortunes to the decisions he makes, and then ask him to make their official positions, some quite unpopular, known. In other words, the "bosses" want Commissioner Bettman to provide counsel and a strategic plan but then stand in front of the media and throngs of avid fans and take the heat for their frustrations.

In February 1993, when he took the reins, the NHL, just four years into its move to New York, featured 24 teams and was in the process of going to 26 for the 1993–4 season. The League added another team in each of 1997–8, 1998–9, and 1999–2000, and two more in 2000–1 to move to 30 clubs, a number it stayed at until 2017 when it added its 31st. Seattle, in 2021–2, brought the League to an even 32. Hopes for a 33rd franchise have been expressed from numerous cities, including Quebec City, Houston, Hartford, Hamilton, and Kansas City.

In the end, whether Commissioner Bettman served 24, 29, or 32 bosses, we would argue these owners have consistently endorsed his performance for 30 years. Figure 1.1 depicts the upward trend (what some business executives would call a "hockey stick" of performance) in total League revenues from 1994–5 to 2021–2, with continued increases forecasted to 2025–6. It shows a 32-year window of data when League revenues have gone from approximately US$500 million to more an expected US$6 billion.

If we dig deeper into figure 1.1, NHL revenues increased more than eight-fold in just under three decades (from US$570 million in 1994–5, just after Bettman started, to 2018–19), to top US$5 billion. Revenues dropped slightly for 2019–20 with a shortened season and bubble playoffs but then dropped drastically for 2020–1 to US$2.9 billion with the shortened season and few fans in venue. The pre-COVID 800 percent increase is an impressive number when compared to an approximate increase in inflation over that same period in North America of about 60 percent. At the franchise level, in 2021, *Forbes'* analysis suggested the New York Rangers were the first US$2 billion NHL club.

Notwithstanding the impacts of COVID, the NHL has created strong business-sector success. League revenues are growing, the League's size has grown, franchises are appreciating in value, more clubs are reportedly profitable than not, and media deals (traditional and streaming) continue to increase in value, all while the game expands globally. Although COVID hit League revenues hard in 2020–1, franchise values were only modestly impacted, with the large market clubs holding or increasing based on future values.[2] The commissioner, as the League CEO, sits at the heart of each of those achievements. The revenue results and projections for 2021–2 and beyond predict strong future financial success.

Additionally, per the collective bargaining agreement between the League and the players' association, revenue sharing is now quite substantial. Although specifics around the details of the revenue sharing are not public, trusted sources and industry reports suggest the top 10 highest-earning clubs share revenue with, as stated on the NHL's website, the clubs "ranked in the bottom half (bottom 15) in League revenues, and that operate in markets with a Demographic Market Area of 2.5 million or fewer TV households." In so doing, the big market clubs pitch in to help small market teams.

Before COVID-19 (i.e., before March 2020), the NHL was enjoying a tremendous 2019–20 season with attendance averaging more than 17,000 per game across the League. *Team Marketing*

Report reported the NHL's average ticket price was US$76 per seat, suggesting each home team was generating on average approximately US$1.3 million per game in ticket sales.

And, while the NHL has established strong roots in the southern United States (Dallas, Tampa Bay, Miami, San Jose), the League continued to dominate as the number one sport entertainment offering in Canada and held high popularity in long-standing northern US markets (Boston, Chicago, Detroit, Minneapolis, New York, Philadelphia, Pittsburgh, and St. Louis).

The League's games were also closely followed internationally in countries such as the Czech Republic, Finland, Germany, Iceland, Norway, Slovakia, Sweden, and Russia.

A Century of Business Decisions

The NHL's rise to its apex is a story revealed through an assembly of decisions, many of which were taken long before Bettman was appointed commissioner in February 1993. In fact, a detailed history beyond the scope of this book outlines the business expansion of the League before 1945.[3] A quick review shows there have been numerous historical drivers. What is important for any leader (in any business) is knowing where the business has come from:

1 **1893**: The Stanley Cup is awarded for the first time to Canada's top amateur hockey club in a challenge format. The trophy is donated by Lord Stanley, then governor general of Canada.
2 **1917**: At a meeting of future club owners in Montreal, the NHL is formed with four Canadian franchises: Ottawa, Toronto, and two in Montreal.

3 **1924**: The first US-based franchise, the Boston Bruins, joins the League. In 1925, clubs in New York and Pittsburgh are added.

4 **1942**: After many franchise changes in the preceding years, the League and its "Original Six" franchises (Boston, Chicago, Detroit, Montreal, New York, and Toronto) solidifies and remains unchanged for 25 years.

5 **1967**: The NHL's first and most extensive modern expansion takes place as six new clubs are added, all based in the United States. This growth doubles the League to 12 clubs by adding teams in Los Angeles, Minneapolis, Oakland/San Francisco, Philadelphia, Pittsburgh, and St. Louis.

6 **1979**: After competing head-to-head for much of the 1970s, the NHL merges with the upstart (but struggling) World Hockey Association (WHA) that had been a strong competitor for much of the decade. The WHA had attracted star players, built a fan base, and challenged the NHL at every turn. The merger includes four clubs joining the NHL: Edmonton, Hartford, Quebec City, and Winnipeg. Although three of the franchises have since relocated, all remain in the League today, in Carolina (Raleigh), Colorado (Denver), Edmonton, and Phoenix. The one franchise that didn't move, the Edmonton Oilers, has won six Stanley Cups since the merger. Note that, while Winnipeg lost its franchise in 1996 to Phoenix, the city regained a franchise in 2011 when the Atlanta Thrashers relocated to the Manitoba capital.

7 **1987**: The NHL replaces its annual All-Star game this year with Rendez-vous '87, held in Quebec City, which sees the NHL All-Stars play the national team of the Soviet Union. An incredible three-game series is played, emphasizing the global nature of the League. Many credit these games, in

part, for opening the door to players from around the world, and particularly Russia, to joining the NHL.

8 **1989**: The NHL head office is relocated from Montreal to New York by the then commissioner of the League, John Ziegler Jr. This move, largely ignored by fans, is symbolic of the growing strategy to drive growth of the League, its clubs, and the game of the hockey in the larger (by population) and more lucrative US market.

9 **1998**: First Olympic appearance by NHL players. In 1986, the International Olympic Committee (IOC) altered its regulations on the professional and amateur status of athletes participating in the Games, thereby opening the door to professional athletes competing in the Olympics. The NBA was the first with the Dream Team in 1992, which attracted worldwide attention for the sport and its athletes to huge success. Notably, Gary Bettman was an NBA executive at the time of the Dream Team. Following decisions to not participate in the 1988, 1992, and 1994 Winter Games, the NHL finally debuts in 1998.

10 **1998**: The NHL signs its first major US national broadcasting contract with ESPN-ABC – a five-year, US$600 million deal.

11 **2003**: The NHL holds the first (of many) outdoor games, which will be heralded by the media as strokes of marketing genius. Dubbed the "Heritage Classic," the first spectacle is held in Edmonton, Alberta, between the Montreal Canadiens and Edmonton Oilers with Les Habs defeating the Oilers, 4–3, in front of more than 57,000 fans. Eleven years later, in 2014, 105,491 fans watch the Toronto Maple Leafs defeat the Detroit Red Wings 3–2 in a shootout at the University of Michigan's football stadium, the most watched hockey game in history. Over the years, more than 30 outdoor games, including the sunshine-delayed Lake Tahoe game, are branded

as the Winter Classic, Stadium Series, and the NHL 100 Classic.

12 **2004–5**: The NHL and its players association endure a divisive player lockout that leads to a canceled season and a gap year for the Stanley Cup (North America's oldest trophy). Off the ice, numerous changes are made that pave the way for future business success, including revenue sharing, a salary cap, and rule changes making the game faster, more fan friendly, and safer for the players. These improvements create a common theme throughout this book.

13 **2010:** Team Canada, behind a magical goal by NHL superstar Sidney Crosby, defeats Team USA 3–2 in overtime to take the 2010 Winter Olympics gold medal in Vancouver, British Columbia.

14 **2011**: NBC (and NBC SportsNet) sign a 10-year deal with the NHL for national broadcast rights in the USA for a reported US$2 billion.[4]

15 **2013**: Rogers Sportsnet signs a record 12-year, CDN$5.3 billion contract with the NHL for broadcast rights in Canada, starting in 2014–15 and lasting through the 2025–6 season.[5] This contract represents a new era of media dollars for the NHL and a market value recognition of its importance in Canada.

16 **2017–22**: With expansion into Las Vegas and Seattle, the NHL reaches 32 teams spread over two countries and joins only the NFL with two conferences of 16 teams each. The creation of the Vegas Golden Knights is hailed by many in the media as an historic embracement of America's gambling capital. The NHL is duly rewarded when the Golden Knights reach the 2018 Stanley Cup finals in their first season (losing to the Washington Capitals and the legendary goal-scorer Alex Ovechkin in five games).

17 **2021**: With the start of the shortened 2021 NHL season, the
League creates sponsorship opportunities for teams and itself
by allowing advertising on player helmets and by attaching
corporate sponsors to the NHL's four divisions. As games
begin that January, big brands such as Scotia, Honda, Discover, and MassMutual become the respective sponsors of the
North, West, Central, and East divisions.

18 **2021**: A blockbuster deal is engineered during a late night
visit by Bettman with ESPN chair Jimmy Pitaro to the tune of
a reported $400 million annually over seven years, along with
$225 million yearly from Turner Sports over the same time
frame. This total of more than $4 billion more than doubles
the League's previous deal with NBC Sports.

19 **2022**: The NHL, due to health and safety concerns, opts out
of the 2022 Beijing Winter Olympics. Arizona Coyotes move
from Glendale to Arizona State University in Phoenix. The
Colorado Avalanche win the Stanley Cup for the third time.

The Commissioner's Role

The commissioner of a professional sport league is a somewhat
unique leadership position. Like a CEO, commissioners have the capacity and obligation to establish strategies and tactics that achieve
competitive values capable of driving league success while advancing goals and objectives. Commissioners are also traditionally responsible for maintaining a league's reputation and not allowing
any activity to bring "the game" (the business) into disrepute.

However, unlike many CEOs, they do not run (nor are they
responsible for) the entirety of the business because of the
league-franchise model. Commissioners set the standard and provide the direction, but each franchise (or club) is its own unique

organization with its own structure, staff, and goals. Further com-plicating matters, each club's owner is also one of the commission-ers' bosses.

Thus, a successful commissioner must build a cultural mindset across the league and ensure owner consensus related to concepts such as rules, rules enforcement, parity, collective bargaining, marketing, revenue sharing, and media management. These must work collectively to benefit each member locally but also centrally (i.e., for the good of the whole).

Concepts that favor one team, region, or, in the NHL's case, one country cannot be allowed. Every effort must be designed to balance the concept of collective growth. For many, this all-for-one socialism makes the capitalistic nature of sport extremely cu-rious. Sport finance professors call this "competitive balance."

Teams that consistently lose are not allowed to go out of busi-ness. There is no relegation (in which a club that performs poorly is demoted to a lower-level league for the following season) like that found in England's Premier League or Germany's Bunde-sliga. In fact, weak North American professional clubs are often rewarded with benefits such as top draft picks or, in some older cases, easier playing schedules.

At the other end of the spectrum, wealthy owners wanting to win championships are able to "break the bank" by paying extravagant player salaries but often find their team forced to play within fixed salary caps or pay "luxury taxes" for exceeding the cap. Constraints such as caps or taxes traditionally infuriate larger-market (usually wealthier) owners who feel capitalism means that small-market op-erators or penny pinchers should not be protected.

In one decision specific to the NHL, Commissioner Bettman included measures intended to manage currency inequities be-tween the US and Canada, particularly when the Canadian cur-rency was historically low. This action created the ability for clubs to lock in exchange rates because the League decided to conduct its business in USD.[6]

The business outcomes of this decision for a small-market Canadian club are considerable. Imagine the impact of the Canadian dollar shifting from nearly 60 cents US in 2002 to parity ($1 US) in 2007 for a club that collects many of its revenues (e.g., tickets, local media rights, local sponsorship, parking, concessions, etc.) in Canadian dollars and pays its main expense (i.e., player salaries) in US dollars.

Ultimately, the NHL commissioner must implement strategies that cover every aspect of the game. Governance, pricing, labor peace, legal liability, communications, supply chain (of talent and administrators), broadcast strategies, social responsibilities, and many other aspects fill every day with challenges.

The commissioner can make some decisions in the best interest of the league or the sport but must always answer to the board (i.e., team owners) who consistently ask if the value of their franchise is rising. This asset appreciation commitment must come while simultaneously protecting the interests of the players (the primary workforce); referees; league/club staff; stadium operators; fans; the media; sponsors; vendors; concessionaires; city, state and provincial governments; and federal tax collectors.

Thus, any discussion of Commissioner Bettman, despite his vocal detractors, must be presented in a holistic fashion and established so readers can see where the "business" puck was and is now likely headed.

For Bettman, a law school graduate (Cornell University) and previous senior vice president and general counsel of the NBA, there is no questioning his stellar financial performance on behalf of his board of governors and all the owners of clubs. For 30 years, he has been retained on multiple occasions. Commissioner Bettman was expected to have his most recent contract extended in July 2022. His previously reported salary, following a series of raises and contract renewals, of approximately $10 million per year affirmed the value he consistently brings to the League. Of course, as every great leader knows, leadership is not limited to the top job, it must permeate throughout the organization, empowered from above and engrained in the culture. Chapter 2, which follows, delves into the next level: leadership traits and characteristics of the NHL.

2

Leadership Essentials

The act of leading others is one of the most researched and discussed management concepts. The list of leadership traits, tactics, and thoughts is varied and empirically assessed. We've learned leaders are not necessarily born; they develop, they fail, they take risks, they empower, they are servants and role models, and, well, you get the idea.

Yes, Studying the NHL's Leadership Traits Can Really Help

Like any professional sport, the NHL and its many "actors" are highly visible. The League and its games are a great source of content, learning, and stories that can serve every business regardless of size.

Hockey is a great metaphor. Both as a game and as a business, it is competitive and fast moving and offers powerful stories and illustrative cases that create learning opportunities for other contexts. In its fullness, hockey allows discussion of the following:

- **Competition**: awareness, knowledge, and understanding of your competitors are vital, enabling proactive response planning and action
- **Courage**: also known as risk in the business context – taking action when reward is possible in the face of potential defeat
- **Focus**: dedicated attention and practice toward an objective (or set of objectives) without distraction. Focus is described in further detail later in this chapter.
- **Group Dynamics**: the ability to emerge as a team rather than as a set of individuals through a balancing of personalities, skills, shared experiences, strengths, and weaknesses of each member of the group
- **Leadership**: the position or role related to directing a group. See *Rick's Recall* "My Dad: A Leader" about Rick's father on the topic.
- **Motivation**: interest, drive, passion, dedication, and enthusiasm for the task at hand. *Norm's Nostalgia* "Two Motivated Authors" outlines the passion we have for our trade and gives you a bit more insight into one of the authors.
- **Restraint**: being smart and able to not react in the face of an opportunity that is not appropriate to pursue
- **Resiliency and Reliability**: the dual ability to stay the course and be able to deliver as expected on tasks, as described in further detail later in this chapter
- **Sacrifice**: the willingness to put the good of the group/team ahead of your own, described in further detail later in this chapter

Each of these constructs is always visible in the NHL, support-ing our "hockey is business" analogy. Indeed, hockey in its many variations (including street, roller, and sledge hockey) has shaped our lives and driven our careers. From 5 a.m. practices as kids to memories of our national teams capturing Olympic or Paralympic medals. From beer league tournaments with lifelong friends to skating on cracks-in-the-ice ponds, the sport has been part of our lives in very meaningful ways. Although each of the bulleted con-cepts described above will emerge in more detail in later chapters, we mention several here. A *Rick's Recall* about leadership, a *Norm's Nostalgia* about motivation, and three additional sections about resiliency and reliability, focus, and sacrifice offer an introduction to leadership essentials at the intersection of hockey and business.

Rick's Recall: My Dad, A Leader

One of my all-time favorite family photos doesn't feature me. In fact, I'm nowhere to be found. It's a photo of my Dad, probably in his late 80s, in his hockey skates with my two older brothers and one of his grandsons. The Burton men are all lined up, Dad with his old stick (no curve) and big blue hat. Behind him, the pond looks right for a quick game of shinny.

I dearly wish I had been there that day in New Hampshire because my Dad, who passed away at 98 in September 2018, was vibrant until he was 96 and then bravely faced memory issues his last two years.

He was a proud Newfoundlander and the most loving, giving man I ever met. A role model and leader to me and many others. He was the also the same father who declared when I was about 10 or so that no son of his was growing up without learning how to play hockey.

Certain things in our house were sacred. I tell this particular story because I think there is much to be learned from our elders. I'm also convinced it takes us a long time to figure that out.

In fact, one of the funnier lines I've heard about aging is how teenagers think their parents are so "clueless" but amazed to find these same people have magically become much smarter when those teens reach their mid-20s.

For me, my Dad was always cool.

Probably because his core values were loyalty (he and Mom were married 79 years!), love of family, truth, and hard work. And, importantly, challenging others, including me, to embrace these traits. Those terms sound quaint in 2022, but I haven't given up the hope that, despite great new technologies and media platforms, love and loyalty will make a big return for my grandchildren.

One of my favorite stories about Dad and his belief in the truth happened when some friends of mine traveled to a famous Cape Cod beach with my parents. My buddies and I wandered down the seashore at one point and came upon a massive sand dune that begged to be climbed. The only problem? A small sign said the "hill" was protected and climbing in the sand was prohibited.

As many readers know, teenage boys don't often need much encouragement to do something foolish or forbidden. So, up we went ... and when we slid back down, a National Park employee was waiting for us. For some reason, I was the chief culprit and the ranger wanted my name and address to give me a warning citation.

Thinking quickly, I gave him a fake name and the address of one of my friends. I figured no one would ever know the difference. The ranger filled out the paperwork and gave me my ticket and asked us to stay off the dune.

For me, it was "no harm, no foul" even though I'd been caught red-handed. What became interesting happened when my friends and I got back to my parents. My Dad had clearly watched the whole episode and wanted to know who we'd been talking to.

I said it was a guy from the beach patrol and he'd given me a ticket for climbing on the dune. Thankfully, I said, I thought quickly and gave him some fake details.

Years later, I can warmly write about the fact my father instructed me to march back down the beach and tell the truth.

"You find that ranger, tell him you lied, and give him your real details."

I was, of course, ashamed, and embarrassed this was happening in front of my friends. They walked back down the beach, mocking me the whole way, while the "culprit" turned himself in.

Years later, when I think of my Dad and see him on his skates in that photo, knowing any kind of fall that day would've broken whichever hip he fell on, I'm proud of how he helped shape me for adulthood. Parenting is rarely easy, and I think the same holds for serving as someone's boss.

Managers, directors, small business owners, and vice presidents are responsible for shaping the people they hire and the employees they inherit. The leader's values become instantly clear to the crew. If the leader is sexist, racist, dishonest, cynical, sarcastic, caustic, angry, abusive, power-hungry, selfish, inconsiderate, and a host of other negative traits, the result will reveal itself via employee turnover; bullying; an absence of diversity, equity, and inclusion; and reduced profitability.

I'd like to think my Dad (with a lot of credit going to my Mom) helped raised three fine sons. I'd also like to think his approach to life and leadership greatly contributed to his parenting success.

We were never wealthy, but we were rich beyond words.

Norm's Nostalgia: Two Motivated Authors

As you get into the book, some of you might be asking, what do two academics have in their heads allowing them to think they can comment so deeply on the NHL and business of hockey, and – even more – provide advice to businesses or leaders based on that knowledge? Let us give you an answer and defend ourselves. At the very least, you should get the answers from us straight rather than somewhere else.

First, let me talk about Rick. He is a very motivated sport business professional. His résumé takes care of this immediately. Former commissioner of a professional sports league (Australia's National Basketball League). Former CMO of the United States Olympic Committee. Former professional (for a dozen years) with major beer brands (Miller Brewing Company). Former vice president for a leading sports and entertainment marketing agency (Clarion Performance Properties).

Not to mention time spent as a professional journalist, a stint running a sports marketing center at the University of Oregon's business school, a noted author, and a professor of sport management in the David Falk College of Sport and Human Dynamics at Syracuse University (where he also served as the Faculty Athletic Representative to the ACC and NCAA). Those credentials seem reasonable for offering some advice.

For me, the task is not quite as easy.

Before becoming a full-time academic, I spent time with Triathlon Canada (the national sport organization/national governing body responsible for the sport in Canada), worked on an Olympic bid (Toronto 2008 [failed] bid), was a senior program officer and senior policy officer for Sport Canada (Canada's government arm responsible for sport), and was an entrepreneur (for a start-up firm in biotechnology).

Then, I got the chance to teach and decided to embark on a doctorate, later taking my first full-time academic appointment shortly after turning 29. Since then, for the past two decades, I've been in a full-time role at universities in Canada and the United States, in both business schools and health schools, depending on the university.

I have been fortunate to have had the opportunity to do media, keynote presentations, and consulting work and write trade publications, which – in turn – allowed me to stay engaged and informed on the "real" business of ice hockey. This includes media appearances and media-supported research, such as the *Why Not Canada* six-part series with TSN and the *Globe and Mail* that is highlighted in *Norm's Nostalgia* "Dreams Can Come True!"

At the consulting level, like many business professors, I spend time every year on these activities. In addition to being good for me, it also creates opportunities for my students in terms of job hunting, research data sources, internships, and locating funding for student thesis work.

For me, this has been all done through my role as an advisor with The T1 Agency, a Toronto-based agency with which I have worked for more than a decade. T1 has a long roster of past clients that includes brands and properties from within and outside of sport.

Specific to hockey, my past work has included projects involving Hockey Canada, the CHL, many NHL and CHL clubs, and a number of organizations for whom hockey is "part" of their business (e.g., USports, Ontario University Athletics, school athletic departments) or places where hockey was a targeted investment (i.e., sponsors, event-promoters, investors). I've had the wonderful opportunity to work with the women's national team and Hockey Canada during my time at Sport Canada or as a researcher.

Neither of us are impressed with our credentials and don't believe for a second that they make us experts at handling problems you, your department, or your business might face. But we would like you to believe if we were sitting in your office, we could be "real" enough to offer suggestions you might consider.

Nothing more than two very motivated people passionate about our trade.

Resiliency and Reliability

From our list in "Yes, Studying the NHL's Leadership Can Really Help," the traits that came to the fore during 2020–1, at the height of COVID-19, were resiliency and reliability. When global and regional leaders and public health experts sought to guide their nations, states, provinces, and cities through a health crisis unseen since the Great Influenza pandemic killed more than 17 million people between 1918 and 1920, professional sports leagues found their arenas and stadiums closed and their seasons delayed, postponed, or canceled.

Around the world, COVID-19 delivered a devastating reduction in game-related revenues, marketing, and sponsorship, and every aspect of a league's sporting life was disrupted. Commissioners like the NHL's Gary Bettman and the NBA's Adam Silver were forced to suspend their seasons just before their playoffs began while other leagues, notably Major League Baseball (MLB), were obligated to put the start of their lengthy 2020 season on hold.

As March stretched into July of 2020, with no games played or televised, the media quickly descended on North America's four commissioners wanting to know when games would return and the specifics of in-person viewing restrictions.

What interested us in watching strategic decisions unfold in real time was comparing the success of MLB's Rob Manfred with the NHL's Bettman. Where Manfred and his players (represented by their union, the Major League Baseball Players Association) struggled to find common ground on the number of games to be played and whether full salaries would be honored, the NHL was first to announce, on May 26, it would immediately end the 2019–20 regular season and launch a 24-team playoff concept in two easily accessible hub cities.

On-ice training camps began early in July and the playoffs were held in the hub cities of Edmonton and Toronto in empty arenas in August and September, ending in early October. In contrast to baseball, the NHL and NHL Players' Association (NHLPA) jointly agreed on a four-year contract extension during this crisis time.

The 24-team playoff scenario meant that, for the first time ever, 12 clubs from the League's two conferences competed for the Stanley Cup. This approach ensured teams just outside the playoff bubble in March 2020 (when the League shut down) couldn't suggest they would have made the playoffs when the regular season was scheduled to end April 4.

In other words, every team that held even a remote chance of making the playoffs was "in." The inclusion of some large and important hockey markets (e.g., Chicago, Montreal, New York) from the clubs ranked 17 to 24 created an ancillary marketing benefit of this format. Yes, for the first time, the fans of 24 NHL clubs were part of the Stanley Cup playoffs.

Seven teams (Anaheim, Buffalo, Detroit, Los Angeles, New Jersey, Ottawa, and San Jose) did not qualify and immediately began preparing for the NHL's annual entry draft and a "fresh start" when the 2020–1 season began in January 2021.

The NHL's understanding of its fans, players, owners, and partners and its quick-thinking proactivity likely played a major role in the NHLPA voting in late May to accept the League's season-ending plan.

The shared decision allowed League and union executives to move collectively toward protecting the health of players, coaches, officials, team administrators, and fans but also to begin negotiations with ten cities capable of hosting 12 teams and playing multiple games a day (à la the NCAA's famed March Madness format) during a compressed playoff window.

Even before the official announcement, the candidate cities were aggressively positioning themselves for selection. They badly wanted games played again.

"If the NHL wants to play without fans, we want to be a (host) city," said Butch Spyridon, the president and CEO of the Nashville Convention and Visitors Corporation. "We have the practice facilities, the game facility, the walking distance of hotels. I think we're as well-equipped (as anyone), when you add in our geographic location for teams to get here."[1] Perhaps, even though fans were not likely to be in attendance, bid cities felt that the long-term benefits would make it worthwhile.

At the time, Commissioner Bettman told the media that completing the NHL's 2019–20 season was what "our fans are telling us overwhelmingly they'd like us to do, because people have an emotional investment in this season already."

But for anyone who thought finishing a disrupted season was easy, the logistics were mind-boggling. A 24-team playoff meant four opening round series (best-of-five) between the teams seeded 5–12. Those four winners advanced to meet the top four seeds. In the East, that was Boston, Philadelphia, Tampa Bay, and Washington. Out West, the defending Cup champion St. Louis Blues were joined by Colorado, Dallas, and Las Vegas.

Since the top four squads in each conference could not start quarter-final contests ice cold, round-robin games also needed to be scheduled (at the same time as the 5–12 games) to determine playoff seeding. This was an interesting concept, not (to our knowledge) previously seen before in sport, where clubs played essentially meaningless exhibition games that were not part of the regular season or the playoffs.

On top of playing those games, safety required the NHL test every player every night for COVID-19 (producing test results by the next morning). Entering the bubbles, the NHL estimated it would need to supervise between 25,000–30,000 tests at a cost of more than US$2 million dollars.

Additionally, dozens of League employees would focus on government relations (involving visas, border crossings, quarantines, isolation, and testing), ticket sales, sponsor activation, advertiser leveraging (using NHL imagery and trademarks), arena security, broadcast partner access, team transportation and accommodation, training rinks, game ice, and a host of other challenges normally handled by "home teams."

Each element needed League approval and carried notable liability for the NHL if any aspect of traditional game management was inefficient or compromised. The tiniest details could have derailed the NHL finishing the 2019–20 season.

In times of stress and crisis, attention to detail is paramount and determines reliability. It explains why we seek to hire the best talent (employees) and train them for the times when the unexpected confronts us.

Few individuals in late 2019 predicted that a pandemic was imminent. But every professional sports league knew an act of terrorism, a tornado, an earthquake, or building failure could derail the standard operating procedures. Most have contingency plans for such an unwanted occurrence in the form of emergency preparedness protocols, which determine in advance which individuals will comprise their "quick-response" team and what actions that group will take if necessary.

This resiliency and reliability are hallmarks of professional sports leagues and help explain why fans in 2020 were so thrown off by the suspension of every scheduled sport. The games had always been played. Night and day. In every time zone. From the Newfoundland Growlers of the East Coast Hockey League (ECHL) to the Vancouver Canucks. Postponements or cancellations were largely unheard of at any level or in any setting.

A commitment to stability helps explain why Commissioner Bettman, with an eye toward safety for all, moved as staunchly as he did during May and June 2020. He needed facts and guarantees to guide his decisions governing the health of his sport, the players, the coaches, and the trainers. Not to mention the NHL's brand image and his owner's financial assets. All called for a flexible and committed workforce producing viable solutions to every challenge.

The NHL was guiding 24 teams through training by July 2020 and the Stanley Cup was finally awarded on September 29 (with the Tampa Bay Lightning hosting the trophy). Studying this experience revealed to us how the NHL painted a clear picture of collaboration, focus, and cautious planning during a time of crisis.

What was achieved, the completion of a key task despite a massive disruption, impresses us and, we argue, can be replicated in the office when organizations commit to aggressive sustainability of surviving and staying in business for the foreseeable future.

Focus: A Complete Commitment to the Objective

Whether in a global pandemic or a wartime conflict, focus is a trait that we consistently observe in great leaders. In his magnificent book *The Captain Class*, author Sam Walker told of spending years researching the most dominant teams in sports history and articulating what made them special. For his project, a labor of love, he roamed the world looking at every major league club, national team, and Olympic squad that met his rigorous standards. In the end, he identified 16 dynasties from 10 countries (Australia, Brazil, Canada, Cuba, France, Hungary, New Zealand, the Soviet Union, Spain, and the United States) that fit his championship criteria.

What, he asked, was the common denominator that each of these elite teams held in common? The answer was the team captain. The leader of the club. And when it came to his consideration of the NHL, only one unit stood out to Walker: Maurice Richard's 1955–60 Montreal Canadiens, the only NHL team ever to win five straight Stanley Cups.

With Richard, Walker found an enigma. Among the 16 captains featured, the "Rocket" was the outlier. Most of the featured captains led by athletic example or used special verbal skills to inspire their fellow players. But Richard was different. He rarely talked to his teammates. And while he scored fabulous goals at an amazing rate, Richard lacked visible physical strength, wasn't a great stickhandler, and wasn't even all that fast of a skater.

What he showed outwardly was something his coach Dick Irvin could only describe by using words like "fury, desire and intensity." Richard's fiery stare even caused author (and occasional journalist) William Faulkner to suggest the eyes of Montreal's Hall of Fame right winger featured the "passionate glittering fatal alien quality of snakes."

Walker even noted that opposing goalies were often "spooked" by Richard's snarl and seemingly demonic approach. "When he came flying toward you with the puck on his stick," said Hall of Fame goalie Glenn Hall (as recounted on page 182 of *The Captain Class*), "his eyes were all lit up, flashing and gleaming like a pinball machine. It was terrifying."

One reason we include this story of Richard in this section on focus is because of a single sentence Walker used in describing NHL players and their approach to the game. On page 182 of *The Captain Class*, Walker noted that "in a supercharged environment like the NHL, where the challenge to the athletes is both mental and physical, this deeper form of communication – based on displays rather than words – seems to have been a perfectly effective substitute."

Wouldn't you like to work in a place with such focus and drive? We certainly would.

Richard reportedly did not need verbal assurances to convey his commitment to his teammates. In fact, on long train trips to away games, Richard could sit for six hours and not say a word. On game days, he might only reach ten words spoken. In the locker room, after he fixed his icy stare on each member of the team, his statement was usually no more than "Let's go out and win it."

Business leaders and contract negotiators have long known that "silence intimidates." And in an age of social media when the "noise" of the world tends to drown out all reason (and often the truth), we may achieve our best outcomes when our focus on the single over-riding objective is clear to everyone. In short, leaders could learn much from "The Rocket" and his quiet style, not to mention his relentless drive.

In the NHL, as Richard consistently showed his teammates, the absence of words, of meaningless chatter, was used to motivate or make clear the need for intense focus. Think about it: in the face of a pandemic or market recovery, we should not need to discuss what needs to be done next. Or how important it is that we hit our sales target or make great sales calls.

We need only to do it. You do not need me to give you a pep talk every day. You know our objectives. As Nike's advertising has stated for so many years, "Just do it."

As Richard probably thought to himself any number of times, "I don't need to explain how important this final period is. Or tell the team to dig deep or fight harder for the puck. You don't need clichés from me. Or words. You can see where I'm coming from. Do your job."

Silence often makes employees uncomfortable because, for younger generations, constant encouragement from parents and teachers has led to settings where everyone gets a participation medal. We've created settings where no one is ever at fault, where no one ever does a second-rate or half-completed job. In this 21st-century world, many employees regularly expect repeated pats on the back and statements of praise shared with everyone in the department. And these accolades are expected (often) despite lackluster performances.

This "softness" would never have existed in Richard's years as captain and serves little purpose in the modern NHL. Watch any game and when a goal is scored, goaltenders are traditionally left alone. While everyone on the ice is dealing with +/− measurement (i.e., the NHL statistic assessing how well a player does in terms of goal differential when they are on the ice) and blame for a goal may belong to the defenseman who screened the goalie or the inept forward who failed to clear the puck out of the zone, it's the goalie who gave up the goal.

Said another way, when the lamp is lit, the goalie stands alone, amidst the cheers and jeers. There is no need for a defenseman to skate over and say something like, "We'll stop it next time" or "That was a lucky shot" to boost the keeper's confidence. Instead, an unspoken dialogue begins. "We have work to do. This stops now. Shut out the noise."

So too in business, contemporary leaders must learn to motivate subordinates with a clear understanding of the moment and organizational goals still to achieve.

Let's take the example of an annual performance review. A supervisor might start the discussion by asking the employee to sum up their performance during the last year. Regardless of what that individual recounts, the supervisor, the unit leader, must remain clear on whether the challenge was successfully met.

Similarly, the employee receiving the review must reconsider whether they have done enough, whether they could have done more, or whether they made the organization as strong as possible. The review should initiate a discussion that identifies areas for improvement.

We all want affirmation and for others to know we have "done our jobs" but when employees are conditioned to expect flowery praise for the simplest of achievements no matter how well accomplished, the leader diminishes their power and influence. Standards drop. Credibility disappears. Learning halts. Passion wilts.

In hockey, the difficulty of winning the Stanley Cup is so great, the odds of any hockey player ever seeing their name on the trophy so low, that non-winners routinely leave a room if the Cup is brought in. That silent statement is language enough.

In an era when Maurice Richard's Canadiens won five straight Cups and won or drew nearly three out of every four games they played during that period, a goal, a great save, a penalty killed, an opposing star player neutralized … none of it needed comment from Richard. There was the Stanley Cup, and the rest was "noise."

Richard's true focus on the desired goal never wavered.

A Willingness to Sacrifice Self for the Team

A third leadership characteristic that we would like to highlight is a willingness to put the team ahead of oneself, as exemplified by Terry Sawchuk. When Newfoundland poet Randall Maggs created his remarkable conversational saga *Night Work: The Sawchuk Poems*, about the life of Hall of Fame goaltender Terry Sawchuk, Maggs worked hard to capture the pained life of a 21-year NHL veteran still considered one of the greatest goalies of all time.

The imagery in that remarkable poetry came solely from words. Not from the flesh and sinew of a Winnipeg-born goalie who frequently bled for his sport.

To say the least, it's difficult explaining to modern readers just how many injuries, cuts, or severed tendons Sawchuk sustained during his career. The list is too long, and his creased face, when seen in black and white, is too horrific for modern sensitivities. Indeed, one of the pictures Maggs selected to show the crouching 5-foot-11 goalie is truly macabre.

Still, the accolades for the professional goalie who died tragically at 40 remain. Four times the Cup was inscribed with Sawchuk's name. Four times the Vezina went to the old man whose face bore more than 400 stitches (including three in his right eyeball) from flying pucks and slashing sticks.

On 103 occasions, Sawchuk shut out the opposition. It was an NHL record for career shutouts and stood for more than four decades. Yet, as Maggs wrote in the poem *An Ancient Fire*, Sawchuk lived his life in pain.

In the deep slump of his body you see his agony
And sagging spirit ...
The signs of defeat are clearly there. The taped-up
hand that holds the damaged arm. The body that only
wants to curl into itself.

In a different poem, *No Country for Old Men*, Maggs illustrated Sawchuk, playing for Toronto in the 1967 playoffs, a season when Sawchuk helped lead the Maple Leafs to their last Stanley Cup championship with a 40-save, 3–1 clinching-game win over the Canadiens. The poem imagines the Leafs players looking at their battered netminder in disbelief:

Someone breaks the silence. The whole room
gapes at the hammered chest and belly. Easy to count
the darker nine or ten from Hull. They can't even look
at the shoulder.

Why include Terry Sawchuk in this chapter? Why write about a journeyman goalie who developed lordosis and was unable to sleep more than two hours at a time?

The simple answer is that every business must ask employees to make sacrifices for the good of the organization. It may mean working late or coming in on a weekend. It may mean not getting an annual pay raise when a pandemic has knifed a company's profitability. It could take the form of working double shifts for someone who can't (or won't) report to work.

None of those sacrifices compare to those made in war or a pandemic ... or by NHL players during the playoffs (when the hitting is more intense and win-or-go-home pressure ratchets up). Hockey fans acknowledge playoff beards, heightened commitments, and brutal forechecking because the pressure is real. The playoffs and Cup require every active NHL player pledge to figuratively (if not literally) bleed for his teammates, for his club.

Strangely, in our current age, it often seems many employees are unwilling to make sacrifices for the "team." Is that because they've never been made to feel part of a cohesive unit?

Sports Physical Therapy CEO Lynn Steenburg frequently tells university students that research consistently suggests the number one intangible that most employees crave is to feel appreciated. Not to get a pay raise or improved working conditions. Rather, they want appreciation for their work. Want to feel like they are "in" on things. Can get sympathetic help when they fall behind. That their sacrifices are appreciated.

How do leaders teach senior managers to think about subordinates? To hold employees accountable to the most important firm objectives and encourage making a sacrifice for the team toward those outcomes, yet still help them feel like they matter? How do bosses, in challenging times, ask the rank and file to go above and beyond the norm?

Perhaps the NHL's unspoken code is something we can draw from. Anyone who has ever played hockey at an elite level knows the game demands a selfless egalitarianism. It requires players skate with their band of brothers or sisters as if their lives depend on that game's outcome. They must skate, backcheck, and block shots with an "all in" mentality. Channel their inner Maurice Richard, Terry Sawchuk, or Steven Stamkos.

Why is that? Is it because "winning" or "losing" is determined in 60 minutes? And what of the belief that commitment in hockey is somehow greater than that found in professional baseball, basketball, or football? Could that be true? We believe part of the answer comes from hockey's unique game form.

Baseball features complete half innings where players sit on a bench waiting for their turn at bat. Football is structured such that specialists only take the field to play offense or defense. If these warriors are not on the field, they are resting.

Basketball is more demanding but generally features small rosters where the top seven players generate most of the minutes. In fact, on many teams, it is not unusual for five "starters" to play 80 percent or more of all available minutes. In recent years, teams invest most in "the big three," or the idea that having three stars is the secret to on-court success. The substitutes are used sparingly but, when they do compete, fill customized roles designed to give the stars a breather.

Even European football (soccer), with its global appeal, only pits 11 versus 11 with very limited substitution (three per team per game). In fact, no more than 14 players will play for either side and often, when the ball moves to the far end of the pitch, players slow down significantly in preparation for their next burst of speed. It is rare that substitutions happen before the final 20 minutes of the game.

None of those conditions exist in the NHL. In the world's fastest game, players change lines on the fly and every player, regardless of line, must commit to intense physicality for the 45–50 seconds of each taxing shift. Often, the best teams roll four lines of forward and three duos on defense. There is no whining, phoning in sick, excuse-making, criticizing of teammates, demands for more minutes, or anything else associated with privilege.

For those 47 seconds (the NHL average), top players will skate their legs into jelly and do so while expecting to take 30–40 full-tilt shifts each game. There is no hiding on an NHL bench. The NHL's legendary history is filled with stories of players competing on broken legs, of skating to the point of passing out, of cracked ribs and devastating slams into the boards. For many years, no one in the NHL, not even the goalies, wore protective headgear. While that ancient time has passed, every NHL player still goes through an apprenticeship of getting hit, checked into the boards, high-sticked, tripped, blindsided, cross-checked, clobbered, and, usually, punched.

If actor Tom Hanks famously suggested to his team that there was no crying in baseball (in the movie *A League of Their Own*), then surely the equivalent for the NHL and any business is this: there is no bellyaching. Players like Terry Sawchuk knew about sacrifice all too well. We can extrapolate the same for today's modern business world where so much is different than it was just five years ago.

Hockey has always been a demanding sport. Similarly, leaders need to anticipate and forecast the unique demands of the future marketplace. Executives must work harder at inspiring employees but also at getting them to make the sacrifices each business unit needs. This may involve helping nervous staffs understand *taking one for the team* (a very NHL concept) because nimble organizations must produce sustainable bottom lines while serving as good corporate citizens.

These traits (competitiveness, teamwork, discipline, motivation, and leadership) can be worked on and mastered by any employee. Likewise, every leader, at every level, must acknowledge the need to develop those NHL "habits" and deliver them daily. As if every day, like every NHL game, matters.

All of us, in the years following this brutal pandemic of 2020–2, must work on our focus, resilience, and sacrifice (for the organization) and acknowledge leadership starts at the top and permeates throughout the organization. In the chapters that follow, we'll do our best to share examples and learn from the NHL's greats.

3

Why Many of the World's Business Leaders Use Sport to Drive Themselves

Sport. Such a simple word. But such a terribly complex construct.

And yet business executives use sports language and metaphors all the time to motivate employees. "It's crunch time." "It's third period, gang." "Who wants the puck on their stick when it matters?" "We have to go into the corners this month."

Historically speaking, sport, by some estimates, has interested humans for at least 4,000 years. Like war, it produces winners and losers. Like combatants preparing for battle, sport involves planning or strategies for achieving success.

Perhaps the single greatest difference between war and sport is found in knowing that forms of sport were frequently used as preparation for conflict. War killed people. Sport, on the other hand, prepared warriors by allowing them to learn which skills produced victorious results and which wouldn't. Sport was competitive, passionate, religious, and would allow complete commitment without requiring the ultimate sacrifice.

That's not to say there hasn't been blood sport through the centuries (e.g., hunting, gladiatorial combat) but when authors and journalists write about sport, they invariably draw distinctions and focus on modern sport by referencing the ancient Olympics (believed to have first been staged in 776 BCE) and professional sports leagues of the last 100 years.

Still, if business leaders use sport for inspiration, are they talking about professionals or amateurs? Or is it professionals, Olympians, Paralympians, and grassroots kids? What about community sport? The Special Olympics? College sport? From a hockey perspective, are we talking about women, men, boys, girls, trans, or nonbinary participants? How are we playing the game—on ice, sledge, roller, street, underwater, table, or air?

The truth is this: talking about sport never grows old for business leaders because the foundations of sport are vast, diverse, and almost always about pride and winning. Taking a high-performance approach to business, the same way an athlete does, will generally work. Athletes seek to win for a variety of reasons. Some simply love competition and the individualistic feeling that comes from winning. Others want to win for their parents, guardians, team, school, or community; they want to win for others. Thus, sport sets us up to understand our own personal motives or to realize the utility we gain from serving the larger whole. In short, competition makes us feel better about our unique place in the universe.

Norm's Nostalgia: Apply a High-Performance Athlete View to Business

Many of us want to be a professional athlete, be an Olympian, compete at the Division I NCAA level, or even win a state or provincial championship in our age group. The reality is that the odds are very low that few of us will ever do so.

Consider the Summer Olympic Games, held every four years with about 10,000 athletes competing, drawn from a world population that approaches eight billion people. In the NHL in the 2021–2 season, reports indicate 473 Canadians and 294 Americans played at least one game. More than 750 players.

To give context, in 2019–20, official membership levels of boys and girls were about 607,000 for Hockey Canada and about 561,000 for Hockey USA. Of the many who want to play, some really try hard but very few succeed. Even fewer realize the dream of becoming a professional, an Olympian or Paralympian, NCAA champion, or member of their country's national team.

I'm one of those who dreamed and – by most accounts – tried hard. First as a hockey player, but it didn't take me long to realize it wasn't going to happen. So, although I kept playing, I tried many other sports, eventually finding some talent on the bike, then in cross-country skiing, and finally in triathlons.

I got into triathlon and cross-country skiing, won some youth and local races, raced in some national championships, qualified for a few national teams, won a (team) university (Ontario) championship, and had a 10-year period of my life where high-performance sport was one of the main priorities of my existence.

During this time, sport was my priority, my love, my passion, my number one focus.

In turn, this rendered school and my studies to number two. Most times, I was able to balance both getting good grades, learning and (by some accounts) excelling at my athletics, along with building a social life. But … and I didn't realize that this was a flaw until later on … I was not taking the right approach to my career or my life.

The biggest example of this happened during a biology final exam in my first year of university. I was coming off an intense ski season and was ramping up for a summer of triathlons. It was April and I was working through my six final exams for the semester. As I'd often done, I'd "cram" for a few days before the exam, studying day and night, go in, and usually walk away with a very good grade. And the first five were all like that, but number six – biology – was the exception.

I was training, studying, not sleeping, and pushing myself hard. Bottom line, I ran out of gas and, while passing, I ended up with a poor biology grade, one that I view as embarrassing. It is the only subpar grade in my many years of schooling.

Disappointed and distressed, I knew I needed to change. After some reflection, chats with mentors and my parents, I put my finger on it. I needed to treat my studies (and later my career) like I did sport. I would never stay up all night before a major competition to work on my skills. Or allow myself to get massively dehydrated and malnourished before a training session.

So, why do that with something as important as my career?

My solution? From that moment forward, I decided to apply the same approach to my career as I did to my athletic efforts.

What Business Leaders Can Learn from the Duality of Sport Engagement

Sport has two major engagement forms, spectators (watchers) and participants (players). Spectators seek entertainment, social interaction, and group affiliation. Players seek health, competition, and self-actualization.

We can talk about sports with fans or sport participants. We compete or we are passive. With certain sports, we do both. We know well this point that there are two very different mechanisms from the viewpoint of sport organizations seeking to find avid fans or grow their youth participant base.

Take the NFL, North America's most popular sport for spectators. It features a game very few (a small percentage point of one percent) of the more than 100 million fans who watched the 2022 Super Bowl ever competed in at any level. Lots of fans but very few who have ever played.

Similarly, and conversely, if we polled the 50,000 finishers from more than 140 countries of the 2019 New York City Marathon, we would find few who could name the male and/or female winners of the most recent Olympic marathon, let alone the national champions from their home country. Many participants but few fans.

This helps explain why it is hard to define sport. Our sense is many have tried, and no one has really succeeded. In fact, many governments and associations opt to define what it is not (as opposed to what it is). For instance, you can include or (not) competitions involving an automobile (e.g., Formula I, NASCAR), an animal (e.g., equestrian, horse racing, modern pentathlon), or skill without heightened physical exertion (e.g., chess, darts, billiards).

At its simplest form, business is about generating revenue from the sales of some product or service. At its most complicated, it is about an extensive ecosystem of organizations, stakeholders, individuals, and groups that compete and cooperate in a performance-based environment with political, technological, social, demographic, economic, and competitive realities changing dynamically. But, before we provide specific concepts that business leaders can learn from sport, let's dig a bit more into sport and describe a bit about how we view it and why it is worth understanding.

The Sport Industry Ecosystem

Sport is entrenched in society from Argentina to Zambia. And from Zimbabwe to Australia. Media – social, digital, televised, print, or otherwise – is, by far, the most observable place to view sport's intertwined importance in societies all over the world. From elite athletes performing at the Stanley Cup finals to social issues on display thanks to sport (e.g., retired NHL player and NHL commentator Anson Carter's words and videos in support of the Black Lives Matter movement of 2020), sport is everywhere. For instance, a Google search for "Anson Carter Black Lives Matter" on June 20, 2020, generated 1.46 million hits.

Much can be written showing how sport is an exemplar of society. Coaches and general managers get fired (often). Athletes are caught in scandals. Esports is growing. Championships are fleeting. Heartbreaking losses are common. Gambling on sports and fantasy sports are on the rise. Local heroes drive fan interest and revenues. International celebrities include athletes. The list goes on. Parades, social causes, collective bargaining agreements, and more.

Billions follow sport and revel in the competition, the celebrity, the incredible highs of amazing victory, the devasting lows of defeat. It is entertainment, an escape, even a proxy for international competition. Communities (national, regional, and local) rally and build around their teams and athletes. During certain

FIFA World Cups and Olympic Games, sport has even stood in as a substitute for war.

Millions are active in sport. They are weekend warriors or body sculptors. Weight-loss wizards or average individuals wanting fun ways to socialize or kill downtime. They participate as families, friends, individuals, and as competitors. We see young kids competing (with parents watching) to senior citizens competing as master's athletes fighting the aging process. All of them seek the physical and mental health benefits that result from sport.

Sport's ecosystem is comprised of numerous stakeholders who are directly or indirectly linked to sport and the business of sports. These stakeholders are found in professional, grassroots, and Olympic/Paralympic sport.

Our published representation of the sport industry noted sixteen stakeholders in the business of sports, comprised of four "target" groups and twelve "business" groups.[1] Such complexity is representative of the sport ecosystem and briefly explained here. First, the four target groups of fans, cities, communities, and participants emphasize sport as entertainment, for health purposes, and as a community builder.

Second, the twelve stakeholder business groups are highly illustrative of sport's deep reach (i.e., governments, leagues, federations, associations, clubs, teams, universities, colleges, events, facilities, arenas, stadiums). There are those who set the rules, create assets, provide venues, compensate athletes and coaches, and grow sports.

There are those (i.e., players, coaches, general managers, agents, player associations, physicians, trainers) who create sport and keep it happening, including organizations who provide the apparel and equipment required to make it happen. Finally, there are stakeholders who let the world know about sport (i.e., networks, agencies, sponsors, bloggers, video game publishers, ticket sellers, and more).

Sport Drivers for the World's Business Leaders

The sport ecosystem traditionally inspires leaders and provides guidelines for others to follow. We offer a few suggested drivers here:

1 **Innovate and Expand Asset Value**: Sport organizations have been exceptional at this for many years. Take, for instance, the International Olympic Committee (IOC), rights holder of the Olympic Games. Despite some highly publicized governance scandals, the IOC has innovated repeatedly to expand its asset value. Examples include (i) launching the Youth Olympic Games to target the younger demographic; (ii) building the TOP Sponsorship Program, arguably the most successful (and most copied) sponsorship model in the world; (iii) continually altering its program of sports to fit with host cities and changing demographics; and (iv) aligning its values and positive role in the world with all of its activities. In the last case, similar examples from the professional sport world of innovations to expand asset value include club-owned regional sport networks (e.g., YES Network), league-owned esports (e.g., NBA 2KL), and player-owned fashion lines (e.g., S by Serena).

2 **Brand, Brand, Brand**: Yes, we wanted that repetition in the heading because this is a reminder for most in business that brands really matter. Brands are what people attach to, follow, love, hate, punish, and support. How sport can help here is the highly illustrative and immediate examples of how brand

shifts can happen up and down due to a variety of things that happen. Tiger Woods and Lance Armstrong are two "brands" that lost equity and suffered financially due to their negative off-the-field behaviors. Roger Federer and Michael Jordan are examples of brands that have consistently grown and shown an ability to thrive.

3 **Focus on Value Creation for the Stakeholders That Matter**: The commissioners of North America's major professional sport leagues should be an inspiration to leaders everywhere, with the long-standing leader of the NHL, Gary Bettman (1993 to present), having served the longest of the active commissioners. In addition to Bettman, the list is long and includes Don Garber (1999 to present) of MLS, the late David Stern of the NBA (1984–2014), the NFL's Pete Rozelle (1960–1989), Paul Tagliabue (1989–2006), and Roger Goodell (2006 to present). Further to this point and as described in chapter 1, commissioner is a position that provides a significant salary but also considerable responsibility. Ultimately, what has made many of these leaders successful is a laser focus on the stakeholder group most important to them, namely the owners of the clubs who make up the board of governors for the league. Yes, many of these commissioners have had their reputation with players, players' associations, fans, media personalities, and coaches damaged, but they have kept their jobs by performing well in the eyes of the owner stakeholder group by growing their leagues (attendance and team profitability), improving league revenues (subsequently shared with the owners), and protecting the interests of the owners (by shielding them from unwanted negative publicity).

4 **Follow the "Revenue" and "Value" Pucks**: In business, like sport, success is driven by a focus on what counts as success. In sport, it is individual performance and winning. In business,

it is group performance and winning. Just like Wayne Gretzky was given accolades for his ability to follow the puck and "know where it was going before it got there" (an ability to not get caught up in defenders seeking to deter him), business leaders have to build value for their customers (and potential customers) and generate wins (revenue) supporting the ongoing operation and growth of the enterprise.

5 **Integrity Matters**: If we can learn anything from the major doping and match-fixing scandals that have plagued sport in recent years, it is that fans and consumers care about what they invest their free time and discretionary income in, and they want it to be ethically upstanding. Sports that initially turned a blind eye to doping, such as Major League Baseball, eventually learned to regret that decision. Thus, industry leaders need to remember that "win at all costs" is a thing of the past, in sport and in business.

6 **You Don't Live in a Fishbowl**:[2] This is an example of what someone can learn *not* to do from sport. Sport is special in that it draws media attention, often to the detriment of making rational business decisions. Yes, the coach of a major New York sporting club may get fired due to the pressure on ownership and executives to appeal to a rabid fan base's discontent about the club's performance. In most businesses, leaders have the time and privacy to plan, research, and act proactively (not reactively).

7 **Your Boss Wants to Make Money**: This is another example where learning how *not* to do something comes from sport. Big-time sport is one of the (very) few places where organizations, individuals, and syndicates invest in ownership of a club for reasons other than financial gain. Let's review the Deloitte financial reports for the Manchester City club in the

FIGURE 3.1 *The eight drivers from sport for the world's business leaders*

English Premier League as an example. The team's owners want to win (seemingly at all costs) and they have spent irrationally on talent to do so. This is (most certainly) not the case for you as a business or unit leader. Your organization likely has a primary focus on making or acquiring money (e.g., tickets, media rights, sponsorship, merchandise). Don't forget that.

8 **Make Your Key Staff into Stars**: Although it is an extreme, take a page from the major sports leagues – we're talking about the big four in North America (NFL, MLB, NBA, and NHL) and the big five in Europe (English Premier League, La Liga, Bundesliga, Serie A, and Ligue 1) – and treat your stars like stars. In each of these nine leagues, public reports suggest that players receive between 45 percent and 70 percent of total league revenues, depending on the year and the league. We are not suggesting (at all) that you do this, but we are taking a page from any strategic human resources book to say that you need to invest in, respect, share, and recognize your key talent (stars) and view them as business assets.

Sport Drivers of the World's Leading Organizations

Just as the sport ecosystem can guide leaders, it also provides valuable guidance at the organization level. Here, we offer a second set of suggested drivers for decision makers but this time at the level of the organization rather than the individual leader. As you'll see in the sub-sections that follow, we have supported many of these recommendations with widely respected core business concepts.

1 **Consider Experiences as Your Product Focus**: Although experts have long known that "experiences" are a key driver of business for many organizations,[3] this really became a mainstream realization during the COVID-19 pandemic, which took many lives and stopped the sport (and other live experiences) industry almost completely for an extended period of time. During COVID-19, many sport organizations learned that they were very traditional in their offerings and business models, heavily reliant on the live experience–generated revenues (e.g., ticket sales, concessions, parking), and not overly innovative. This led to most sport organizations canceling or postponing their activities, with an eye to planning and pivoting for a different future, seeking safe ways to offer experiences to their fans or spectators. Examples during the height of the pandemic included NASCAR offering simulated races with their drivers and UFC holding competitions in locations without fans.

2 **Major Innovations Should Be Prioritized over History**: We know this may be a bit controversial, but the point of this list is showing business organizations what we can learn from sport. It's well-known that innovation,[4] and now digital innovation, is a key success factor in any business.[5] This

recommendation is built on an apple-to-orange comparison of MLB versus the NBA. Pro basketball has been on a growth trajectory for decades, while MLB, although still the number 2 league in North America by revenue, has an aging fan base. The NBA's growth is characterized by drastic rule changes (24-second clock, 3-point shot) to make the game more exciting and has used a global focus to foster growth. MLB, on the other hand, has struggled to make rule changes to modernize the game.

3 **Focus on Both the Numerator and the Denominator of Value**: Sport has shown us both that all businesses need to focus highly and separately on the constructs (perceived quality and price) that make up value, a construct known well in major business marketing research.[6] The numerator – or the quality perceived by the consumer/user/fan – is highly observable in sport, spectator, or participant, while the denominator – the cost – is similarly evident in the behavior and spending by fans and participants. Importantly, value needs to be understood by business managers as a customer perception that is based on their views of the value of the time and financial investments they made in spectating/participating, as well as the personal meaning they accrued from said investment.[7] A classic example is Tough Mudder, a sport participant adventure run that experienced fast success and revenue growth, followed by decline, much of it attributed to the fact the personal meaning achieved by participants was more of a "one-and-done" view, and the desire to return to do the event a second time was low for most participants.

4 **Focus on Trust with Your Customers**: An area of vast empirical study in business research and one that is highly observable in sport is trust. We know, without question, that trust is challenging to build in consumers (i.e., repeat purchases, brand

building, awareness, avoiding quality problems, etc.) and very easy to lose (e.g., bad experience with product or service).[8] There is no place where this is more obvious than sport. Take, for instance, the Cleveland Cavaliers of the NBA. During the past 15 years, they have featured and lost locally born superstar Lebron James twice. The Cavs ultimately won a championship with James but after he left a second time, Cleveland dropped to the bottom of the league standings. As an indicator of trust, the year after Lebron James left the club (2018–19), local regional sport network television ratings went down 58 percent from the year before.[9] What can you do about it? Take a page from Larry Tanenbaum, chair of the board and one of the owners of the Toronto Maple Leafs, who apologized publicly for the club's performance following the 2011–12 season, a season where the club had a rough final two months dropping out of a playoff position, thereby missing the post-season for the seventh straight year.

5 **Create Advocates for Your Brands**: One of the most powerful marketing techniques is advocacy or word of mouth[10] whereby a fan or customer becomes an ambassador for you and markets your product to others. It is a well-established element within effective relationship marketing.[11] Once again, sport and the "super-fan" or the "die-hard participant" offer a tremendous example of advocacy where these individuals can do more for your marketing than many costly, time-consuming programs could. Active bloggers with large followings (10,000+) are great examples and increased in value during the pandemic.

6 **Embrace Strategic Agility and Adaptability**: Another example of an important learning for businesses from sport that was emphasized during the COVID-19 pandemic was that those organizations that produce an experience (i.e., leagues,

FIGURE 3.2 *The six suggested sport drivers of the world's leading organizations*

associations) *must* be able to pivot during times of environmental pressure or change, with a global pandemic or a war being extreme examples.

By *agility*, we mean an efficient rationale and a logical shift in a product or channel offering, often driven by technology by an organization.[12] With the word *efficient*, we mean timely, as in being quick and nimble enough to protect (at least to some extent) revenues that may have otherwise been lost to the effects of the external change.

In using *rationale*, we mean the pivot must make sense for the organization and its customers. For example, if you are seen to be taking advantage of the pandemic, there could be a negative result (i.e., lost sales, image damage, etc.).

By *logical shift*, we mean that if a company has the resources, expertise, and internal support to make the shift, it must do so. An example would be music artists, post-pandemic, moving to a model of small-venue concerts with digital sales (i.e., pay-per-view) for mega audiences, if large-venue concerts are no longer possible.

Strategic Agility and Adaptability: The Example of the NHL's Response to COVID-19 to Save the 2020 Stanley Cup Playoffs

As mentioned earlier, the NHL successfully staged the 2020 Stanley Cup playoffs in two bubbles – Edmonton and Toronto – where 24 clubs fought for the Cup. Why do we suggest this was a *success*? To have staged as many games as possible and crowned a champion, with no positive COVID cases or deaths, would by most accounts be considered an incredible positive.

As quoted in *Sports Business Daily* in August 2020, NHL Deputy Commissioner Bill Daly reported the League was then cautiously planning for a December 2020 start to the 2020–1 season with hopes of getting in a full season, perhaps even in front of some fans. In that same article, Daly gave praise to the NHLPA and felt the players and owners had worked well together. He was even quoted as saying that this collaboration "really reached unparalleled heights during this pause … we have one common enemy, right? Which is the pandemic. Everybody is kind of in the same boat. Everybody is looking to achieve the same results. So, everybody has kind of been working together and carrying their share of the load … I like having the union on my side and helping us move the sport forward."[13]

Learning Made Easy for Business and Everyday Leaders

It is, of course, easy to suggest there is much to learn from sport. Sport is much appreciated by fans (and participants) and we believe it makes life tolerable. Sport writ large is generally about improvement, attainable goals, and, in most cases, winning. It is different from "playing." The two lists of sport drivers – one for leaders and one for organizations – are incentives where you can deconstruct an element of sport and think about how to leverage that specific element in your business.

Figures 3.1 and 3.2 are tools we are sharing for your strategic planning and implementation. Certainly, not all 14 drivers will apply to you or your organization, but we feel confident more than a few will.

The matchups won't always be perfect, and a couple of conceptual models cannot replicate the exact challenges you or your organization faces. But we heartily believe the NHL can serve as an inspirational proxy for any business because almost every sector or service we've ever analyzed faced competitive threats.

Or, to use the transitive law, we might end with this logic: If sport equals competition and business equals competition, then sport equals business. In applying this outcome to the NHL, it leads us to the League's best coaches, who are arguably some of the greatest experts in transformative leadership ever.

Coaches as Leadership Exemplars

While there are a few dozen elite and intelligent NHL coaches who come to mind when one reads the title of this section (e.g., Al Arbour, Ken Hitchcock, Punch Imlach, and Pat Quinn) and a few active ones who might one day get there (e.g., Jon Cooper, coach of Tampa Bay since 2013 and winner of the 2020 and 2021 Stanley Cups), one name rises above all others: Scotty Bowman, the quintessential transformative coach. He won the most games of any coach in NHL history and guided teams to nine Stanley Cups.

More impressive is noting that during his nearly 30 years as a professional coach, he never endured a losing season. Many reports have characterized his coaching style as (i) highly analytical, (ii) based on intense study of his competition, (iii) always seeking to build trust in his players, and (iv) having a consistent goal to transform those players into winners (which he did). There are many anecdotes published related to Bowman's dedication to preparation and building trust with his players.

Bowman's results consistently spoke volumes.

You may not agree with our simple approach, but we believe there are solid linkages any leader can take from the NHL's historic decisions as well as its day-to-day decisions (i.e., borrowing $1 billion in 2021 for distribution to each of the NHL teams to offset COVID-driven financial challenges) and, by way of transformation, bring them into the workplace. We also believe the disruptions of 2020, 2021, and 2022 (including the January 6, 2021, insurrection at the US Capitol) made all too clear that every business needs the capacity to pivot on short notice. We will look at these realities in our next chapter.

4

Why Hockey Mattered during Extreme Global Challenges

Between 2020 and 2022, thanks to multiple major global events, the world of sport – including pro hockey – went through a challenging period.

In fact, we would argue 2020 was the most challenging year ever for the NHL and for businesses.

In 2020, the deaths of George Floyd, Breonna Taylor, and Ahmaud Arbery, plus the shooting of Jacob Blake in Kenosha, Wisconsin, led to a heightened social awareness of systemic racism and resulted in global civil unrest. COVID-19 (a pandemic that killed more than six million worldwide at the time of writing and caused widespread economic damage) was also a landmark event. Operating within this context, the NHL faced and responded to numerous challenges. Yet, four timeless characteristics or drivers of the NHL (see figure 4.1) helped the organization to remain resilient and should be considered by any business: passion, force for good, citizenry, and ability to expand:

1 **Ice Hockey Inspires Passion**: As highlighted in the first two chapters, the game of ice hockey is fast, energetic, exciting, and competitive, leading to deeply connected fans who show their passion for the game, their team, and/or their favorite players. A great example is the International Ice Hockey Federation (IIHF) World Men's Junior Championships, held annually in December/early January, where teams of the top under-20-year-old players in the world compete for their country in pursuit of a world championship. Although it involves only amateur players, including many future NHL stars, the event draws enormous attention, especially in Canada and Russia where it has become an annual event on the calendar of many hockey fans. As an illustration of this high level of interest, the 2020 gold medal game (Canada versus Russia) held in Russia drew a reported 17 million viewers in Russia.[1] In 2017, hosted by Toronto and Montreal in Canada, the gold medal game drew a reported 11 million viewers in Canada.[2]

2 **Ice Hockey Breaks Down Barriers**: The civil unrest brought to light by the Floyd, Taylor, Arbery, and Blake incidents led to global protests and increased attention to race-related issues around the world. These events also reinvigorated efforts to leverage hockey's ability to break down barriers, whether related to gender (the rise of women's pro hockey), disability (sledge hockey), culture (English-speaking versus French-speaking in Canada), or race (Indigenous youth hockey). Certainly, the Black Lives Matter movement (a cry heard all over the world in 2020 and ever since) rising from the police-induced deaths of Black men and women made many countries realize they had long supported systemic racism and discrimination, a challenge the NHL continues to address.

3 **Governments Invest in Sport, including Ice Hockey**: Akin to many sports, in many countries ice hockey receives government support for its key administrative organizations. For instance, in Canada, Hockey Canada, the national sport organization responsible for hockey in Canada, receives financial support from the Government of Canada (Sport Canada). Similarly, the provincial sport organizations responsible for hockey in their given province (e.g., Hockey Quebec, Hockey Alberta) receive financial support from their respective provincial governments. Sociologists, management scholars, and political scientists frequently report that most governments support sport for a variety of different reasons, including enriching health, developing elite athletes, hosting major events, providing role models, building community cohesion, and promoting their jurisdiction globally.[3] From a sport management perspective, government investment in sport has been characterized by researchers as delivering a number of important outcomes, including (i) the communication of key values of benefit for society (teamwork, competition, talent, friendship), (ii) the improvement of physical literacy/health of citizens, (iii) pride in elite athlete performance that can bring a country together, and (iv) the idea that sport is a forum to replace other less attractive competitive outlets for inter-country competition, such as war.[4]

4 **Like All Sport (and Most Digital Businesses), Ice Hockey Has No Borders**: In a year like 2020 when most of the world's borders were (essentially) closed, the importance of a sport like hockey was made clear as people expressed how much they missed live sport. In fact, in an April 2020 survey of a representative sample of Canadians by IMI International, 49 percent said they missed live events and 37 percent indicated sadness at what everyone involved with sport

FIGURE 4.1 *Examples of Timeless Influences in Hockey*

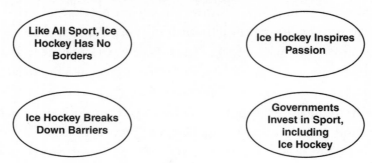

was going through due to COVID-19.[5] In a follow-up global survey of 39 countries in late May 2020, IMI found pent-up demand for sport across the world at a very high level;[6] both Canadians and Americans indicated a desire to increase their attendance and viewing of sport once it returned, including 57 percent of Canadian respondents indicating "excitement" for the return of the NHL playoffs that July. In 2021–2, ESPN+ and TSN Direct began coverage of the Premier Hockey Federation, a women's professional league, where clubs compete for the Isobel Cup, named after Lord Stanley's daughter, thought to be the first female hockey player in Canada.

Rick's Recall: Russian Penguins

How often have you done the unthinkable to solve a problem?

How often have you thought of going someplace you've never visited? A place where you don't speak the language, are culturally ignorant, and might feel unwanted? What if your only connection to this foreign setting was hockey?

A friend of mine, Steve Warshaw, did just that in the early 1990s when he helped build a sport franchise in the Soviet Union around the famed Red Army hockey team. Warshaw's story is showcased in *Red Penguins*, a documentary distributed by Universal Pictures and available for streaming on various platforms.

In this 80-minute film, director Gabe Polsky shows the outlandish craziness of bringing American promotional exuberance to a failing Moscow club essentially disowned by the Communist state – all during the rampant lawlessness brought on by the 1989 collapse of the Soviet Union.

For Warshaw, the jump from the comforts of New York City and America to the life-threatening risks of Russian mobsters and furious army generals in Moscow was challenging but always exhilarating. Exotic but dangerous.

Of course, most of us tend to select the risk-averse side of the coin. We are conditioned to avoid pain, failure, embarrassment, exclusion, or isolation. Instead, we favor long-standing custom, familiar routines, and easy continuity. Even complacency.

Warshaw was never one of those.

A wild-eyed singer in a punk rock band (the infamous Homer Hustler and the Mules) during his days at Syracuse University, Warshaw honed his sports marketing skills as a GM in minor league baseball and basketball, working in small towns like Helena, Montana, and Rockford, Illinois. Warshaw was then hired by sport management agency IMG and generated endorsement deals for Joe Montana, Wayne Gretzky, and other top athletes.

Like many things, opportunity met curiosity. They decided to dance. As former Pittsburgh Penguins owner Tom Ruta says in the film, "The Russians were looking to get a partner. To help them pay the bills. We couldn't believe one of the greatest hockey teams was on the verge of extinction, if that's possible. This was the Soviet Union. This was a vast country with a history of hockey, with an Olympic tradition that went back decades."[7]

History suggests a partnership idea was first presented to Howard Baldwin, a co-owner of the Pittsburgh franchise and the person designated to solve the Rubik's Cube of an American organization joining forces with a storied Russian franchise. The man-on-the-ground solution was Warshaw.

"They were looking for a crazy young guy," said Warshaw, now a sport management consultant, "who wasn't afraid to die in the new Russia. I had the special talent of creating a firestorm inside arenas."

In other words, a non-traditional thinker. A gunslinger for a re-imagined Wild West. A guy with guts who might not understand the risks but also not care. Someone curious about the enigma of a place that few understood.

What happened next? Well, it's better if you buy (or rent) the movie on your favorite streaming platform but as the film makes clear, Warshaw, freakish in his originality (strippers, circus bears, and free beer nights), made the Russian Penguins wildly successful.

Despite death threats from stereotypical gangsters ("the system"), he took the Red Army team from playing in an empty stadium, "a mausoleum," to an "ice palace" offering the hottest ticket in town. From bupkis to bodacious. From empty dasher boards to sponsorships with the world's biggest brands ... and the potential to create a massive deal with Disney.

It might have all kept working except the Russians began staging a political revolution in September and October 1993. Armed forces stormed Russia's Parliament and riots broke out in the streets. After nearly 200 were killed in violent street fighting,

Moscow emerged as a different place. Organized crime and government officials wanted a piece of the lucrative action.

For a while, Warshaw delivered the creativity, ingenuity, commitment, and charisma to make a difficult situation work. In the end, though, it became clear the Pittsburgh Penguins needed to cut their losses before people got physically hurt.

Warshaw's ride in Moscow may have been short but he gave Baldwin and Ruta's ownership group international visibility, dynamic sponsorships, and a sense of how the Penguin brand could be leveraged globally.

There is a lesson in all of that, and it starts with the willingness by owners, leaders, and managers to occasionally attempt bold and daring projects or initiatives. To try something completely off the firm's beaten track.

It may not always involve moving to another country, but it will almost certainly involve visiting the unknown and unfamiliar.

In considering the four drivers presented earlier in this chapter, we need to critically consider each when discussing societal change and hockey. Clearly, the situations of civil unrest and a global pandemic were not 2020's only stories, but focusing our lens on these two situations helps us to illuminate the intersection of the sport of ice hockey with global societal challenges.

COVID-19

In discussing COVID-19, a deadly change accelerant, we refer to the role the pandemic played not only in temporarily reducing the industry of sport to a fraction of its former size but also in encouraging (perhaps forcing) its managers and proactive staff to adapt to a changing world, whether that included digitizing content or finding new ways to operate safely.

So, what happened?

In early 2020, a deadly new virus was reported. Within weeks, a global pandemic had taken hold and it came on with a scale (and impact on society) not seen globally since World War II. By June 2022, the pandemic had resulted in more than a half billion infections globally, and more than 6.2 million confirmed deaths, including 1 million deaths in the US.[8]

Sport, including ice hockey, was decimated. Crushed. And the pandemic was still evident during the 2020–1 season with at least 35 games postponed and more than 120 players placed on the NHL's COVID-19 list. One team, the Dallas Stars, the Western Conference champions, were unable to "officially" start the season when 17 players were found to have contracted the virus.

At the professional level, every league stopped as games/playoffs/major events were canceled or postponed. A few fortunate sport properties had pandemic insurance, including Grand Slam tennis tournament Wimbledon,[9] but most did not, and they experienced major financial implications due to lost ticket sales, concessions, merchandising, parking, sponsorship payments, and all miscellaneous event-related revenues.

In the case of the NHL, on March 12, 2020 – just a day after the NBA was the first major league to see one of its players test positive – the two-country hockey League paused the 2019–20 season that was near completion and set to start its playoffs. It caused Commissioner Gary Bettman to announce:

In light of ongoing developments resulting from the coronavirus, and after consulting with medical experts and convening a conference call of the Board of Governors, the National Hockey League is announcing today that it will pause the 2019–20 season beginning with tonight's games. We will continue to monitor all the appropriate medical advice, and we will encourage our players and other members of the NHL community to take all reasonable precautions – including by self-quarantine, where appropriate. Our goal is to resume play as soon as it is appropriate and prudent, so that we will be able to complete the season and award the Stanley Cup. Until then, we thank NHL fans for your patience and hope you stay healthy.[10]

This announcement led to a string of cancellations across the hockey world, with the KHL, CHL, AHL, NCAA, and minor hockey of all levels shutting down. Access to arenas – both indoor and outdoor – around all of the hockey-playing countries was also shut down.

What followed, from mid-March to late July, was the NHL focusing on supporting the efforts of healthy isolation and virus prevention. The League, players, and NHLPA became engaged in numerous charitable initiatives. The game went to the back burner as North American began grasping what the new "normal" would look like.

On May 26, without specific dates and locations confirmed, the NHL announced it would return to play and produce a late summer Stanley Cup playoff involving 24 of the League's 31 active clubs. A Stanley Cup playoff followed from August to October, played in two hub cities. The start of the 2020–1 season was delayed until January 13, 2021, when a shortened 56-game season began.

Societal Change

While in the midst of the COVID-19 pandemic, the world was rocked by the shocking death of American George Floyd, a

46-year-old Black man, in Minnesota as a result of police brutality. This incident led to a worldwide civil rights uprising. Society's reckoning with systemic racism was echoed in business organizations such as the NHL. Given hockey's traditional white demographic and the fact that about 95 percent of the NHL players are white, the NHL clearly has work to do. Whether we discuss the US federal omnibus known as Title IX (enacted in 1972) or the NCAA moving to add women's sports in the 1980s, we must realize society and sport are intertwined. The same holds for discussions about Americans Tommie Smith and John Carlos and their powerful display for Black rights at the 1968 Mexico City Olympic Games.

Specific to hockey and the NHL, in the fall of 2019, we observed what we hope was a major turning point when two major (and controversial) decisions were made. The first involved the firing of Don Cherry, the long-time and legendary commentator on *Hockey Night in Canada*, for anti-immigrant comments he made during a national telecast. We will go deep into the Cherry situation in chapter 12 but reference it here as an important example of the strong sport and society association. Rogers Sportsnet, which produces *Hockey Night in Canada*, made the challenging decision (given the broadcaster's popularity, stature, and long association with the NHL) that Cherry's decidedly right-wing comments warranted his termination.

The second example, which followed almost immediately from a timeline perspective, was the resignation of the Calgary Flames head coach Bill Peters, in part following accusations he made inappropriate racial comments about former Black NHL player Akim Aliu. In the Canadian and US contexts, unfortunately, race-based discrimination (as well as discrimination involving country of origin, sexual orientation, religious beliefs, gender identification, and physical/mental ability/disability) holds long histories.

A third example, which came to light in the fall of 2021, involved the Chicago Blackhawks and a player claim of sexual assault by a coach that led to numerous resignations, firings, and fines more than a decade after the incidents occurred around the club's 2010 Stanley Cup run. Indicative of a change in how the NHL responds to sexual assault, this situation led to a US$2 million fine to Blackhawks and the resignations of multiple former Blackhawks administrators, including Stanley Cup–winning coach Joel Quenneville, who was coaching successfully with the Florida Panthers at the time of his resignation.

One-Off Accelerants or Ongoing Drivers?

In considering the impacts on a single sport, these influences can be considered as one-time accelerants of change. That is, they are incidents and events that – although potentially short-term in nature – are profound in their impact on hockey. And they shaped many industries and organizations beyond hockey as well. No reader of this book could have escaped those two game-changing realities nor underestimated their power and the pain both generated.

These examples illustrate that major federations (e.g., global leagues and major franchises) were required to adapt and evolve quickly. So must you.

The Global–Local Nexus Is Hockey

The two global issues, four timeless drivers, plus *Norm's Nostalgia* "Apply a High-Performance Athlete View to Business" show clearly hockey's impacts are strong at the local level (e.g., an old man's championship), at the regional/national level (e.g., the deep desire for a return of play of clubs in the NHL and other leagues), and at the global/societal level (e.g., racism, COVID-19).

But let's focus specifically on the NHL, the one League in hockey with the ability to reach fans and people in all corners of the globe.

The 32 NHL clubs have vast followings, players who act as role models to many, and – for the most part – a place in their local community that is among the most important and most recognized assets their city has. And, like any business, this global–local nexus is the reality in which they operate. And, since entertainment options – like the NHL – are easily substituted, the League must continue to market and act at this level and remain vibrant.

There are numerous ways historically the NHL has stayed relevant or enhanced how much it matters to its fans. Here are seven:

1 **The NHL Brand**: Like any league, the NHL is responsible for its brand. If a player behaves badly on or off the ice, the NHL is tasked with responding, and if studies show the NHL brand is sagging, it is the League's responsibility to build that equity back up. Over the past 18 years, since the lost season of 2004–5 (due to labor issues), the NHL has done a tremendous job of building its brand, promoting the League logo, strengthening its relationship with its Players' Association, and building a marketplace image of strength.

2 **Revenue Sharing**: Also, since the lockout season of 2004–5, and as introduced in chapter 1, the NHL has – with that collective

bargaining agreement (similar to that of the NFL) – built in a mechanism where the top revenue-generating clubs share with the low revenue-generating clubs that are based in small markets (i.e., less than 2.5 million homes) in order to provide strong competitive balance across the League.

3 **Owned Properties**: Over the past decade or so, the NHL has built its own group of properties, namely its outdoor games (e.g., Heritage Classic) and the Stanley Cup playoffs.

4 **Creating Player Wealth**: During Commissioner Bettman's tenure, the average salary of players has gone up nearly 10-fold from US$350,000 to US$3.5 million. Plus, League efforts to support the development of its stars through sponsorship, video games, and digital media have increased.

5 **Esports and the NHL**: The EA Sports NHL Game, in its 31st version in 2022, has been a successful video game for two decades and serves as the basis for the NHL working with EA Sports to build a comprehensive esports environment (tournaments, games, star players, etc.). In June 2022, the NHL held its 5th World Gaming Championships in Europe and North America.

6 **Sports Betting and the NHL**: The NHL, like the other major North American professional leagues, has embraced gambling on its games through partnerships and sponsorships. MGM Resorts was named the official gaming partner and resort destination of the NHL in 2018, the first time such a partnership was formed. A multi-year extension was signed in February 2022, including the BetMGM product.

7 **Ability to Adapt and Change**: Having moved through more than 20 percent of the 21st century, League executives have needed to recognize the ever-pressing move toward "digital bodies," artificial intelligence, virtual reality, data analytics, surveillance technology, modern policing, mental health therapy, and evolving athlete rights.

These are just seven examples showing that hockey matters but always with an eye toward workable solutions. This holds true for your work or efforts for your firm, start-up, or department. In simple fact, we think hockey matters because meaningful games are played. And because hockey lessons and abstracts are notably beneficial when studied or modeled.

We see the work ethic of NHL players and intense efforts they put into every shift. Games and names are frequently forgotten but on any given night in any NHL arena, there are players giving everything they have and not worrying about whether they will be remembered as the best player on the ice.

They are, in large part, just grateful to have reached a place, the NHL, where their efforts are appreciated. More often than not, their achievements give meaning to others around them.

Looking at your own life, you may not feel you have achieved your dreams or reached your potential. You may think you can never achieve the equivalent of skating just one shift in the NHL. But trust us, you have more to give. More water in your well.

Let the NHL be an inspiration. If you are watching a game, know that the NHL is inspirational because of the stories hidden inside every sweater. Every one of the players in the arena had doubts they weren't big enough, fast enough, accurate enough, tough enough, skilled enough, or hungry enough.

And yet every single player on the ice made it through Juniors or the NCAA, through the SHL, Professional Hockey Federation, AHL, or the rough-and-tumble leagues in Sweden, Russia, or Finland.

It reminds us of the Slater Brothers movie *Odd Man Rush* that came out in September 2020 about an injured hockey-playing collegian knowing he will never reach the NHL but deciding to play professionally in Sweden. He has everything going against him but guts it out.

We hope you get our point. We must want to improve and must adapt to the challenges we face. In the 2020 to 2022 period, the NHL faced major hurdles. They weren't easy to address and revealed weaknesses. Critics complained. Cynics doubted.

Still, the NHL came back. As it had after brutal lockouts and pandemic bubbles, it consistently filled stadiums to show us hockey matters a lot during tough times. The NHL evolved with the times.

WINNING THE DRAW

5

Smart Copycats Can Run with the Big Dogs

When we were kids, having someone call us a "copycat" was usually an insult. It meant we lacked originality. Couldn't think of something funny on our own. It almost always stung.

But what if acting like a copycat was a good thing? What if adopting a copycat strategy allowed us to run with the big dogs?

The copycat strategy in business is often the smartest thing an organization can consider and cost-efficiently construct. Nike built its brand through endorsement deals with the world's greatest athletes. Today, all of its major competitors (e.g., Adidas, Li Ning, Puma, Reebok, New Balance, Under Armour) have employed that approach. Google Home followed Amazon Echo. The list goes on.

Let's look at an example where the NHL borrowed smartly from the mighty NFL.

On February 16, 2005, NHL Commissioner Gary Bettman canceled the 2004–5 NHL season. The 2004–5 season was supposed to be the 88th in League history and not a single contest of the planned 1200+ games were ever played.

No Stanley Cup awarded. Fans enraged. Employees laid off. Owners lost any popularity they once held. And money as well. Players missed a season of their careers and all the stats, salary, and accolades associated with those performances.

By all accounts it was a disaster for everyone.

But now, more than 18 years later, we can look back with a very different view and suggest – in our humble opinions and from a business perspective – that hockey's "lost" season was worth it because of a copycat approach.

We're not saying the NHL fan in us agreed with or liked what happened. We don't. We really don't. In fact, we hated it and wished the Stanley Cup had been contested and awarded.

Perhaps that was the year a Canadian team (Calgary or Ottawa) would have won the first Cup since the Montreal Canadiens in 1993. Or, perhaps San Jose's Sharks – one of the most successful clubs of the past 20 years without ever winning the Cup – would have broken their curse. Maybe Martin Brodeur and his New Jersey Devils would have captured their fourth Cup.

The Impact on Players of Lost Opportunity

Let's also not forget lost personal accolades. As an aging Alexander Ovechkin continues fighting Father Time (as of July 2022) and keeps scoring goals at a high rate in pursuit of Wayne Gretzky's all-time record, let's remember 2004–5 was supposed to be his rookie season.

Could he have added another 40 or 50 goals to his career tally? What if that extra season of NHL experience had created a cumulative impact over time and added an additional 100 goals to his record? Is that possible?

And what was the impact on the retired player front? One favorite example is Jaromir Jagr, the NHL's second all-time leading scorer, who was playing in his prime that year. He scored 123 points the following season, so arbitrarily adding another 123 to his total would have put him over 2,000 points, a milestone achieved only by Wayne Gretzky.

If you also consider Jagr spent three of his "young" years playing in the KHL and another one of his "prime" seasons was reduced to 48 games (from 82) due to a labor dispute, the "lost season" debate (related to his career achievements) intensifies. Forecasts are run. Debates rage.

Another fact is that a set of mega-stars in their 30s and early 40s never played again. Some of them may have already been thinking about retirement, but the full-year break certainly pushed some legends away from the game. Names like Mark Messier, Adam Oates, and Ron Francis (all top 10 all-time leading NHL point scorers) and elite defensemen Scott Stevens and Al MacInnis – both (at the time) top 10 all-time leading scoring defensemen in the NHL – chose to retire.

The list is almost endless, and we imagine by now you've added your own favorite players (or team outcomes) to this story.

Quite simply, lost games are painful on many levels because a season voided (or halved) is a gap in history. In the worst case of a lost season, for the players involved, there is no record of their official involvement in that season.

Similarly, the two truncated seasons for the NHL due to COVID-19 left players short of their historic goals. Each club lost between 11 and 14 games in the 2019–20 season, and all played a 56-game 2020–1 season (a reduction of 26 games each). They lost shifts, minutes, goals scored, games played, assists, penalty minutes, fights, and shutouts. Add to this the many players who lost games due to COVID-19 protocols and many who lost another half-season from their career.

For example, if Ovechkin retires short of Gretzky's career record, or even 50 (the total he scored in 2021–2) behind, some of us will forever wonder "what if?" when it comes to discussing the number of times the NHL wasn't in session. As of the end of the 2021–2 season, he had lost two full seasons of potential games due to COVID and collective bargaining.

Consider the Messier case. He officially retired in September of 2005, just before the start of the 2005–6 NHL season but nearly a year and a half since he'd last played (due to the 2004–5 lockout). At the time, he was just 11 games shy of setting the NHL record for most games played (then held by Gordie Howe and now by Patrick Marleau). Many of Messier's stats were so close to new levels (e.g., six goals shy of 700, seven assists below 1,200, and just 13 points from reaching 1,900). They are all levels few players have ever reached.

The Most Important Part of the Story

You can see why the fan in us is bothered. But let's stay focused on the business side, which is, after all, the focus of this book. Here we offer a different view and return to our copycat.

If you look back on NHL history in the 21st century and use a baseball term, the NHL decision in 2004–5 was the equivalent of a home run. And not a home run down the foul line that just sneaks over the fence, but a massive "moon shot" into the far upper deck of a deep stadium. A near 500-foot drive. That kind of home run.

How could a painful lockout be so important to the NHL? Well, we would argue it was a brilliant example of the NHL using the copycat strategy.

One need only look at the NFL's collective bargaining agreement (CBA) for 1993, which was extended in both 1998 and 2002 and ultimately was maintained (in essence) during the 2006, 2011, and 2020 agreements.

Why would the NHL copy the NFL's blueprint for a revenue-sharing/competitively balanced league? Easy. Because the NFL is the most financially successful professional sports league in North America and arguably anywhere in the world. Its franchises are balanced, and its owners are all in strong financial positions.

For the NFL to reach that platform, a lot of groundwork was laid. And like those competitors seeking to keep up with Nike, Netflix, Amazon, Disney, and Apple, why shouldn't the NHL consider copying a best practice from a competitor? If the NHL's owners were struggling (and many were) and the NFL's owners and players were enjoying the benefits of record revenues, was there something in the NFL's CBA to emulate?

To start, the NHL's 2005 CBA was structured to set the stage for revenue sharing (hockey-related revenues), competitive balance, and the subsequent creation of new assets designed to bring more dollars to the entire League. To all NHL constituents (including the players).

Although the early days following the new deal did not see much of a change, during the next 15 years, the NHL steadily increased numerous financial metrics, including its sponsorship revenue. IEG reports that NHL sponsorship revenues increased from US$367 million in the 2010–11 season to US$559.5 million in the 2017–18 season[1] to US$676 million in 2020–1.[2]

Similar arguments can be made for media dollars following the signing of League deals with Rogers Sportsnet (Canada) and NBC Sports (USA). The Sportsnet deal was the largest media deal ever signed in Canada, at CDN$5.2 billion for a 12-year agreement (2014–15 season to the 2025–6 season),[3] while the new ESPN/

Turner Sports agreement with the NHL – at seven years and more than US$4 billion – follows the previous NBC–NHL contract, which was a 10-year extension that ran from 2011 through to 2021 and was worth a reported US$2 billion.

Second, the new CBA resulted in rule changes designed to make the game faster, reduce "clutching and grabbing" (i.e., a tactic used by defenders to slow down a fast forward), increase the number of goals scored, and produce a more exciting on-ice product.

Next, the CBA was finally re-designed to build a culture of competitive balance, where any club in any market – big or small – held an even-playing-field chance to compete each year from a financial perspective. The primary method to achieve this was putting in place mechanisms to control individual player and team-level salaries. This was accomplished by setting both a maximum (i.e., a salary cap) and a minimum (i.e., a salary floor).

That meant each club saw its spending controlled (ensuring competitive balance across all clubs, including those with lower revenues and operating in smaller markets) and all clubs were required to spend a minimum amount (meaning players are more similarly compensated across the League).

For instance, in the first year of the CBA, the floor was US$21.5 million and the cap was US$39 million per club.[4] For the 2019–20 season, prior to COVID-19, those numbers were expected to reach $60.2 million for the floor and $81.5 million for the cap.[5]

Additionally, the new NHL CBA, for the first time in League history, put a lid on individual player salaries within the larger club salary cap. This amount was set at 20 percent of the club-level salary cap. In a similar approach to the club cap, this change was accompanied by the introduction of a minimum NHL player salary, initially set at $450,000 annually.[6]

Thus, the theme of top performers giving up some salary so that the majority (and the lower-paid ones) could benefit came through and was formally recognized. Entry-level salary maximums (i.e., "rookie salary caps") were also added to control salaries in the first few years of a player's NHL career.

The CBA was also designed to balance the players' share of League-wide revenues with overall League revenues. To achieve this parity, a scale was approved whereby the players' share would range between 54 percent and 57 percent depending on composite League revenues in any given year.

The new CBA de-emphasized performance bonuses in lieu of base salary and included expanded provisions for unrestricted free agency for players later in their careers. Signing bonuses were also addressed, with a cap put on the size of a signing bonus and its amount allocated over the contract's total length and included within the salary maximums.

Finally, the revenue-sharing aspects of the new CBA were big shifts from the previous agreement between the League and its players. For instance, subsidies were included for clubs in the bottom half of the League in terms of revenues and for clubs that exist in small markets (measured by population).

Although there is some argument about the validity of the *Forbes* published data on major sport league financials, our contacts tell us the relative nature (i.e., club-to-club) of the data is worth looking at and that the main concern is how some revenues are counted or allocated. The only other league in the world that possibly compares to the NFL for efficiency and competitive balance is Germany's Bundesliga, but it is an ocean away and less profitable, making the NFL the obvious best practice to emulate.

If readers take a quick visit to www.forbes.com/lists and peruse the MLB, MLS, NBA, NFL, NHL, and club-level data, they will see quickly the NFL produces, by a significant margin, the most profitable set of owned franchises. According to this data, no NFL club has lost money for many years and many of the clubs record significant profitability. Now read Deloitte's annual review of football finance of the five leading European leagues (https://www2.deloitte.com/uk/en/pages/sports-business-group/articles/annual-review-of-football-finance.html) and the NFL's profitability story emerges. Based on *Forbes*' and Deloitte's analyses, the story for the clubs in all the other leagues is very different from the NFL, with many teams reportedly losing money even large market teams with on-field success stories.

The Green Bay Packers, the smallest-market NFL club, is publicly owned and discloses its financials each year, and this data showcases the amount of central revenues that each club receives under revenue sharing. For instance, for the 2020–1 fiscal year, the Packers received US$309 million as part of the revenue-sharing agreement, meaning that each of the 32 NFL clubs received that same amount from the shared revenues from that year.[7]

Clearly, profit is not always the primary motivator for owners of professional sport clubs. In fact, instead of trying to make more money, some owners focus their energies on benefits such as community goodwill, owner ego, or club sustainability.

Although some NFL owners are not solely focused on profit (i.e., it is more important to win a Super Bowl), NFL clubs are all very profitable (according to *Forbes*) and their asset (the value of the franchise) has appreciated (i.e., grown in value) significantly.

Thus, if the NHL leadership in the early 2000s had decided to make a change to improve the financial situation of the League, the NFL's benchmark model would have been the one to study. Whether it is called "best in class" or a "best practice" or a "case study," the most profitable league's approach to business was worth copying.

Numerous famous quotes capture this approach, including "if you can't beat 'em, join 'em" and "imitation (mimicry) is the highest form of flattery." There is a reason those clichés exist.

As detailed earlier in the chapter, the "socialist" changes to the CBA, based on the NFL approach, were highly evident in the 2004–5 NHL CBA and could be described as evidence of a copycat strategy that worked.

In summary, a logical view holds that the NHL copycat strategy implemented during the 2004–5 lockout (which led to the loss of an entire NHL season) transformed its entire business model. The CBA that emerged after that painful work stoppage allowed the NHL to generate a new set of expanded revenues and generate terrific growth for the League during much of the next two decades.

We also argue the change toward the NFL's model made the NHL and its on-ice product far more sustainable despite the short-term public relations cost/damage and revenues/income lost by both the League and NHLPA membership.

Would everyone agree with that choice? No.

As of 2022, traditional NHL fans were still angry their game was taken away from them and no Stanley Cup was awarded. The ire is particularly real to those fans in markets where a contending team existed in 2005. They will always feel that was "their year."

But the flip side of the coin has some very positive aspects. In addition to the new CBA structure, new/young fans started to see an improved product (i.e., less fighting, more scoring, faster pace) that made the NHL's business more sustainable (and able to weather the financial storm brought on by the pandemic of 2020 and 2021).

For anyone looking for examples of things to adopt from the NHL for their own professions, organizations, and industries, this example may stand out. If a model of excellence exists in your local market or sector, if a competitor is achieving prioritized objectives, there is no disgrace in copying (even if it means modifying an original effort to fit specific needs).

There exist multiple instances of successful copycat strategies from other industries, with major players, such as Apple/Samsung, Coke/Pepsi, McDonald's/Burger King, Guinness/Heineken, and Visa/Mastercard/American Express, frequently copying strategies that kept one firm's growth from leaving the other party far behind.

Think about the development of the Apple iPhone. Its existence forced competitors to build their own version that provided similar customer benefits or risk failing (e.g., Blackberry). Additionally, as copycats entered the mobile communication marketplace, Apple (and others) were obligated to create improvements (think the Apple 13) to provide product differentiation. Xiaomi, Chinese manufacturer of the Mi phone, was perhaps the best example of an Apple copycat.

Long ago, in the soda wars, Pepsi decided to show customers Pepsi's taste was as good as or better than Coca-Cola's. Despite trailing Coke in market share in the United States, Pepsi's advertising agency developed a campaign built around a "Pepsi Challenge" where blindfolded soda drinkers sampled both brands. The advertising suggested Pepsi had a preferred taste.

How Do Copycats Do in the End?

Despite an impregnable position as the long-standing number one cola, Coke responded to Pepsi's challenge and decided it would introduce New Coke while retiring traditional Coke. That calculation is generally considered to have massively backfired and Coca-Cola quickly retreated by once again fully supporting and promoting "classic" Coke.

In the footwear wars, when Nike developed "visible air" for the Air line of shoes (Air Jordan, Air Max), it watched with interest as Reebok created its Pump line. While pumping "air" as a concept did not catch on (a copycat approach that did not work), it was clear people buying sneakers were interested in the use of "air" for heel cushioning and a snug fit. Nike had a concept and Reebok did not.

Norm's Nostalgia: Helping Sledge Hockey Join the Big Dogs

We've both had career journeys in sport that featured interesting stops, major challenges, and geographic diversity. For me, one of these stops took place while working with the Government of Canada in the department (Sport Canada) responsible for supporting (amateur) sport in Canada.

After the passing of the *Fitness and Amateur Sport Act* in the Parliament of Canada in 1961, a dedicated government department to create sport policy and support sport programs was created. In the early 2000s, I had the wonderful opportunity to work for Sport Canada, combining my patriotism and my passion for the job. Similar to many Sport Canada employees, I was given the task of being the representative for a few national sport organizations, including Hockey Canada and Sledge Hockey of Canada.

This was a classic example of a big dog represented by Hockey Canada and a very small puppy by Sledge Hockey of Canada. But, and as Rick would say, Hockey Canada was the 200-pound Newfoundland dog at Canada's National Sport Organizations' bowl. With more than a half-million members, an event-hosting program that brings in tens of millions of dollars, a highly trained and sophisticated staff of more than 100 people, and a set of great media partners and sponsors, Hockey Canada was (and remains today) an operation that is the envy of almost every sport organization in Canada.

Sledge Hockey of Canada during the early 2000s was your classic "kitchen table" organization, comprised of devoted (and unpaid) volunteers, many of whom were also players or coaches, who literally ran the national organization out of their homes.

Hockey Canada (founded in 1914) and Sledge Hockey of Canada (founded in 1993) were separate organizations in 2000. One of the duties of my job was to work closely with both and, on behalf of the minister responsible for sport in Canada, and to push for the integration of the Paralympic version of hockey into Hockey Canada. It was actually a very easy exercise as Hockey Canada was open and supportive, and Sledge Hockey of Canada wanted "in." We accomplished this goal with an objective of increasing support and legitimacy of what would become known as para ice hockey with formalized operations under the Hockey Canada banner. Looking back nearly two decades later (and by most published media accounts), this has been achieved.

With roots dating back to Sweden in the 1960s and its Paralympic debut in 1994, sledge hockey is a wonderful game. It is fast-moving and aggressive, like its able-bodied cousin. Played on the same ice surface and with very similar rules, players sit on small sleds that have skate-like blades under them and use hockey sticks that have metal "teeth" at one end so they can be used like ski poles to propel the players. The other end are traditional hockey stick blades designed for passing and shooting the puck.

The Canadian men's national team has competed at 11 World Sledge Hockey Championships, called the World Para Ice Hockey Championships since 2016, winning four, and eight Paralympic Games (capturing the gold medal once in 2006). In an epic match at the 2018 Paralympic Games, the United States beat Canada in overtime to take gold, with the US again taking gold over Canada at the 2022 Paralympic Games, in a 5–0 victory. The US is the dominant country today, having won the past four Paralympic Games. Women's sledge hockey began developing the United States and Canada around 2008 but is not yet a Paralympic sport.

To be sure, copying an existing idea is usually not enough. That's because the originator generally holds a marketplace advantage. Concepts like the "leadership curve" are routinely taught in many graduate business schools because a leadership position allows innovative brands to leverage their home ice advantage where market followers cannot.

On the other hand, if many copycats enter a shallow market, the original innovator is not assured of maintaining market share if it does not competitively respond to the modifications imitators introduce. This is particularly true in the service sector where there is less of a product to emulate and the point of difference is service.

In the last decade, during an age of online retailing from giant providers (like Amazon and Walmart) disrupting entire supply chains, customers have made their position clear. Strong examples can be found in customer-centric tactics like "free shipping," "no-questions-asked returns," "24-hour helplines," and "guaranteed service call-backs in minutes." The COVID-19 pandemic further accelerated movement in digital supply chains and accentuated customer-centric delivery. Companies that didn't instantly offer the same services were almost immediately "punished" by ever-more sophisticated consumers who could switch their online shopping preferences in a flash because Company X offered a service Company Y had not yet added.

We will close by acknowledging that while a copycat may sound like a diminished position, it is not always a negative and it has been shown to work as an effective business strategy to drive growth or to maintain competitive parity.

And, if we seek a warm pop culture smile at the end of this chapter, it's imagining everyone wants to keep up with the cool cats and big dogs. Or as the slogan on a famous T-shirt once noted, "If you can't run with the big dogs, stay on the porch."

6

Brand New Offerings with Creativity

"What's in a name?" is a cliché originally penned by William Shakespeare and, like many phrases the bard coined, is used far too often by journalists. We won't give you the *Romeo and Juliet* back story, but we will argue with Juliet's suggestion that monikers don't matter. They do.

For the NHL and its 32 owners, naming teams is a relatively new pastime (warranting a complex League approval process) largely because 11 new teams have joined the League since 1991. Those 11 have created winners and losers but collectively show how important a name is for a new product or business.

Historically, the NHL has enjoyed three long-standing periods in its history when it was consistent in terms of franchise count. The first, a period of 25 years known as the "Original Six Era" existed from 1942–67 when only six franchises played in the League. This period of stability followed a quarter-century of ongoing growth and contraction and preceded a period of massive expansion during the late 1960s and 1970s.

The second stable era, when the League featured 21 clubs, lasted a dozen years (1979 to 1991) and followed a merger with the rival WHA. It too was followed by a flurry of expansion and relocations in the 1990s, leading to a 30-club League. The League was then a 30-team entity for 17 straight years (2000 to 2017) prior to adding two clubs to join the NFL as a 32-team League.

In reviewing the list of new clubs that joined in the 1990s following the second consistency period, a series of creative, contemporary, and – dare we say – "cool" club names and brands were created for the nine new clubs. We'd also suggest the two newest nicknames (2017's Golden Knights and 2021's Kraken) carried on this smart trend of inspired creativity.

There is certainly a lesson to be learned here for leaders outside of hockey and this is most obvious, as noted, in the NHL's two newest additions: Las Vegas and Seattle. But before we discuss these two, let's offer a quick review of the nine additions from the 1990s.

- **1991**: The San Jose Sharks, located in the predominantly wealthy Bay Area of Northern California, became the 22nd NHL club. Following a public call for names, the club adopted the name "Sharks" because it both offered a ferocious theme and fit with the team's location near the Pacific Ocean.

  Reportedly, the option with the most votes (Sharks was second), the Blades, was vetoed by the club's owners because they felt it could be linked to violent weapons.[1] The logo (a shark biting a hockey stick) and colors (teal, black, and white) were very popular and despite a very weak team on the ice (winning only 17 of their first 80 games in their first season), they set NHL records for merchandise sales across North America, including in faraway Canada where demand was very high for the distinctive jerseys.[2]

A *New York Times* article at the time reported the Sharks accounted for 27 percent of all NHL merchandise sales that year and only Michael Jordan's Chicago Bulls (of the NBA) sold more across all North American professional leagues.[3] Of the 10 teams to follow the Sharks, few would enjoy more profitable associations from their name selection.

- **1992**: The Ottawa Senators and Tampa Bay Lightning joined the NHL as the 23rd and 24th clubs. The Senators opted for a historical branding strategy, adopting the name and logo of the original Ottawa Senators NHL club that existed (intermittently) between 1883 and 1934, winning 11 Stanley Cups. The Senators name also fit with Ottawa, Canada's capital and home to the Canadian Senate. Tampa Bay, alternatively, opted for a strategy like the San Jose Sharks, with an active logo (a bolt of lightning) and colors of blue, black, and white. To some, the Tampa area is known as "lightning alley" and it got that moniker since it reportedly receives the world's most bolts (or strikes) of electricity each year.[4]

- **1993**: The 25th and 26th NHL clubs were added the following season (1993), both with truly unique and creative approaches. First, and most interesting, was the Mighty Ducks of Anaheim, a southern California club owned by the Disney Corporation and named after a series of hockey-themed movies known by the same name (*The Mighty Ducks, D2, D3*), starring Emilio Estevez and released sequentially in 1992, 1994, and 1996.

  Clearly, cross-promotion was part of the team's approach but more important to the NHL was drawing the Walt Disney Corporation into the hockey family. Disney would ultimately buy ABC Television and cable sports giant ESPN in August 1995 and that synergy could only bode well for a League that would ultimately need to enhance its media presence during future broadcast negotiations and network contracts.

The second club added that year – the Florida Panthers – was named after a rare species of big cat that once lived in the metro Miami area where the club plays in Florida. In fact, the panther is Florida's state animal and was facing extinction with only a few remaining. Picking Miami was further evidence of the NHL's desire to fill in open areas on the national map. The Panthers thus became the NHL's southernmost team. This was also the year the Minnesota North Stars relocated to Dallas, emerging as the Dallas Stars (keeping the "Stars" part of the name and some use of the color green but dropping the "North" since Dallas was deep in the heart of Texas).

- **1998**: The NHL's 27th club adopted a strategy very similar to the of the San Jose Sharks with a similar result. In 1998, the Nashville Predators joined the League with a very popular saber-toothed tiger logo and a modern color scheme. The origin of the logo reportedly came about because Nashville was one of but a few archeological sites in the world where the remains of such a tiger had been found. The club selected the logo after an open fan competition led to the selection of the name "Predators."

- **1999**: The Atlanta Thrashers, the 28th club, hit the ice for the first time in 1999 and lasted until 2011 before moving to Winnipeg for a re-birth as the Jets. The Thrashers struggled on and off the ice, and their choice of a brown bird did not enjoy the same kind of merchandising success that other teams leveraged.

Interestingly, the Thrashers were the second failed Atlanta franchise after the Atlanta Flames, a 1972 expansion team that moved to Calgary in 1980. The name "Thrashers" was reportedly the second choice (after Flames) during club-naming deliberations in 1971.[5] Of the 11 new entrants to the League since 1991, a case can be made the Thrashers were the worst ... although the name's relevance and success may have had more to do with the re-selection of Atlanta following the failure of the Flames.

- **2000**: Columbus Blue Jackets and Minnesota Wild brought the League to 30 teams with their launch in 2000 NHL season. In the case of Columbus, the club ran a "name-the-club" contest and received more than 14,000 applications,[6] with the Blue Jackets selected at the end of the process by Columbus's ownership and the NHL.

The name was in honor of the many contributions made by the state of Ohio to the United States, with the logo and its 13 stars representing the 13 original colonies of the United States.

In Minnesota, the Wild was chosen from a set of finalists as a reflection of the Minnesota outdoors and incorporated a bold color palette meant to showcase a forest landscape and the silhouette of a "wild" bear (which is often not seen unless the viewer looks for a silhouetted profile). Also evident in the design is an elongated North Star to honor the previous NHL team (the North Stars) that played in Minneapolis from 1967–93.

What Have We Learned about Club Brands?

Of the nine new clubs added between 1991 and 2000, all but the Thrashers continue today in their original cities and have built appealing brand equity. How and why did these brands emerge as they did? Here is where the learning lies for contemporary organizations.

Specifically, and as described in the following section and captured by figure 6.1, we point to the following five concepts:

1 **Creativity Flows from the Ownership Group Down**: The San Jose Sharks and Ottawa Senators, two of the earliest of this new batch, are also based in high-tech clusters, known as Silicon Valley (San Jose) and Silicon Valley North (Ottawa). San Jose's founding owners were the Gund brothers (George and Gord), astute businessmen from the Cleveland-based Gund family with a passion for the sport business. One of the brothers, Gord, played hockey for Harvard University.

   In the case of Ottawa, founding ownership was a syndicate led by real estate developer Bruce Firestone who leveraged real estate assets and the high-tech growth in Ottawa's west end to win franchise selection in an NHL expansion competition where Ottawa was thought by most to be a long shot at best. Ottawa's win came – by many accounts – because of a poor bid effort by a favored group of buyers in Hamilton.[7]

2 **A Good Brand Will Fit with the Local Market**: Sharks and the California coast. Senators and Ottawa, Canada's capital. Mighty Ducks and Disney. Panthers and Florida. Lightning and Tampa. Blue Jackets and Ohio's state capital. Wild and the Minnesota wilderness. All, in our opinion, work. All hold regional benefit that fits the psyche of the people most likely to emerge as fans.

   This is important because while customers (i.e., fans) are not owners in the financial sense of that word, they are stakeholders and dictate the success of a club as much as the selection of players and the individuals sent onto the ice at any given moment. Your family name, if you run a small business, may not mean anything to local customers but your history in a particular village, town, or city is important.

It's why, even if your company was established only yesterday, many start-ups use language like "Serving Toronto since 2020" even though it shows they have no long-standing presence in the community. The goal is to create permanence and suggest a dedicated commitment to the local stakeholders.

3   **A Good Logo within a Brand Is Important**: The Sharks, again, are the best illustration here. The legendary saber-toothed tiger and Nashville. Even part of a logo can work here – the eye of the bear in the logo of the Minnesota Wild is shaped as a star in honor of the first Minnesota franchise (the North Stars).[8] There is not much sense in bland, boring, and mediocre. Yes, logo or brand design cost money (or time with people working for free), but bad graphics suggest a weak product and a lack of investment in the operation.

4   **A Good Brand Can Fit with the Trends of the Time**: Predators and the popularity of dinosaurs (driven by the movie and theme park ride *Jurassic Park* in the 1990s) have been more than evident (think of the NBA's Toronto Raptors as well). Joining that group in late 2021 was Seattle's Kraken, based on a famed science fiction ocean monster from the film *Clash of the Titans*, Dungeons and Dragons, Greek mythology, and Norse tales.

5   **A Good Brand Has Exceptional Creativity**: While a great city and name that fits are important, the delivery (the marriage) of those components via quality creativity (think logos, colors, third jerseys, a mascot, etc.) is just as – if not more – important. Not everyone is cut out to think about marketing or is talented when it comes to explaining the ideas in their heads. But not to think holistically is a mistake. When the Sharks launched to unparalleled merchandising success for an expansion club, the new club brand was full of attractive coloring, a very appealing logo, a cool mascot, an overall team theme around the "Shark," and well-thought-out marketing from top to bottom.

FIGURE 6.1 *Five Characteristics of a Successful NHL Club Brand*

With the above noted, let's review the NHL's two newest franchises, including the unquestionable success of the Las Vegas Golden Knights. The Knights launched in 2017 and enjoyed one of the greatest years ever for an expansion team. Seattle's Kraken were born in July 2020 and started play in 2021. In both cases, the teams exemplified points number one (creative ownership) and number five (exceptional creativity).

The Golden Knights' first year is one of legend, as far as the first year of expansion franchises go. Most first-year squads, filled with castaways and tired veterans, do not make the playoffs and are lucky not to finish dead last. Instead, the Golden Knights expansion season is, in our view, the most successful (by a wide margin) in major North American professional sport.

Las Vegas had a tremendous regular season (first in their division; fifth overall) and made a "fairy tale" run in the Stanley Cup playoffs, winning three demanding multi-game series over Los Angeles, San Jose, and Winnipeg before losing in the finals to the Washington Capitals. In total, the Knights won 13 playoff games that year, a record for an expansion club. The club's success continued in the following three seasons, with the club for the post-season year posting a winning record and winning a second division title in 2019–20.

A few important activities characterize the success of the Golden Knights. First, the NHL and the Las Vegas ownership group deserve credit for moving quickly and becoming the first major professional league and ownership group to set up operations in the attractive Las Vegas market, ahead of the NFL's Raiders, who began play in 2020.

Las Vegas is a growing tourist destination of renown, with the city's population nearly tripling between 1990 and 2020 and its reputation as a center for gambling, entertainment, conferences, and events on the rise as one of the most popular cities in the world.[9] We imagine it is only a matter of time before the NBA, MLB, and Formula 1 follow the NHL's successful lead.

The business case of people traveling to Vegas to gamble, see a show, and catch their favorite hockey team was a common feature of reports on the Golden Knights' successful bid. The Knights were first, they did it right, and did it with an eye toward sustainability.

Second, the club's management showed they held the ability to draft and trade to put together a team that was immediately competitive. The club's principal owner, Bill Foley – a Texan who grew up in Ottawa (where he fell in love with hockey) – is a successful businessman following time in the US Air Force.

A graduate of the famed West Point academy, where the athletic teams are known as the Black Knights, Foley altered that moniker to Golden Knights. Although not as creative as linking to the market or current trends, the owner's prerogative is another naming strategy that exists in the NHL.[10] In the case of the Las Vegas, the "Golden" could be perceived to fit with the casinos dotting that city's famous strip and the perceived wealth of the local market.

Foley's background in management and sport could also be given some credit for the success of the expansion club on the ice. He selected George McPhee as general manager and Gerard Gallant as head coach, both of whom performed superbly in a rookie season.

Leading into the expansion draft, the club's strategy (and numerous reports have been published supporting the team's success) included acquiring a top goaltender (Marc-Andrew Fleury) with their top pick and leveraging their position in the expansion draft to acquire playable or tradeable talent.[11]

Third, just before the onset of its season, on October 1, 2017, Las Vegas was rocked by a tragic shooting when a gunman opened fire on a music festival from his hotel room, killing nearly 60 people and injuring more than 400 others.

Following the tragedy, the city of Las Vegas and its citizens responded by rallying in many ways, including mass blood donations for the victims. The Golden Knights opening home game, just a couple of weeks later, paid tribute to the victims, served as a show of strength for the city, and was reported by some of the players during a documentary film called *Valiant* to be a huge motivation for them as individuals.[12]

Fourth, marketing – call it *smart* marketing – has been a cornerstone of the Golden Knights success off the ice, amplifying strong links to Las Vegas. "Sin City" is a bright-light, go-big-or-go-home, anything-can-happen place. Perceptions have long suggested the inhabitants are daring, sexy, camp (sightings of Elvis still abound), spontaneous, and, above all, entertainment-minded. An operator that doesn't put on a good show won't last.

This town brings a gambler's mentality to the table and every night the regulars and the tourists expect fireworks, splashy water fountains, show girls, and top-notch singers. For a team to play in Vegas and not understand the market, or grasp what its fans want, would be foolish.

Rick's Recall: Cool Minor League Names

I went for a workout recently and, needing something ratty to wear, reached into my locker and pulled out a Jacksonville Lizard Kings t-shirt. First reaction? Greatest brand name ever for a minor league hockey team. *Ever.*

The Lizard Kings (undoubtedly named in honor of legendary Doors singer Jim Morrison) operated in the ECHL from 1995–2000 before folding. Whether the target market was kids, hipsters, or old rock and rollers, their savage green lizard logo (a reptile wearing a crown and brandishing a hockey stick) was perfect. Heck, even the screenwriters for Marvel movies would love it.

But were the Lizard Kings the best named minor league hockey team ever? This conundrum calls for a list and this Recall seems like the perfect place to discuss the value of creativity when it comes to inspiring sales or building corporate pride.

To that end, here is my top 10 all-time minor league hockey team names:

1 Jacksonville Lizard Kings (ECHL)
2 Orlando Solar Bears (IHL/ECHL)
3 Amarillo Gorillas (CHL)
4 Rockford IceHogs (AHL)
5 Austin Ice Bats (WPHL/CHL)
6 Louisiana Ice Gators (ECHL)
7 Lowell Lock Monsters (AHL)
8 Quebec Rafales (IHL)
9 Greenville Swamp Rabbits (ECHL)
10 Roanoke Rail Yard Dogs (SPHL)

And a bonus extra for the end of the list? Well, I'd have to include the team whose jersey I'm proudest to wear due to family. A black Newfoundland Growlers, ECHL Kelly Cup 2019 champions sweater. As everyone should know, the Growlers logo features a tough-looking Newfoundland dog … a great, loafing goalie when playing pick-up hockey on a frozen pond.

You may think this exercise foolish but our reason for including the above team names is to salute the efforts local operators put into making hockey relevant (albeit briefly) in places like Louisiana, Florida, and Texas.

Selling tickets for professional sports teams is often difficult and, in an era when competition exists in hundreds of formats (TV, streaming devices, the internet, movies, concerts, the beach, etc.), we salute every organization that understands it faces significant competition by responding with creativity and all-out hustle.

It is convenient to suggest naming a minor league hockey team is easier than running a tool-and-die shop or operating a landscaping business. But what if you could start again and name your organization anything you wanted? What imagery would you select? Would your company have a mascot? Would your office reflect the dynamic energy of the Cleveland Monsters? The whimsy and hip attitude of the Solar Bears? The fierceness of the Ice Gators?

Many people go through life, trudging to work, dreading the monotony of their everyday chores. That's why we look to sport for entertainment. But can you leverage a concept like the Swamp Rabbits or the Lock Monsters? Can you imagine an accounting firm or hardware store offering a more dynamic branded relationship for weary customers to consider?

So, tell us … if you could pick your company's mascot, what would you use?

And don't you agree the Lizard Kings is the greatest name ever for a hockey team?

The Rise of the Kraken

Finally, to conclude the chapter, a few words on Seattle, the newest NHL franchise, and one that has clearly set the stage for its business success in the 2021–2 season, its first. The booming city, home to Amazon, Microsoft, Starbucks, and Getty Images, is a dynamic place where the mountains meet the ocean, and two of the key factors (ownership and brand) checked off easily for owners when they introduced their Kraken logo.

The first success factor in the Kraken case is about Seattle's ownership syndicate and management team, a group that features a dynamic set of entrepreneurs who have a deep background in entertainment and professional sport ownership.

David Bonderman, billionaire businessman and minority owner of the Boston Celtics (NBA) and Jerry Bruckheimer, legendary film and television producer, are the two majority owners. Tod Leiweke is the founding CEO of the club and brought vast experience across numerous professional sports during his more than 35 years in the industry.

This group, along with the NHL and civic leaders, worked to create a successful bid, including a major renovation of the former Key Arena that was quickly named Climate Pledge Arena after Amazon (as the naming rights sponsor) began calling for environmental awareness.

On top of that, the team's sales staff engineered a pre-launch ticketing effort that delivered more than 40,000 deposits for future tickets! We think even the coldest cynic would allow that is highly impressive.

The second factor, branding, also came across as smart and creative. As noted earlier, the Kraken (a mythical giant octopus) fits with both the local fish market (oceanside city) and current trends (high popularity of science fiction) and was accompanied by attractive colors of deep-sea blue and ice blue (with a touch of red). The Marvel Studios folks would be pleased.

The team was instantly rewarded when the Kraken made Seattle the best-selling expansion team in NHL merchandising history. In fact, one industry source (Fanatics) reported the Kraken topped the previous merchandise sales record by more than 50 percent.

Interestingly, the club has both a primary and a secondary logo, with the secondary including the city's famed tower, the Space Needle.[13] Further, in taking a page from the Ottawa Senators and Minnesota Wild, the Kraken logo includes the "S" shape, reportedly a tribute to the long-defunct Seattle Metropolitans, a highly successful NHL club that played from 1915–24 and qualified for the Stanley Cup on three occasions, winning in 1917 before facing the Montreal Canadiens in the 1919 finals.

That best-of-five Cup was tied at two games each (and one tie) when the series was abruptly canceled prior to the sixth game due to an outbreak of the Spanish flu that touched most of the players and led to the death of a Canadiens player on March 29, 1919.[14] Yes, about 101 years to the day before COVID-19 first impacted the NHL.

That the Seattle Kraken would honor a historic ancestor from a century earlier was notable and expressed the sincere goodwill of a local business wishing to show allegiance to its dynamic hometown. One other historic commitment made by Seattle's ownership, beyond a fierce commitment to front-office diversity, equity, and inclusion, was selecting Everett Fitzhugh as the first Black play-by-play announcer for any NHL franchise.

Like many NHL expansion teams during the previous 30 years, the Golden Knights and the Kraken have continued a trend of selecting strong names and designing dynamic brands capable of benefitting multiple stakeholders.

7

Innovation: How the NHL Has Thrived in This Space

Hockey, and specifically the NHL version, is one of the fastest and most aggressive games on earth. To play, even at a lower level as we have, is to get a taste of this. To watch, whether sledge or able-bodied, male or female, is be entertained.

At the NHL level, it moves. It's physical and hard hitting. Mentally demanding.

You must be fast and strong to play at this level.

The little black rubber disc is fast. No one can outskate the puck. For added value, the puck flies. Leaves the ice. Sometimes at more than 100 miles per hour. In fact, NHL defenseman Zdeno Chara, who is featured in a later chapter, long held the hardest shot record at just under 109 mph.

Spectators, many of whom have never played the game, love what hockey represents. The courage and commitment, the unspoken rules, the respect players must show the game. And then there are larger-than-life concepts like Country (the Winter Olympics) and Cup.

Still, some parts of the NHL's game have been slow to evolve.

Innovation was not originally seen in hockey the way it was in other major sports. Equipment, for instance, was particularly slow to evolve. Wooden sticks have been used for nearly 100 years, most of them straight (and many not lasting beyond a few games). Although, to be fair, we must point out some players sing the virtues of the wooden stick. Al MacInnis, Hall of Famer and the third highest scoring defenceman in NHL history, retired from the game in 2005 using primarily a wooden stick. MacInnis, who split his career between Calgary and St. Louis, said the trade-off of lost accuracy for a few more miles per hour was not worth it. Of note, on six occasions he won the hardest shot competition at the NHL All-Star game.

Even current sticks, composed of composite materials (e.g., aluminum, carbon fiber) and producers of very hard shots with wicked movement, break at a high rate, with negative ramifications for the game.

How often did the greatest goal scorer of the current era, Alexander Ovechkin of the Washington Capitals, shatter a stick and skate to the bench to retrieve a new one while play continued and scoring opportunities were lost? Some reports suggest NHL players break their customized sticks so often that team administrators are left scratching their heads for both financial and on-ice performance reasons. Yes, stick destruction is costly for clubs and breaks often happen at inopportune times.[1]

Goalie pads and masks, skate, and helmet technology were also slow to change. It was not until the 1970s that goalies wore masks and the late 1990s before players fully (and regularly) protected their heads. Even today, many players do not wear protective visors, even though preventable injuries have happened around them. Sometimes career-ending ones.

But this reality is more about player culture, individual comfort, tradition, and resistance to change rather than innovation.

Many reports suggest the very first goaltender to wear a mask was a woman, Elizabeth Graham, who was attempting to safeguard her teeth. In the NHL, the first goalie to regularly wear a mask was Jacques Plante in 1959 and this was against the wishes of his coach, Toe Blake.

The coach might have gotten his way that November if he'd been allowed to carry a backup goaltender, but NHL teams didn't make room for substitute goalies at the time and if Plante refused to continue (he'd just been struck in the face and stitched up), the Canadiens would have forfeited the game. As Plante started wearing a mask, his bravery and even his dedication to the team were questioned.

We tell these stories because many businesses are slow to seek change or even accept it. They cling to outdated concepts or inefficient protocols because of fear, cost, or naivete. This type of thinking can't continue, especially in the economic environment of 2022 where inflation is high, supply chains are constrained, talent is scarce, and interest rates are rising.

There are numerous modern examples where companies resisted computers, email, the "cloud," drones, online retailing, website marketing, and health regulations designed to protect employees (like providing masks or face shields). These "resistance" snapshots may seem unimaginable but every older employee remembers the legendary naysayers who complained bitterly about having to learn how to use computers and type their own memos.

Areas of NHL Innovation

The point of this chapter is to emphasize areas where the NHL has embraced innovation (often in the face of "traditional" fans, not the League, resisting change). Herewith are a few of our favorites, some old, some new:

1 **The Glowing Puck**: When US Network FOX covered the NHL, it introduced – in 1996 – its FoxTrax technology, or a "glowing puck" to allow fans to find and follow the very small puck on their TV screens. And, although the innovation received considerable backlash from long-time fans (who were used to a fast-moving black dot), it was a success with new fans, particularly in the southern United States (where the NHL was attempting to grow the game).

Prior research showed that those newcomers, as they were exposed to the NHL, had difficulty following the action (or specifically, knowing where to look). Keep in mind this was before HDTV and large screens in most homes. Thus, some fans resisted "liking" hockey because it was too hard to watch. Now, looking back, perhaps the best testament to the NHL's experiment were the many copycats (see chapter 5) that followed in other sports, such as the glowing first down line in the NFL and the glowing strike zone in MLB.

2 **3-on-3 Overtime**: For almost a century, the NHL awarded ties. And these tied games happened frequently. For instance, Montreal's famous 1976–7 season was, by many accounts, the most successful in NHL history. Of their 80 regular season games that year, the Canadiens only lost eight. They scored an impressive 387 goals while allowing only 171. They swept the best-of-seven Stanley Cup in four straight games (with three of the four games decided by two goals or more). But the rarely discussed aspect of that legendary Montreal season record was the existence of 12 ties. They tied 15 percent of their games.

Yes, in 15 out of every 100 games (on average) the fan left with a feeling of dissatisfaction.

At the time, if an NHL game ended in a tie score after 60 minutes of play, it was recorded as a tie and each club received a point (versus two points for a win). Montreal's epic season produced a 60–8–12 record or 82.5 percent of all possible points.

Considering the strength of the Canadiens club in 1976–7, it seems likely Les Habs would have won most (if not all) of those tie games if they had of gone to overtime, so perhaps a 70–10 season would have been possible, even 72–8.

The overtime experiment that started in 1983 was the inclusion of sudden death overtime (also known as "the golden goal") that incorporated a five-minute extra period where the game would still be recorded as a tie if no goal was scored in that overtime period.

In 2005, the League added a shootout to decide any game that was tied following overtime, thereby eliminating any ties as possible outcomes (although the overtime/shootout loser would be awarded a single point). Most importantly, this increased fan satisfaction.

Then, in 2015, to increase the number of goals in overtime and reduce the number of shootouts, the NHL added 3-on-3 format for overtime (as opposed to the typical 5-on-5 format of NHL games) to again increase excitement, scoring, and wins. The result was successful because the best players stayed on the ice, with lots of room to move and little help for goaltenders. Again, the fans won.

3 **The Department of Player Safety**: In 2011, in a then bold move (that looks brilliant in hindsight), the NHL named former NHL player Brendan Shanahan – a long-time Detroit Red

Wings star and a respected "tough" player – to lead the newly formed Department of Player Safety. The mandate of the department was to reduce unsafe actions on the ice and reduce injuries. Readers might respond by saying, "That isn't very innovative." And they would be right. But the innovation at play here was not in the "what" but the "how."

As with any social change effort, the change agent has numerous tools available, grouped broadly as law, education, and marketing. As an example, if a government seeks to reduce drinking and driving, it can put in place large fines and jail time for perpetrators (i.e., legal sanctions), can launch a nationwide communication campaign to inform people of the perils of drinking and driving (i.e., education), and/or can convincingly "market" to "drinkers" an outcome that is produced by a change in behavior (e.g., videos of the scenes of car accidents with victims shown).

This is where businesses can take a card from the NHL's playing deck. Shanahan could have increased the volume and frequency of suspensions, increased resources to review game tapes to find more instances where penalties were warranted, or visited each team at their pre-season training camp to educate players (with a smart ex-pro) about player on-ice safety.

He could have done some of these things but the action taken, which still resonates (and remember this was 2011, not 2022), was using video explanations for each of his decisions, with each video played on the major telecasts of NHL games in Canada (CBC *Hockey Night in Canada*) and the USA (NBC *Game of the Week*). In those settings, he explained in detail his decision, how he reached his conclusion, what he was trying to prevent, and why (or why not) a suspension was given. With repeat offenders, he explained the increased penalty that resulted.

This practice continued with former NHL players Stéphane Quintal (2013 to 2017) and George Parros (2017 to present) succeeding Shanahan. Although the protocol has undergone challenges (namely dealing with criticism of favoritism or inconsistent decisions), the use of video explanations, mainly for transparency, was an innovation that truly benefitted the League.

Norm and Rick on Rule Changes as Innovation

As we were writing this book, as we've often done in our 12 years as a writing duo, we held countless phone chats, Zoom meetings, and email exchanges on key subjects for the book. The innovation topic was one of those and as we dug into it, our curiosity led us to ask, "How often does an organization change its rules?"

We ask because many hockey fans may believe leagues like the NHL never change their requirements or governance. That the game is always, if not mythically, the same. In fact, for the NHL, it's quite the opposite.

Since the League was founded in 1917, the professional game has undergone hundreds of alterations and not long ago, Jordan Epstein of Fox Sports chronicled the biggest rule changes during the first 100 years of the NHL's history. They include:

- Permitting goalies to drop to the ice
- Painting two lines on the ice, creating three zones
- Introducing a penalty for passing the puck backward into the defensive zone
- Enhancing forward passing rules
- Refining the offside rule
- Creating the penalty shot (with goalies not allowed to move more than one foot forward)

- Establishing icing rules
- Modifying the penalty shot rule
- Resurfacing ice between periods using icing machines (Zambonis)
- Discontinuing regular season overtime periods (due to WWII)
- Introducing red line to reduce offsides calls (and speed up the game)
- Releasing a player from the penalty box (on a minor infraction) after an opposing goal is scored
- Prohibiting bench-clearing during fights
- Creating a sudden death overtime period for games during the regular season
- Employing video replays for goals
- Managing offensive players in the goal crease
- Redefining high sticking
- Contesting sudden death overtime with four players and a goalie
- Eliminating the center line and adjusting offsides rules (again!)
- Downsizing goaltender equipment
- Not allowing icing to facilitate line substitutions

Clearly, the 2022 version of the game is drastically different than the 1917 edition. As recently as the delayed start of the 2020–1 season, a new offside rule was put in place to further speed up the game. Prior to 2019–20, a series of new amendments tied to expanded video review, enhanced player safety, and the encouragement of offensive prowess to aid goal-scoring were approved, with additional secondary rules modified for coaching challenges tied to offside calls, goalie interference, and goals scored.

In other words, the NHL is not standing still, relaxing poolside with a flawed perception its product is perfect. It is changing on the fly. The commissioner's office is charged with protecting the game but the product, the entertainment service the NHL provides to its fans, plus the safety of the players, can always stand a review to determine what is working and what isn't.

That's why groups like the NHL use a rules committee to constantly assess and optimize their operating manual. And those rules are written or upheld with a 360-degree view of every constituent. They are reviewed often with an aim to make the game as appealing as possible for fans and safe for players.

Is your company doing the same?

4 **Outdoor Games**: This concept might be the most successful innovation created in North American professional sport since the turn of millennium. First held in 2003 and now an annual occurrence, these games turned back the clock to the roots of the game and touched on a nostalgia that fans have shown they value. For any former player from the northern US or Canada, they'll remember those glorious winter days of playing on a perfectly frozen rink, pond, or lake. See *Norm's Nostalgia* "Outdoor Hockey with My Kids" about just such a story.

These are some of the greatest memories people have. But the innovation was much more than a single game. There was variety on numerous levels: the first was business and economic vitality. The games, often played on holidays, were a resounding success, selling out much larger baseball and football stadiums across North America while attracting strong TV ratings. These contests now include (i) the Heritage Classic (a game hosted by a Canadian team in a Canadian city), and (ii) the Winter Classic (an annual game hosted on New Year's Day in the United States).

Often, these games attracted fans who previously had not attended a hockey game in a large outdoor stadium. Second, innovations required stadium hosts to address winter weather (or sunshine) while managing highest quality playing conditions for an official regular season game where statistics are recorded.

In some years, the games have been held in southern locations (e.g., California) with warm temperatures. This required innovative steps turning the field into a giant freezer capable of keeping ice on a 70-degree day, often with the sun shining on the ice for hours prior to puck drop. Both Los Angeles (MLB's Dodger Stadium) and the Bay Area (Levi's Stadium of the NFL's San Francisco 49ers) of California have hosted outdoor games. The net result? Massive crowds, new fans exposed to the game, healthy TV ratings, and a New Year's Day holiday-type occasion created for NHL fans rivaling the one-day excitement football fans feel for the NFL's Super Bowl.

Norm's Nostalgia: Outdoor Hockey with My Kids

In the fall of 2015, I fulfilled a lifelong dream when my wife and I purchased a cottage.

Having grown up in "cottage country" north of Toronto, it was something I'd always wanted and dreamed about. Additionally, my wife – who is from France (where buying a cottage is only for the very wealthy) – bought into my dream.

Over the course of many years, we searched but were always limited by our financial resources and career movement. For a decade, we never found anything we liked or could afford. Finally, in the summer of 2015, we visited Mont Tremblant, a renowned ski resort north of Montreal, for the Ironman Triathlon and found a spot on a lake about 30 minutes from Tremblant (Lac Chapleau) just by the small village of La Minerve.

It was a triathlete's playground in the summer (ideal for me), with a lake perfect for swimming, quiet hilly roads and trails for biking or running, and a wonderful location for raising a growing family.

In the winter, Mont Tremblant is arguably home to the best (and biggest) ski resort in Eastern North America, attracting thousands of downhill and cross-country skiers each year. Additionally, due to the latitude and elevation of the area, skiers generally get plenty of snow from December to April.

One thing I had not realized was just how buying a cottage in Quebec would also create an amazing source of hockey nostalgia! And that flood of warm memories hit me just weeks after our purchase was approved, when we arrived in early December to find a perfect natural skating rink. It was our lake, stretching for miles, frozen perfectly.

Literally within minutes of arrival, we were skating, then playing hockey – all six of us – on a rink that was all ours. Boots for nets, snowbanks for boards, wooden sticks, and 3-on-3 glory for each family member.

Ever since that first outing, big outdoor hockey games have become a staple of our winter visits to the chalet, including an annual New Year's game with as many as 20 people playing.

Hockey outdoors? It is so special it is hard to believe the NHL did not attempt their Winter Classics 50 years ago.

5 **Hiring Gary Bettman**: Think back to the early 1990s. The NHL
was clearly the number four league in North America. League
revenues were less than US$500 million dollars and the aver-
age player salary hovered around US$350,000. Although televi-
sion coverage in Canada was very good, it was sporadic at best
in the United States and the League lacked a national deal.

Enter Bettman, whose hire was certainly out of the box. He
was an NBA lawyer with no hockey background. And he switched
leagues at a time when the NBA was expanding rapidly under the
leadership of David Stern. Bettman was one of Stern's lieutenants.

Although Bettman has endured his detractors due to issues with
work stoppages and clubs leaving Canada, the numbers (taken
in aggregate) speak for themselves as both total League revenues
and average player salaries have increased more than 10-fold during his 28 years at the helm.

FIGURE 7.1 *Five Examples of the NHL Being Innovative*

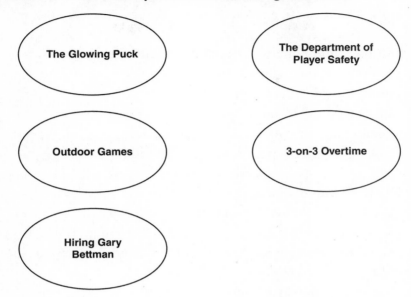

It is often suggested that while many individuals think they would like to lead, they would never agree to the loneliness found in making hard decisions nor survive the criticism fired at them from all directions. Commissioner Bettman was an innovative hire and one to whom much credit for the League's growth must be offered.

Each of these five examples is summarized in figure 7.1 and illustrates how the NHL's innovations can be adopted in other contexts.

Figure 7.1 captures five examples of NHL innovations. These highlight a few key points:

1 Don't always just listen to your core (or traditional) customers. Think also about how to engage new ones (e.g., the glowing puck). Yes, the traditionalists are the bread and butter of anyone's business but failing to attract new customers will ultimately cause new problems the traditionalists can't solve.

2 Prioritize fan (customer) satisfaction over tradition or "the way it's always been" (e.g., 3-on-3 overtime). Great products need enhancements to keep from getting stale and this requires constant (and honest) review if the brand or event is to stay relevant as local, national, and global environments (and economies) morph and change.

3 Invest sufficient (if not major) resources toward infrastructure and put influential people in charge of your biggest challenges (e.g., Department of Player Safety). People, especially leaders, make a massive difference in every field but they also need foundational support to change perceptions.

4 Take big risks with your best product (e.g., Outdoor Games). Except for monopolies (which are generally illegal), big brands need big ideas, and your best product likely has the most revenue potential.

5 Hire your leaders from outside-of-the-box places (e.g., Bettman) by understanding what your organization wants to become (i.e., mission, vision, values, goals) and by finding a candidate who fits with that vision and mission.

We willingly admit it is often scary to embrace new employees and emerging technology and many long-standing or bureaucratic employees consistently resist change. Indeed, change management is one of the most important areas of modern business thinking. We understand some companies can't afford to innovate because of the capital cost ramifications. We recognize that following on the heels of a major disruption, many businesses are simply trying to keep their current workers employed.

But consider this: following almost every downturn, economic depression, technological disrupter, or pandemic, companies that invested in themselves and their workforce saw notable gains.

Nothing can stand still (sometimes strangely stated as "nature ab-hors a vacuum").

All things (people, places, policies, politicians, probates, pric-ing, promotions, and protocols) change. Some quickly and some more slowly. Some change for logical reasons and others because the market dictated the change. Some evolve and some die.

Every organization should anticipate disruption and find ways to welcome it. A perfect example may be the NHL and NHL-PA's decision in late June 2022 to sign a partnership agreement with non-fungible token (NFT) distribution platform Sweet. This made Sweet the official NFT digital collectibles marketplace and an official NFT partner of the NHL, NHLPA, and NHL Alumni Association (NHLAA). It also meant NHL fans could start cre-ating digital collections composed of cinematic, high-definition game highlights from past and present NHL seasons and dozens of other cutting-edge features sought by NFT collectors. Sweet's platform was expected to give hockey fans an ability to buy, sell, collect, and trade in a newly created NHL marketplace.

We think the NHL continues to evolve and has done so for more than 100 years.

8

Marketing and Promoting the NHL Way: Relevant to the Day

As the NHL has continued its global success and growth over the past three decades, we observed numerous opportunities and examples where NHL-inspired marketing or promotion could be adapted and used in a variety of other contexts. Importantly, many of these tactics were perfect fits with the issues and environment of the time. Arguably, they were best practices.

In other words, businesses can learn something from each of a handful of NHL examples relevant to specific situations.

Why is this concept of "relevant to the time" so important?

First, time is a variable in almost every model that predicts financial markets, stock prices, firm value, and sales price. And, in many cases, time is simply the most important variable. Think about the life cycle of a firm: outcomes are very different during the start-up years versus the point considered market maturity. Think about the impact of points in time on business decisions (e.g., COVID-19, Black Lives Matter, the 9/11 attacks, Cold War, World War II, World War I).

Second, in the timeframe we're talking about, the 1980s to 2020s, things changed socially and culturally at the fastest rate in the history of humankind. To stay on top of these seismic shifts (or aware of them) has been vital for every firm and, we would suggest, all professionals.

For instance, in the early 1980s, a cigarette brand could sponsor sport. Today that is not an option for a sport marketer. However, in the 1980s a sport wagering entity could not sponsor sport. Now brands like Draft Kings, Fan Duel, PointsBet, and BetMGM are highly evident.

We'll start by investigating a series of activities and takeaways. These examples are random (far from exhaustive) and presented in loosely semi-chronological order. By offering this list, we comment on familiar moments when advertising, endorsement, promotion, and special events utilized hockey imagery to build a brand and, in turn, reinforce the NHL's importance.

1980s to Today: Tactic 1 – If a Sport Property Fits with Your Brand, Own It

Tim Hortons has become synonymous with hockey in Canada and now in some parts of the northern United States where hockey is big (e.g., Michigan, New York, Ohio). In Canada, Tim's sponsors the NHL, all seven NHL clubs, the Hockey Hall of Fame, the CHL, some of the CHL's clubs, star athletes (e.g., Sidney Crosby, Nathan MacKinnon), youth programs, learn-to-skate programs, and much more.

It is often difficult to amass that much "association" and some would say that "placing all of one's eggs in one basket" is risky. But when a game is ubiquitous in a country (i.e., hockey in Canada, soccer/football in Europe), a strategy to go "a mile wide and a mile deep" can ensure a competitor's entry into a market (in this case doughnuts, sandwiches, muffins, and coffee) is difficult.

Tim Hortons will never be a monopoly when it comes to quick-serve restaurants but its many challengers know if Tim Hortons stands for anything, it stands for hockey.

Rick's Recall: Vegemite and Darwin's Ice Hockey Team

During the northern hemisphere summer of 2019, my wife and I joined with 11 other friends to participate in a carefully planned 4WD road trip that ran from Darwin, the capital of Australia's remote and tropical Northern Territory (NT), along the notoriously rough Gibb River Road, to Broome in the extreme northwest corner of Western Australia.

Leaving town (and driving south toward humid outposts like Humpty Doo and Rum Jungle), we went past a sign advertising the Darwin Ice Skating Centre. That premise made us all smile because Darwin sits in the tropics, 12 degrees south of the equator.

Seeing the rink, I thought back to 2011 when a mythical Darwin ice hockey club became famous in Australia because Vegemite (a spicy yeast extract) created a laugh-out-loud TV commercial about Darwin's ice hockey world champions. It was a claim the fictional Darwinians made because no other team in the world had ever come into the NT to play them.

The beauty of the advertisement was in avoiding ever showing the Darwin players on ice. Instead, they lounged in pools or hot tubs talking about their undefeated status. The commercial ended with a player firing a slap shot off a sandy beach toward a goalie and net set up in front of the Timor Sea.

For Vegemite, the concept tied into "toasting the nation" and showcased the versatility an advertiser could take in creating a promotion based on a global game that traditionally requires ice. But rather than seeing ice as a required prop or limitation, Vegemite's creative marketers leveraged hockey's unique (and beneficial) positioning.

Numerous examples abound and for various career reasons, I've carried many of them in my head over the decades. During Nike's advertising heyday in the late 1980s, the footwear giant's ad agency Wieden & Kennedy created a legendary sequence of ads featuring multisport hero Bo Jackson. In one version that was shown only during baseball's all-star game, *Adweek* reviewer Barbara Lippert called the "Bo Diddley baseball" commercial "a celeb sports orgy set to great music" that "cleverly nurtures the myth of its beyond-mere-mortal subject, Bo Jackson."[1]

Jackson, a two-sport athlete who played pro football and baseball, was depicted competing in various sports with a different celebrity saying, "Bo Knows … ." The first famous player was Rams quarterback Jim Everett saying, "Bo Knows Football." He was followed by the Dodgers' Kirk Gibson, then Chicago's Michael Jordan, and finally John McEnroe, showing apprehension, indicating Bo knew baseball, basketball, and tennis, respectively.

The funniest moment of the ad came when a quick cut showed Bo on skates checking an opposing player into the boards. Seconds later, Wayne Gretzky came gliding into the frame and simply said, "No."

Interestingly, the footwear Jackson was promoting was a cross-training shoe that could be used for practically any sport including weightlifting and cycling. But not hockey. With Gretzky in the ad, however, Nike supplied the NHL with credibility at a moment when the game didn't naturally fit the script.

Similarly, during the COVID-19 pandemic, viral quarantine hockey challenges sprang up across YouTube as various groups tried to stay fit or reveal their love of a game they temporarily couldn't access. In fact, in one video, players from all over the world engaged in a quarantine puck pass with footage featuring players in Australia, Egypt, and France.

The key point is understanding businesses may see limitations in what they sell or service, but creative people almost always see opportunity. They imagine solutions. They creatively solve problems.

Think of it this way: if the NHL restricted itself to only indoor arenas, it would never unlock the power of outdoor stadium games. If it thought the game was only relevant to individuals with skates, it would overlook the excitement and reality of street, roller, sledge, and Nerf hockey.

Creativity is, for many, a challenging concept. I read one time that many of us, when we don't color between the lines as children or fail to draw elaborate, beautiful pictures, get told we're not very creative. That misapplied conclusion seems to cause many people to forever believe they aren't creative. All because they drew like a five-year-old.

The truth is this: all of us are creative but feature different kinds of creativity. And, like any human movement or task, we have to deliberately practice trying out ideas. We have to look for inspiration and motivation in unusual places. Practice, and I mean a lot of it, makes perfect.

Advertising has traditionally been a great place for creative minds and numerous ads have leveraged the unique commitment of hockey fans to sell their products. In 2015, *Sports Illustrated* went so far to select the 12 best hockey ads of all time.

Who can forget Verizon's crazed hockey fan (a new father) pounding on the glass-windowed maternity ward like a demented hockey fan in one of the corners? Or *Sports Illustrated*'s number one selection: a Budweiser moment where the brewer brought in a huge crowd of vocal hockey fans to surprise two beer league teams with a loud, cheering throng.

As you read this chapter, loving hockey and the NHL, let your mind wander and think about whether there are new ways to do something bold. It certainly worked for Vegemite and I can only imagine the World Champions are still lounging comfortably in their Darwin swimming pools.

Early 2000s: Tactic 2 – Investigate Media-Driven Properties

Hockey Day in Canada, launched by Canadian broadcaster CBC in 2000 and most recently held in January 29, 2022, as Scotiabank Hockey Day in Canada, is a television-driven property that shows a slate of back-to-back games involving all Canadian NHL teams with related celebrations. The broadcast is based in a non-NHL Canadian city (in 2022, the location was Scarborough, Ontario) and sometimes includes other Canadian hockey properties, such as a CHL (junior-level) game. Prior to the Winnipeg Jets returning to the NHL in 2011, Hockey Day in Canada featured a tripleheader of games featuring each of the six Canadian NHL franchises.

Following the Jets return as the seventh Canadian team, US-based clubs were included to have an eighth team as part of a four-game slate. The lead broadcast team (until 2019 it was the legendary duo of Ron MacLean and Don Cherry) is based in a non-NHL Canadian city (e.g., Iqaluit, Red Deer, Scarborough,

Shaunavon, Stephenville, Stratford, Windsor, Whitehorse) that serves as the broadcast hub for the day. That location often includes other associated events (e.g., all-night pick-up hockey games, NHL legends games, World Pond Hockey Championships). An alternative format was used in 2021 due to COVID-19.

Scotiabank's role as title sponsor is indicative of the value of this property. As one of the five major banks that dominate the Canadian financial industry, Scotiabank has built its marketing, in part, around being Canada's "hockey bank" characterized by high-profile partnerships with the NHL, clubs, and venues. In 2018, its reported CDN$800 million naming-rights deal for Canada's (and one of the world's) busiest arena in downtown Toronto was the largest naming-rights deal on record. As title sponsor of Scotiabank Hockey Day in Canada, Scotiabank benefitted from supporting the celebration of Canada's most popular sport and league in smaller cities across the country, all of which have Scotiabank branches.

1990s: Tactic 3 – Seek to Be Positioned alongside Bigger Properties

The NHL has long held the number four position among US professional team sport leagues. Thus, any chance to be associated with the top three leagues (NFL, MLB, NBA) could be considered – by us (and likely by the NHL brass) – to be a good thing. Competition cannot be avoided, and most businesses embrace how competition makes them stronger. As always, the risk for any brand is falling into a state of irrelevance and greater inefficiency.

The hiring of Commissioner Bettman from the NBA is one example of this tactic. The inclusion of Montreal Canadiens legendary player Bernie "Boom Boom" Geoffrion in the famous Miller

Lite "Tastes Great – Less Filling" television commercials that ran from the 1970s to the 1990s is another. Geoffrion's role, alongside athlete celebrities from other major sports, highlighted the NHL hockey's status as an elite sport. That campaign won many awards and *Advertising Age* once named it one of the top 10 campaigns of all time.

A final example is Wayne Gretzky (see Tactic 5 below), the star who helped elevate the NHL. His joint *Sports Illustrated* cover with Magic Johnson and his appearance in Nike's well-known "Bo Knows" commercials are two examples of him elevating the NHL alongside the other major leagues. In other words, defeating your rivals may not happen until another day … but working hard to show you are skating with the big dogs is important to your reputation.

1990s and 2000s: Tactic 4 – Even if It Didn't Last, Getting Nike's Attention Was Valuable

The story of Nike's investment in, and then withdrawal from, Bauer is not normally associated with success, but there is a clear positive outcome from the experience, namely that it gave the NHL a very deep association with global marketing leader Nike, one of the world's most celebrated brands.

As a quick recap, Bauer is an iconic Canadian skate manufacturing brand that started in Kitchener, Ontario, in the late 1920s. In 1995, Nike purchased Bauer. In 2005, it was rebranded as Nike Bauer. But, in 2008, Nike divested its ownership, reportedly selling for about half of the original purchase price. On one level, Nike's acquisition of Bauer was not a long-standing success story, but the investment of the world's largest apparel brand into the sport of hockey sent a message the sport belonged on the big stage.

Nike is, of course, not the only big global brand that matters. Others, such as Amazon, Coca-Cola, Imperial Oil (Esso), Maple Leaf Foods, McDonald's, Microsoft, Tim Hortons, Skoda, and Visa, also matter. Not surprisingly, it is the job of the commissioner (as CEO) and the NHL's leaders of marketing and fan engagement to seek ways to bring the biggest and best marketers closer to their product. The same holds at the local level.

1999 to Present: Tactic 5 – Once a Great One, Always a Great One

Michael Jordan and Wayne Gretzky have a lot in common. They are both championed as the best to ever play their respective games. Both earned the famous GOAT ("greatest of all time") acronym. Both won multiple championships and were leaders of dynasties. Both set scoring records while transcending their respective sports. Most relevant here, they were two of the first athletes to show their endorsement/sponsorship value could extend long past the end of their playing careers.

In Gretzky's case, similar to Jordan's, his marketing acumen and business success continues today, more than 20 years after his retirement. Examples include Gretzky being chosen in 2011 as the face of the video game *NHL Slapshot* for the Nintendo Wii,[2] signing a sponsorship deal with shoemaker Skechers at 50 years of age,[3] having long-standing partnerships with major brands including Breitling watches, EA Sports, Ford, Samsung, and TD Bank. He also launched businesses (after retiring from hockey) in restaurants and wineries. Global giants like Samsung signed Gretzky for the 2010 Olympic Games[4] where the Great One held an administrative role with the Canadian team. This showed the value of Gretzky not only as a player or historic legend, but also as an administrator, business owner, and Canadian ambassador.

As previously shown, Gretzky's 1989 appearance in a commercial built around Bo Jackson and Nike's cross-trainer shoes benefitted multiple entities, including the LA Kings and NHL. Both entities gained valuable visibility in advertising where hockey could have been left out. And it also proved Gretzky, the Great One, belonged on the same stage as Michael Jordan, John McEnroe, and Bo Jackson.

Early 2000s: Tactic 6 – If the Fit Is So Good, Wear It

As discussed in chapter 12, Don Cherry, legendary commentator on *Hockey Night in Canada*, suffered through an unfortunate ending to his career. However, prior to that point, he enjoyed a more than 30-year career as a celebrity and a major attraction on the weekly national telecast of NHL games, drawing high ratings and considerable fanfare.

Among Cherry's popular characteristics was his attire, namely his outlandish, stylish, and colorful suits. The suits were characterized by custom colors, high collars, and pin ties. Reportedly very expensive and custom-made, this led Moore's Menswear to sponsor "Coach's Corner" (Cherry's featured segment on *Hockey Night in Canada*). A Canadian retailer of men's business wear and formal clothing, Moore's has more than 100 stores across the country and their ads with Cherry ran for several years in the early 2000s.

Although Moore's pricing of suits was less than what it would cost for a custom suit and their positioning targeted middle-class men, the linkage between Moore's and Cherry worked because Cherry's commentary consistently suggested that he was a blue-collar guy who made it big. The fit (pun intended) was clear and well-designed.

2005 to Today: Tactic 7 – Where You Can, Control Your Own Content

Like many major sport leagues, the NHL, in partnership with NBC Universal, launched its own network, the NHL Network, in the United States in 2007. The Network was a channel devoted to ice hockey content and is majority owned by the NHL. By establishing the network, the NHL ensured all games were televised and its content was accessible by fans both live and as recorded. Although the NHL Network is no longer widely available, it set the stage for the digital sharing of NHL games, which is now largely delivered via ESPN+.

Much like similar networks for the NFL and the NBA, the NHL Network was designed to complement League and club deals on other networks. More importantly, given the NHL's high popularity and TV coverage in Canada, it allowed the NHL to simulcast, in the US and around the world, *Hockey Night in Canada* productions by Rogers Sportsnet.

Always: Tactic 8 – Talent Counts

In talking to one of our former students, an entrepreneur, he admitted that for one of his first hires, on a limited budget, he screwed up. He hired the wrong person. And then he was forced to jump in and do the job himself, costing himself valuable time and money, not to mention adding unneeded stress. This has probably happened to all of us, often with negative and costly outcomes.

Even NHL coaches and GMs get it wrong but who in the NHL has been good at this? Well, let's go to a leading publication, *Sports Illustrated*, and their ranking of the all-time list of greatest talent managers in hockey: head coaches.

These coaches identified talent, picked teams, knew when to cut someone, understood how to motivate performance, suggested to GMs when it was time to trade someone, knew when to bench someone, learned how to juggle lines, and understood team dynamics.

In writing about elite coaches, it was obvious why *Sports Illustrated* put Scotty Bowman as number one on their list: Bowman's record as the head coach with the most wins of all time, in both regular season and the playoffs with nine Stanley Cups won.

Not surprisingly, Bowman ended up as a "strategist" for 989 Sports when it was promoting its NHL Face Off 2000 for PlayStation.

Always: Tactic 9 – Language Matters

As every marketer learns – sometimes the hard way – language matters. And although a huge proportion of the world's population has at least a limited familiarity with the English language, it does not mean they live in that language or it is their first choice when they consume content.

People prefer to communicate in their mother tongue (or one of their mother tongues for those who are truly bilingual or trilingual), so smart marketers offer their content and services in as many languages as they have sufficient target markets.

For instance, Coca-Cola offers its website in more than 45 languages and Nike presents a "your location" portal with links showing 81 country/language options. As early as 1933–4, NHL radio broadcasts were available in both English and French, Canada's two official languages, in Canada, the United States, and Newfoundland (which joined Canada in 1949).[5]

For TV, in the case of the NHL in Canada, games have been broadcast on television since 1952 in both English (*Hockey Night in Canada*) and French (*La Soirée du hockey*). Two legendary broadcasters, famous at the time in Canada, Foster Hewitt (English) and René Lecavalier (French), were associated with this programming. In 2015, NHL programming moved from CBC/Radio Canada to Sportsnet/Téléviseurs associés (TVA) and réseau des sports (RDS). The programming has continued in both languages, with continued high ratings in English[6] and French.[7]

In the early 2000s, CBC started trialing televising *Hockey Night in Canada* in languages in addition to English and French. They included Cantonese, Hindi, Inuktitut, Mandarin, Punjabi, and Tagalog. In 2008, a regular broadcast of NHL games in Punjabi (Canada's third most spoken language) started and has continued, with only a few periods of inactivity, ever since. Following the Rogers Sportsnet deal with the NHL, the Punjabi version of *Hockey Night in Canada* has been carried on Omni TV, Roger's multicultural channel.

In the United States, for the first time since 2004, the 2021–2 season included televised Spanish language content on ESPN Deportes. This follows a number of years when Spanish audiences could not access NHL content in their preferred language.

As of 2022, through partnerships with networks in other countries, NHL games were broadcast in dozens of countries. The NHL maintains a public list of its international partners,[8] which includes France's Canal Plus Sports (covering French-speaking markets globally) and Viasat Hockey and Nelonen Pro sports channels, which provide NHL games in Denmark, Finland, Norway, and Sweden.

Interestingly, as new media platforms emerge, online hockey forums and weekly video calls are giving fans new ways to create access to the greats of the game. One example is the Lora Evans and Paul Patskou Zoomcast beaming out of Toronto on Thursday nights. This hockey-focused program uses author and Hockey Hall of Fame employee Kevin Shea and limits the number of guests but leverages access to some of the biggest names in the game.

Always: Tactic 10 – Pay Homage to History in the Right Spot: Location Matters

The top three North American pro sports (baseball, football, basketball) feature Halls of Fame in historic locations that have become tourist destinations, including Cooperstown, New York (population 1,800) for MLB; Canton, Ohio (population 73,000) for the NFL; and Springfield, Massachusetts (population 153,000) for the NBA and NCAA.

But the Hockey Hall of Fame sits in the heart of its largest and most passionate market, Toronto, Ontario (metro population 6,400,000). And, by "heart," we truly mean the downtown center of Canada's largest city, where the Hall is walking distance from Union Station, Bay Street (Canada's Wall Street), and Scotiabank Arena, home of the NHL's Maple Leafs.

Stated another way, access and proximity matter when a business is trying to continuously attract new customers, users, or fans. In the digital age following COVID-19, this is even more evident, and Halls of Fame needed, after staggered re-openings, to prioritize virtual tours and online access that kept their game and collections relevant.

Increasing over Time: Tactic 11 – Big Brands Like Integrity

Sidney Crosby, arguably the NHL's biggest star during the past decade, makes a reported $4.5 million annually from his partnerships with Adidas CCM, Gatorade, and Tim Hortons.[9] Given his salary was reportedly about $9 million per year, this means sponsorship added another 50 percent to his annual income.

That's significant for a hockey player. It also indicates the growth of the game and fits "Sid the Kid's" list of accomplishments, which includes two NHL MVPs (Hart Trophy), three Stanley Cups won with Pittsburgh, and two Olympic Gold medals for Canada, including scoring a golden goal in overtime to end the 2010 Vancouver Games.

What makes Crosby special in his endorsement work is his integrity and authenticity. Crosby seems to know that, in the scheme of things, hockey is just a game and, while he is one of the NHL's elite players, he chooses not to rest on (or promote) his laurels. That humility, in a league like the NHL, plays with fans uninterested in someone saying, "Look at me!"

Today: Tactic 12 – As the Game and Conditions Change, the Marketing Must Change

Emerging from the COVID-19 pandemic, numerous media voices went to great lengths suggesting no entity could ever return to the old "normal." That the old days were gone.

The "new normal" or "new different" certainly demands a deft hand, the ability to move nimbly, and the recognition that consumers everywhere had their lives upended. Digital offerings, mental health support, pivoting business strategies, and planning for 2023 and beyond were (and remain) top priorities for many.

In discussing the impact COVID-19 created, we can make clear that professional hockey outside of the NHL was wiped out in 2020 and much of 2021. From the elite leagues in Europe, and the AHL, the song was the same. All were canceled. Not postponed or played to media-only audiences in empty venues but flat-out canceled. No champion awarded. No complete season for the record books.

At the amateur level, from the NCAA to the CHL to junior/minor hockey for girls and boys, all were completely devastated. No games. No practices. Arenas closed.

Hockey stakeholders such as sponsors, advertisers, and merchandisers were scrambling. For a while, no new marketing was possible. Advertising agencies and corporate executives couldn't meet in person. Zoom meetings and interviews replaced conference rooms and cubicles.

The impacts of COVID-19 inspired many new innovations in hockey. For example, in May 2021, the New Jersey Devils became the first NHL team to sign a non-fungible token (NFT) deal, starting a trend around investing in unique digital assets (e.g., memorabilia). In two other examples of digital proactivity in mid-2021, Maple Leaf Sport & Entertainment (MLSE) began using vendors to develop second screen digital arena products to enhance and expand the fan experience and the NHL announced a streaming partnership with HBO Max.

On the sponsorship side, no fans were admitted into venues to drink, eat, test-drive, or socialize during a professional game. As a result, activation opportunities and budgets were wiped out. The SponsorshipX studies[10] indicated major cuts to sponsor investment in rights fees and activations – anywhere from 30 percent to

FIGURE 8.1 *Market the NHL Way*

60 percent reductions in 2020 budgets. In the end, marketing and promotion were forced to change and those directional shifts will likely influence trends for the rest of the decade.

Summarizing the 12 Tactics to Market the NHL Way

Readers of this book will know the race may not always go to the swiftest (i.e., the first mover), but it almost always goes to the entity most able to adapt, evolve, and survive, as illustrated by figure 8.1. Most importantly, success accrues to those who can evolve in ways relevant to the current era. This will hold for 2022 and well beyond as advertisers, sponsors, endorsers, event managers, and the League itself learn how to speak to customers, vendors, participants, and fans.

Marketing Coming Out of COVID-19

In concluding this chapter and bringing specificity to the world's collective COVID-19 reality, we offer the following top 10 list for business leaders. Many items were inspired by a set of surveys around sponsorship and COVID-19.[11]

1 A "return" to "normal" sponsorship, merchandising, and other hockey-related revenues are tied to society's ability to re-engage with live events when safety is not an issue.
2 There is nothing wrong with waiting, saving, and planning during the lengthy tail end of COVID-19. Yes, this pandemic has dragged on, but the time to innovate, change, digitize and re-tool is constant.
3 Don't fall into the pit of trying to move quickly to the "theme of the season." Be focused and clear on the future. Do not panic but don't try to be too clever. Partners (i.e., sponsors) and customers (i.e., fans) will reward you later for a steady hand.
4 Mental health during COVID-19 became a major problem and a societal challenge we will all face for many years to come. This has important internal (employee health) and external (corporate social responsibility) impacts for organizations.
5 People missed live sports, which never really went away, but when the games stopped, marketing to those sports fans shifted to be fully digital. If you are a consummate "scorer" for your firm or company, watch closely for the rebound.
6 For sports getting played without fans in the seats, powerful connections were still made but many of them were made virtually. How virtual is your organization? Are you digitizing as fast as your competitors?

7 In long-term planning, realize that things change, they change often, change is uncontrollable, and sometimes things change permanently. Adapt or get stuck in the tar pit (the supposed fate of dinosaurs).

8 Employees and co-workers matter. Do not make the mistake of viewing the world autobiographically and assuming everyone suffered through COVID-19 equally. Some struggled mightily. Others did not. For many, particularly those with young children, working from home was hell. For others it was a paid vacation (albeit one that often looked like the Bill Murray movie *Groundhog Day*).

9 In crisis (and COVID-19 most certainly counts as a modern crisis), power bases often shift and the decision makers emerging from the rubble may not resemble those in power when the bombs started falling. Leadership is often tested in the crucible of crisis, which means new traits, skills, and confidence often emerge when the smoke clears. Be alert to those transformations in yourself but also in those above and below you.

10 Don't get too comfortable. Soothsayers will suggest global pandemics only happen every 100 years. The influenza of 1918–19 and the pandemic of 2020–2. The reality is knowing another fast-moving pandemic is imminently logical. The next one will be different, but it won't hurt to start talking about the next disruptive game-changer, pandemic or not.

9

Women's Professional Ice Hockey and the True Value of Inclusion

Women and girls make up a large proportion of participants in ice hockey in countries where it is popular. For instance, prior to the pandemic, in the United States, 14.1 percent of the membership of USA Hockey was female (USA Hockey, 2019), while in Canada it was 13.9 percent (Hockey Canada, 2019).

There are about 80,000 female members in each country. Women's hockey also joined the program of the Olympic Games in 1998 and has been a featured event of every ensuing Winter Olympiad. Exhibition or "Rivalry Series" matches between the Canadian and US teams have drawn as many as 13,320 spectators in the US (Anaheim, California, in February 2020)[1] and 16,347 in Canada (Ottawa, Ontario, in December 2009).[2]

The highest attendance at a women's hockey game was more than 55,000 outdoors at Camp Randall Stadium in Madison, Wisconsin, on February 6, 2010, as part of an NCAA double-header involving the women's and men's University of Wisconsin Badgers hockey teams.

However, outside of these few positive points, the game remains largely male at many levels. This has led to notable pressure placed on administrators to become more inclusive from a gender perspective.

Women in Hockey

This chapter seeks to explore this challenge and discuss ways contemporary businesses and organizations can think more broadly about "sticky"' (or uncomfortable) concepts like "diversity," "equity," and "inclusion." For some readers, those words carry a whiff of political correctness. They are handy words for throwing around and many executives talk about wanting more diversity, equity, or inclusion but then fall back on a belief that achieving those aspirations is not realistic (for a variety of flawed reasons).

Of course, following the social unrest incidences of 2020 and 2021, we understand that such an approach to diversity is not just ill advised, it is fully wrong. And words without action may be worse. Diversity today is broad, vital, and multilevel, described often as DEI (diversity, equity, and inclusion). For us, we operationalize diversity as involving people from a full range of social, ethnic, gender, and sexual orientations and backgrounds. Equity is treating all fairly. Inclusion is about putting resources toward and writing policy to guarantee equal access to those who could be marginalized without such.

Take the NHL as a concept. It is a League that has only featured a single female player in a single exhibition game (a story we will dig into shortly) and very few players of color or non-European ethnicity. If the NHL wanted to promote concepts like diversity, equity, and inclusion (let alone move toward such a culture), it would still face a difficult time changing the feeder pool of talented hockey players targeting the NHL as a destination.

But what about the NHL's executive ranks or its players? Could the NHL achieve DEI in the front office before it achieved DEI on the ice? We think so and want to use this chapter to explore the conundrum of an organizational focus on DEI but with a player population that is not diverse.

So, let's start with gender. In thinking about women in professional hockey, thoughts often go to stories illustrating the two themes that emerge when a women's professional sports hockey league fails. The league as a business concept wasn't feasible. And, as far as anyone could tell, sponsor, media, and fan interest were lacking.

Learning from Failures

Capitalism mandates that inefficient entities fail, so if a pro league can't or doesn't cut it – think the short-lived Alliance of American Football (AFA) or the second iteration of the XFL – there's really no harm, no foul. Sports fans will take their passions elsewhere.

However, the AFA and XFL were men's sport and conditions are never the same when discussing the fair treatment of women's sport. Certainly, the two aforementioned themes could apply to the dozens of North American soccer leagues, the first round of the XFL, the United Football League (UFL), the United States Football League (USFL), the International Hockey League (IHL), and the WHA, but in each of those cases, women's sport was not part of the equation.

In fact, of particular interest as we researched defunct sport leagues was finding stories about the Colored Hockey League, a league with only Black players that operated from 1895 to 1930 in Nova Scotia and Prince Edward Island, peaking at eight teams before its demise.

So, what if previous presumptions and assumptions were wrong in the case of women's sport? What if a better business concept could have been developed (making millions for many) and if by not doing so, men, women, and children were actually hurt by yet another failed attempt at inclusion, gender equity, and societal advancement?

If you are like us, you're used to hearing about people who doubt diversity works. But, unlike us, you probably don't read the voluminous academic literature clearly supporting the opposite: that diversity, equity, and inclusion (in all forms) lead to better decisions, stronger groups, and more profitability. These same doubters tend to believe gender equity is not good for the bottom line and suggest homogeneous groups are more effective.

In the minds of those proponents, "inclusion" is just a politically correct phrase they have grown tired of hearing. For them, making the world a better place is not everyone's job. It might be good for human rights advocates but not for large or small business operators seeking profit and market share.

Once again, the litany of academic research on the topic is not widely read. The civil unrest of 2020, however, opened the world's eyes to centuries of persecution and bias.

That is why we think these doubters are wrong, particularly in the case of inclusion around women's professional sport. We can start by looking at a sporting example of a successful women's league.

Learning from the Success of Others

Look at Australia's successful women's pro football league. To start, if some North American readers consider Americans or the French chauvinistic, it's possible they haven't visited Australia in the last 50 years. This is a country where men and women often sit at different tables during dinner parties. While some Aussies may disagree with that assessment, evidence exists that the folks Down Under are not as progressive in matters of gender equity as some other developed countries.

And yet, Australia's largest professional sports league, the Australian Football League (AFL), launched a highly successful women's league in 2017 and is consistently showing the world that inclusion not only works but can drive profitability and growth.

Based in Melbourne, the AFL women's league (AFLW) started with eight teams but quickly expanded to 14 by 2020. It will reach 18 teams in 2023 with a women's team aligned with every men's team in the AFL. The AFLW also started generating meaningful TV ratings (despite canceling the 2020 season due to COVID-19) that slotted in nicely with the men's league in terms of time slots and media-based revenues. What's interesting about the AFL, according to 2019 research by Dr. Tony Ward, a research fellow at Melbourne University, is how the AFL leveraged data showing more than 40 percent of the fans for the men's game were women. In the US, the NFL has long enjoyed similar levels of interest from women but continually felt no need to act on those statistics nor start a women's league.

It begs a research question: what if a big, established league (the AFL) launched a league for female players – something the NFL, NHL, and MLB had never done – and invested in the concept so that it worked? What if the league modeled its line extension on the Women's National Basketball Association (WNBA), a successful women's professional basketball league in the US?

Ward, who looked at 20 years of data, boiled it down to this: "The AFL has been much more successful at attracting female fans." He also saw that where 16 percent of women who were fans of the AFL during their 20s, that number dropped only to

15 percent for women in their 50s. In other words, women who started as fans of the AFL stayed with the AFL.

That data probably played a small role in helping the AFL determine a women's league could make sense. If women liked the AFL, might they not also like the AFLW? And as a bonus, could the creation of an AFLW help women like the AFL more?

Additionally, what if the AFL's business managers spread two "footy" seasons over one calendar year? Could costs be managed (think economies of scale) so the AFL revenue pie was made larger? A bigger pie usually means more revenue and team-based profits.

To inform our points here, we talked to a few experts and researched a few points about the AFLW.

1 Samantha Lane[3] tells the story of the AFLW and describes it as something that is more importantly about society and not just sport. In her book, she tells stories about the AFLW's women and the challenges they've overcome. For the women featured, the AFLW is an extraordinary achievement and a victory in a life full of obstacles for women in sport.

2 Despite the AFLW's success, including the signing of a collective agreement with the players in 2018[4] that includes provisions for salaries never before seen in women's sport in Australia, the existence of a significant pay gap between the female players and the male players has been well documented in all sports[5] and in the AFLW in particular.[6]

3 Contacts/colleagues in Australia have suggested that despite initial indications the AFLW game would be identical to the AFL game, a number of rule differences were put in place, including having 16 players on the field in an AFLW game, as opposed to 18. In our view, any difference like this upholds stereotypes. It is no different than men having a decathlon and

the women a heptathlon in the Olympic Games, or the "marathon" Nordic skiing racing at the Games being 50 kilometers for men but only 30 kilometers for women. Countering that view, however, is the WNBA's choice to play with a ball that is smaller than the NBA ball because the women's ball gives WNBA players greater control (their "handle"), thus producing a better game (or entertainment product) for fans.

4 A comment heard from multiple sources is that despite the acknowledgment the AFLW is a progressive move, why didn't it happen 20 years earlier?

5 A second thought-provoking aspect to the AFLW is that initially tickets to games were free. In the past, we would have criticized this as a mistake (i.e., setting the value of a game at $0 establishes in peoples' minds that the game has no "value"); however, today we wonder if this is a precursor to an emerging wave in professional sport where ticket prices for many teams are variable based on access to secondary market sellers or market demand. Further, where professional games in 2020 and 2021 (in many places) could not feature fans, would spectators be willing to return en masse if ticket prices skyrocketed in the future?

6 Although the AFLW generated high levels of popularity and interest initially, will it fall back, over time, to base levels like the W-League (soccer) and Women's National Basketball League in Australia, both of which have been around for a long time but rarely draw crowds or media attention?

7 While AFLW teams play at smaller stadiums/ovals, receive less media coverage, have fewer major sponsors, and pay female players far less than their male counterparts, the existence of the AFLW means women have more opportunities to emerge as celebrities and role models. Thus, as the league grows and gains are seen, the arrow for the traditional narrative of male dominance is further shifted toward equal standing.

Interestingly, Ward also compared female data with other Australian leagues (which the Australians call "codes") and found with
rugby league, the fall-off by women fans was much more pronounced
as they aged. His speculation suggested female engagement with the
game was tied to off-field arrests of National Rugby League (NRL)
players (all male) and their boorish/controversial behavior.

Ward's conclusion: it was a "likely reason [why] women turned
away from" the NRL. Could that suggest female fans care more
about the "holistic" side of athlete off-field behavior than male
fans? Possibly. And if so, did diversity, equity, and inclusion concepts represent dollars and cents at the turnstile?

This point connects mightily with research Syracuse University
Professor Dr. Mary Graham has been conducting over the last decade. She found when NFL teams had a very few or zero female executives, the likelihood of arrests involving players from those teams
was higher than for those teams with a lot of high-ranking women.

Of course, this feels like using a sledgehammer to drive home
a point that could made with a simple tap. If we connect the dots
and talk about inclusion, the facts are very clear. Where women
are included in the management of men's sports teams, there are
fewer arrests. And fewer arrests mean fewer negative stories, less
time (and fees) with lawyers, more female fans, and greater likelihood for sustained revenue and profitability from a key demographic audience.

The Challenge of the Bludgeon versus the Whisper

If diversity, equity, and inclusion help create a respectful workplace, then who could be against an organization working to provide greater levels of respect for all? The answer is stark: many
people think they are respectful but bring their implicit bias

(which HR professionals and psychologists call "unconscious constructs") to work. Those superiority or privileged feelings create the discrimination, harassment, and incompetence that quickly undermines an organization's strength.

Many companies will tell employees that diversity, equity, and inclusion are about celebrating our respective differences. The things that make us unique. The problem is that many people don't start from a position of recognizing differences as a good thing. They start from a position of wanting to fit in and look for homogenous patterns that facilitate assimilation. If everyone is a white male and we hire white males, we might assume onboarding will go quite smoothly. We're all the same, right? Wrong.

Building a hockey team with only goaltenders would never fly. Nor a football team with nothing but offensive players. Sport shows over and over that we not only need diversity, equity, and inclusion but that they grow the game.

That's why a discussion of Jackie Robinson's value to professional baseball or Becky Harmon's contribution to the San Antonia Spurs is almost always about the positive gains the organization realizes. It may explain why the NFL so aggressively promoted the appearance of a female referee (Sarah Thomas) during the 2021 Super Bowl in Tampa.

Another example is American soccer player Carli Lloyd kicking a 55-yard field goal at a 2019 NFL practice – suddenly numerous NFL teams wanted to provide her a tryout for their team. Many men can convert long field goals. But Lloyd would put the NFL in a position to become the first North American professional sports league (discounting Manon Rhéaume playing in NHL exhibition games for the Tampa Bay Lightning in 1992–3) to formally shatter the gender line. And that would be valuable to the NFL.

Positive gains in business have even been acknowledged at the highest level in the US judicial system. Supreme Court Justice

Sandra Day O'Connor wrote in the majority opinion for the Grutter v. Bollinger case: "These benefits (in discussion of the intrinsic value of diversity, equity, and inclusion), are not theoretical but real, as major American businesses have made clear that skills needed in today's increasingly global marketplace can only be developed through exposure to widely diverse people, cultures, ideas, and viewpoints."[7]

Norm's Nostalgia: Dreams Can Come True!

It's true. But often, if we are so fortunate, they rarely happen as planned. In thinking about the dream of a vibrant, high salary–paying, fan-attracting professional women's hockey league, my thoughts drifted to two things that may be helpful in getting us there.

First, they drifted back more than 20 years to one of my roles when I worked for Sport Canada, the Government of Canada department responsible for amateur sport in the country. One of my jobs was being the representative for the government with Hockey Canada. I loved that job. Part of it was a chance to support the Canadian women's team heading to the 2002 Winter Olympic Games in Salt Lake City.

The sport had debuted at the Nagano Games just four years earlier and the Canadian women had come home with a silver medal, the US taking gold. In Canada, this is not an acceptable result, so the pressure was on. A centralized program was set up with the team all training together in Calgary prior to the Games. Hayley Wickenheiser, widely regarded as the greatest female player of all time, was in her prime, scoring seven goals in five games, as Canada captured gold.

What was my role? Well, very minor, but I like to think I had some part in the dream of Canada's first women's hockey gold!

My first job was to facilitate support to the government's funding programs, support programs for athletes and coaches, and liaise between the organizations. But, more importantly, it was to push – internally and externally – for recognition that these women were high-performance athletes worthy of attention, funding, and admiration. Meeting them and observing their training, their 100 percent focus on high performance, and their talent were things the country would fully understand by the 2010 Vancouver Games (when 7.5 million Canadians tuned in to the gold medal game), but in the early 2000s, this acceptance was still a dream.

Second, and this is a personal story of including small markets in the NHL, on Saturday December 11, 2010, at roughly 9 p.m. Eastern Standard Time, I got to do what many Canadian kids dream of. I was on *Hockey Night in Canada*, Canada's most watched regular sport TV show for decades and a Saturday night staple of Canadian television since 1952. (The radio version of the show started in 1931.)

On that Saturday night, a snowy one in Ottawa (where I was living at the time), the two most storied franchises in hockey – the Toronto Maple Leafs and the Montreal Canadiens – were playing in Toronto. Typical of such a winter Saturday night match-up, ratings were high with an average audience of more than 1.4 million (it peaked at just over 2 million) Canadians watching the game.

Of course, I wasn't lacing up the blades to play or standing behind the bench to direct line shifts. In fact, I was nowhere near the Air Canada Centre (now Scotiabank Arena) in downtown Toronto.

I was driving from Ottawa (Canada's capital city) to Lindsay (my small hometown) to see my family. It's about a four-hour trip and I stopped at a small restaurant in Perth, where I was able to tune in to watch the game's second intermission where my segment, an in-depth interview with legendary host Ron MacLean, would run.

It was my crowning achievement in hockey, and thankfully it was pre-taped and shown tape delayed.

Why was I on air? I had led some major research over the previous months on the NHL's return of a team to Canada. Winnipeg and Quebec City were the leading candidates although there was talk of a second team in Toronto or one in Hamilton.

It was big news and had driven daily media coverage. For me, that element was exciting because although hockey is always big news in Canada, it is typically built around the on-ice excitement and not the business side.

Why was it important? Well, about 15 years earlier, two Canadian franchises had, to the dismay of hockey fans across Canada, moved to the United States. Winnipeg had left for Phoenix and Quebec City for Denver.

In both cases, the teams were successful at selling tickets and enjoyed strong fan bases, but they didn't have the media markets and revenue-generating abilities of big US markets like Denver and Phoenix. The strong US dollar versus the Canadian "loonie" did not help either, as – at the time – the Canadian clubs collected their revenues in Canadian dollars and paid expenses (mostly player salaries) in US dollars. With the Canadian dollar trading at close to 60 cents of a US dollar, the economics were deadly.

But as 2010 rolled around, the Vancouver Olympics, a strong economy, and a loonie on par with the US dollar had inspired rising attention around more NHL clubs (relocation or expansion) setting up shop in Canada. Winnipeg would return shortly thereafter.

To appear on *Hockey Night in Canada* during a Leafs versus Canadiens Saturday night game was unforgettable ... a dream ... even if I was wearing a suit (and not shoulder pads) and even if I appeared for only three minutes (not 60).

Sport can showcase diversity, equity, and inclusion but that is not to say it is the first mover. MLB and the NFL for many years featured written or unwritten rules prohibiting Black athletes from playing in those leagues. The NCAA, founded in 1904, originally did not allow women, student-athletes of color, college students from foreign countries, or transgender individuals. Similarly, coaches, athletic directors, and university presidents were always white males. Even in journalism, it wasn't until 1974 that a woman (Robin Herman) first covered an NHL team.

Over the years, each of those barriers has been broken down as Americans came to see, almost exclusively through the heroic efforts of Jackie Robinson beginning in 1946 (his minor league year with the Montreal Royals), that allowing everyone in made the games better and drove larger audiences to the stadiums and via television and radio. We believe 2020 and the civil unrest we've touched on throughout the book will be looked back upon, like 1946 is, as another "beginning" toward a truly inclusive society.

Many books have been written about the importance of Robinson in breaking a color line that had stood since the late 1880s (the time of Syracuse Stars' Moses Fleetwood Walker) but the issue here is not about an individual being a first but rather the growth that comes from the inclusion of a previously uninvited community.

Interestingly, as much as baseball has long stood as metaphor for America (witness James Earl Jones's passionate speech in the movie *Field of Dreams*), baseball was often seen as a first mover in creating opportunities for individuals who did not speak English, players with profound hearing loss (William "Dummy" Hoy), athletes with less than two arms (Pete Gray, Jim Abbott), and women (as seen in the movie *A League of Their Own* or via Little League World Series hero Mo'Ne Davis).

In fact, in Davis' case, her performance in a youth baseball tournament paved the way for her appearance on the cover of *Sports*

Illustrated (knocking Kobe Bryant and the Lakers off the cover) and ultimately for a Fox television show called *Pitch*. What Davis made so obvious in a sport traditionally reserved only for young boys was that diversity, equity, and inclusion made the story so much bigger.

It's difficult to believe everyone involved with MLB, pro football, or college athletics has long tried to protect a subliminal power base. Often, efforts put forth by well-intentioned people are stymied by bias that they themselves do not recognize. In fact, the conspiracy image many people hold in their minds is one of a small group of desperate white men huddling in a large New York City conference room, wringing their hands while saying to each other, "Let's make sure we hold on to this power ... and only elect or hire people who look like us."

It's not accurate, yet anyone who is a member of an underrepresented class of people cannot help but feeling that those very white men do exist and have held those very conversations. The video footage of how George Floyd was treated in the minutes before his death is undeniable evidence enough that such thinking exists and, of course, white power groups do exist and will continue to exist.

The ongoing inference is that leaders of sports leagues (commissioners, owners, team presidents, and general managers) all believe they are guarding something precious. In this instance, we are reminded of Gollum from J.R.R. Tolkien's *Lord of the Rings,* maniacally desiring to keep something precious, the magic ring of power that consumes him.

Throughout Tolkien's story, Gollum is tormented by his overwhelming desire for something, all the while knowing he must release it. This brings us back to thinking that some of the people running pro sports are hoarding an old way of life. Resisting the spreading of wealth. Ignoring the global social justice trends.

Said another way, these elderly "operators" have theoretically worked hard to earn and enjoy their privilege and getting forced to adopt concepts of diversity or equity or inclusion is scary for them. Concepts like diversity, equity, and/or inclusion will ruin something precious. Change is good but only as long as it does not impact my privilege.

You get the idea.

Today, most organizations actively seek diversity, equity, and inclusion in their membership, athletes, and fan bases. But the question for many (and it incorporates an implicit bias that rarely reaches the surface) is whether all of the diversity, equity, and inclusion truly generate a stronger bottom line and help retain the best employees for tomorrow's challenges.

Diversity, equity, and inclusion became a mainstream topic decades ago, characterized by the cartoonists and comedians who frequently "riff" on the topic. One of our favorites is Wiley's *Non Sequitur* calendar panel showing a table full of hungry bears all dressed in suits with the CEO bear suggesting he had not seen the value in diversity, equity, and inclusion but was warming to the idea. The panel's intended "humor" was in showing the one non-bear at the bone-strewn table, a rabbit, was about to get devoured.

If the joke works, perhaps it is because the figurative tables have already been turned. Representation by a lone person of color, creed, race, language group, gender, sexual orientation, or physical ability no longer cuts it when organizations contemplate true diversity, equity, and inclusion.

In an age of social media, with its instant messaging, an entire generation has come of age looking for situations of obvious tokenism. The situations overloaded with one dominating group (i.e., white males) and scarce representation of all others. For a generation that grew up finding "Waldo" in the books of their youth, a workplace setting where someone has been hired solely as a "token" to give an organization a free pass (what the Australians call "ticking the box") is unacceptable.

Thus, when they see CEOs smiling at the cameras and saying they believe in diversity, equity, and inclusion, they launch counterattacks to rectify the lie. These confrontations have moved to a societal level, and rightly so.

We will close here by noting diversity, equity, and inclusion, three completely different words, work not only by spreading the wealth of ideas, talent, and perspective but also in helping an organization avoid internal attacks that lead to workforce turnover, employee dissatisfaction, reduced efficiency, and lost profitability.

No magic wand can make every human see the value in proactively seeking to give large-scale opportunities to those different from the ruling class. But we can comfortably suggest that organizations that do not diversify and fail to include can only blame themselves for the problems they will undoubtedly create.

If capitalism punishes the inefficient, then the absence of diversity, equity, and inclusion, three simple concepts, will surely make an organization less likely to succeed.

10

Conflict Management: What Can We Learn from the NHL?

Fighting is a controversial, exciting, and integral part of the NHL game. Conflict is also part of the business world. When we thought to address fighting, we thought of the lyrics to one of the more unusual rock-and-roll songs ever to feature hockey and believed it might provide the access portal for introducing such a sensitive topic.

The tune? It is a lively piece the late Warren Zevon co-wrote with Detroit sportswriter and award-winning author Mitch Albom. The lyrics tell of a young hockey player named Buddy who reaches the NHL as a fighter despite his desire to score goals. The song is titled *Hit Somebody (The Hockey Song),* and in it, Zevon and Albom describe the challenge facing Buddy, a Canadian farm boy, going up against tough Czechs, Russians, and Swedes.

Although Buddy wants to score goals, his coach tells him, "Buddy, remember your role. The fast guys get paid, they shoot, and they score. Protect them Buddy, that's what you're here for."

We felt this line highlighted a business concept perfectly. Buddy's job was supporting the stars and matching up physically with the most rugged opposing players. Unfortunately, Buddy's coach didn't believe he needed another scorer. Just a strong and willing enforcer.

That rigidity intrigued us because we know that at many companies, some employees get locked into very limiting roles. Many are good in those positions and enjoy leveraging their specific strengths in a very defined space. But stepping outside their perceived expertise (or skill set) exceeds someone else's fixed game plan.

Others (at the very same company) may chafe at getting pigeonholed into a role they believe holds them back. For them, some aspect of their early performance made the organization's leadership believe the employee was happy without growing, maxed-out on upward mobility, and best left unchallenged beyond the rigors of their current position.

We think anyone reading this book and thinking about their workplace should always allocate time for reviewing the capabilities and interests of direct reports. We won't quote social psychology here, but many leadership books reference the power of untapped potential. Of getting more from a given staff or individual.

Drawing from fighting in the NHL, such thinking fascinated us because as fans, we've always enjoyed the hockey stories where a famous coach or legendary captain inspired a player to "dig deeper." To "go the extra mile." To "give 110 percent." Even legendary scorers like Crosby, Gretzky, and Ovechkin have dropped the gloves for fisticuffs when the time was right.

The above clichés about performance are dated, but media coverage has long reported that great athletes were motivated to achieve greater results. But can we model it in business? Yes, but let's agree, it's tricky.

Sports teams generate game-by-game statistics. Goals per game. Plus/minus per shift. Save percentages. Penalty minutes and fights. Team owners and coaches can cut players or send them down to the minors with little worry about long-term business sustainability.

In other words, the team will not fail its way out of business. There is a ruthlessness to professional sport that doesn't translate perfectly to the office, factory, or storefront.

Still, motivation in the business world is the "real deal" (also ideal) and the simplest version is the carrot-and-stick analogy.

The carrot is a raise, a promotion, an increase in responsibility, more power, access to the executive dining room, stock benefits, equity. The extra benefit incentivizes the worker to produce more (or in coaching language, to "reach their full potential").

The stick (often perceived as punishment) is revealed in the form of missing out on a promotion, the removal of privileges or committee membership. The biggest stick, the ultimate "warclub," is likely job termination. Without question, these are moments of conflict that are generally uncomfortable for all involved.

There are, of course, far more varied ways to motivate employees and one of them is showing real interest in the career aspirations of individuals in a work unit. The act of caring about a person, however, takes time and forces the manager, director, or leader to care about the messiness of life.

What if the employee thinks they are better than they really are? What if their goal is to leave the company and get hired somewhere else? What if the individual has no aspirations beyond doing the bare minimum?

The list of questions is potentially endless, but every supervisor can ask one simple question: How much do I care about everyone who reports to me? And, importantly, am I getting the most out of each employee (much the way a coach is paid to get the most productivity out of each player)?

From here, the excuses by leaders often expand exponentially. I'm not paid to care. I'm paid to extract a maximum performance.

There are too many people in my group for me to care about all of them. I care for my staff but only for the ones who take initiative and show me they are worth caring about.

The issue here is leaders who see every employee as a role player and not as part of a holistic assemblage. Hockey teams feature goal scorers and defensive stalwarts. First-line gamers and rarely used bench players. Coaches mold their teams based on how they can leverage strengths, disguise weaknesses, fit the salary cap, create a competitive advantage, and overcome the rawness of inexperienced rookies and the "lost a step" physical reality of veterans.

Everyone has a role to play but great leaders see beyond the perceived limitations. They see capacity. Not the traditional glass that is half full or half empty, but rather a volume that can be doubled.

How many times has the player with a handful of goals for the entire season lit the light wildly in the playoffs? Want names? Fernando Pisani's 14 playoff goals (including a shorthanded overtime game-winner) for the Oilers in 2006 warrants a mention.

So too, perhaps, Petr Klima. His 1990 Stanley Cup short side wrist shot for Edmonton ended the longest Cup game in history (at the time) at 15:13 of the third overtime. On a night when skaters were practically collapsing on the bench, Klima offered fresh legs. This was because Klima had barely played all game. Why? The Czech's perceived role on the team didn't fit the gritty style Oilers coach John Muckler favored. Muckler had started with Oilers coach Glen Sather as an assistant in 1982 before taking up the coaching reins for the 1989–90 season. Having already played a key role in the winning of four Cups, the 1990 Stanley Cup was the first without Wayne Gretzky.

There are hundreds of examples in the hockey world of players stepping up to play a larger role in a big game, but we believe it has always been discussed within the overarching concept of a winning team. In the business world, leaders need to consistently assess whether they are aware of an employee's potential and are giving that employee the chance to grow and show more for the good of the organization.

Finally, if you want to know how *Hit Somebody* ends and why we chose to highlight it, find the song on YouTube. Or look up the lyrics. You'll be pleased to learn Buddy the brawler lights the red lamp.

Fighting in Hockey: A Famous Night

Picture this: it's December 2, 1992. Winter is approaching, the heart of the NHL season. You're sitting in Madison Square Garden, the world's most famous arena. Midtown New York City, arguably the greatest city in the world. Two of hockey's original six teams, the Detroit Red Wings and New York Rangers, are set to battle. You live for these games. Your heart beats fast and your anticipation is high. Jacked.

Just a few seconds into the first period, 37 to be exact, the NHL's undisputed fighting champion, Bob Probert of the Red Wings, the renowned enforcer known for protecting Wings' stars Steve Yzerman and Sergei Fedorov, drops the gloves to square off with Tie Domi, a great fighter and agitator in his own right. Domi is the beating heart and soul of the Rangers, a massive fan favorite.

The two men have been talking this brawl up in pre-game media and the local journalists have loved it. They enjoy building anticipation. The great unwashed and the bejeweled have come. The arena is jammed.

On television, gleeful announcers cannot hide their excitement. In the Garden's multicolored seats, the atmosphere is electric. Already the fans are cheering wildly, standing, screaming.

The home fans beg for Domi to represent them. The handful of Wings' fans, aware of their distinct minority status, urge Probert to do what he does best.

Hundreds of thousands are doing the same in front of their televisions in living rooms and basements across North America. For about a minute, time stands still. The men battle fiercely with dozens of punches thrown. The players on both benches stand and cheer, banging their sticks against the boards like a Scottish ritual of war. Like David and Goliath thousands of years earlier, it is single-man combat. Domi and Probert fight for their countries, their brothers, their teams, their fans.

The referees let the "goons" go until Probert knocks Domi down. The Red Wings bench erupts, much like the Israelites did when David slew the giant. It is as if they've already won the game. For the remaining 59:23 of ice time, the arena will buzz, and the TV commentators will howl. No one can stop talking about yet another infamous Probert-Domi showdown. (This is one of nine times Probert and Domi will fight in an NHL game during their careers, always preceded and followed by much fanfare.)

A key nugget to remember from this story is that this game in December 1992 is reminiscent of many games, where few can remember the final score (the Rangers won 5–3) but many remember the Probert-Domi battle. Interestingly, many NHL fans carry with them the memories of the League's greatest fights and fighters. They are the equivalent of Norse sagas.

The web portal www.hockeyfights.com is evidence of this. A few quick clicks through the site reveal the passion that thousands have for fights. Names like Dave "the Hammer" Schultz and Terry O'Reilly from the 1970s. Dave Semenko, Probert, Domi, and Marty McSorley from the 1980s and 1990s. Georges Laraque and Derek Boogaard from the 2000s. In today's modern game (circa 2020), due to evolving rule and culture changes, players who are specialists as protectors are rare but fights that draw attention remain, and in the contemporary game, there are all-around players who can fight.

In 2019, the Capital's veteran captain and one of the greatest goal-scorers in NHL history, Alex Ovechkin (a noted non-fighter), knocked out 19-year-old Andrei Svechnikov with a flurry of brutal punches that floored the Hurricanes' young rookie and sent him into concussion protocol. Overnight, the fight was one of the most discussed social media topics in all of sport. It went viral with hockey fans all over the world. For Ovechkin, the fight was a rarity. In fact, according to www.hockeyfights.com, it was just his fourth in a career dating back to 2005.

But for Bruins defenseman Zdeno Chara, also a multi-time all-star and League-wide star, fighting has been more common. Chara, whose jaw was broken by a shot on goal during the 2019 Stanley Cup finals, is a feared fighter, possibly, alongside the Montreal Canadiens' John Ferguson, one of the most feared ever.

Like Ferguson, Chara is revered for sticking up for his teammates, changing the tempo of a game (often with a fight), and most notably for throwing his opponents around like "rag dolls." He is a fan favorite. He has fought, as of the end of 2021, according to www.hockeyfights.com, 65 times and – based on voting by fans – has never "lost" a fight.

Fighting: Stay or Go? Good or Bad? Valuable or a Cheap Sales Tactic?

Fighting sells tickets, attracts viewers, and adds an element of unique excitement for fans, or at least certain segments of fans. However, let's be honest: it is violent. Injuries happen in the short term and some of the names noted in the introduction have suffered longer-term mental and physical health problems. Further, as is well documented, violence breeds violence.

Yes, for every fan who loves a good fight, there is another who does not and decides to keep their child away from the game. This has led to much scrutiny and, not surprisingly because of the intense coverage, fighting has become an important issue for the NHL and the sport of hockey today. It has led to an ongoing discussion – keep fighting in the game or not – that has sport and business implications. Interestingly, this decision has yet to be made at the NHL level.

The League has created restraints to reduce fighting (e.g., more severe penalties) and eliminate fighting beyond a 1:1 battle (i.e., suspensions for third player in or leaving the bench), yet it is still allowed in the sport, with a relatively low penalty (5-minute major) for those who fight. The League, via rule changes, also made the game faster such that the traditional goon, the one-dimensional player who fought as their primary duty, no longer exists in the NHL.

The NHL is the only major professional sports league in North America that does not immediately eject a player for fighting.[1] In fact, fighting has been an integral part of the game for more than 100 years, influencing outcomes on the ice and providing "entertainment" to fans beyond the core sport.

Although the fighting rules have been tightened, and the number of fights in pro hockey have declined for more than a decade, this aspect of the game is still integral to the NHL's DNA and was most evident during the 2020 bubble playoffs when 16 fighting majors were assessed (up from six the previous year) after just 44 contests. In fact, two of the fights happened inside the first three minutes of two different games.

The fact that a specific NHL rule is in place (which says that a player must be in three fights in a single game before he is ejected) supports the view that fighting is tolerated and important to the game. The website www.hockeyfights.com reports that the number of fights per game in the NHL in 2001–2 was 0.65, declining gradually over subsequent years to nearly one-third of the previous total (0.17 fights per game to date in the 2018–19 season). Interestingly, that same data source also reports that the number of games with more than one fight was 172 in 2001–2 compared to 22 in 2018–19.

The number of fights trends lower as each year goes by.

A deeper read about the *Hockeyfights* data tells a clear story. The 21st-century NHL features fewer fights, fewer games with multiple fights, and fewer NHL players fighting. In fact, many players do not fight at all. Alex Ovechkin is a classic example of a player who is a very capable fighter yet who very rarely drops his gloves. His focus is on winning games and scoring goals (749 in fact, when this book went to press during the 2021–2 season).

The statistics and anecdotes make clear that fighting in pro hockey is on the way down, if not out. But a declining trend line doesn't automatically mean these "dustups" should be removed from the game or reduced even further by putting more rules in place (such as automatic ejections or multi-game suspensions when they happen).

From a business perspective, the concepts of a "niche market" and a "loyal customer" may help illustrate why this decision is so challenging. On the niche market, there are a set of fans for whom fighting is a highly attractive part of the game, if not the most attractive. Elimination of fighting means a high risk of losing these fans.

From a loyal customer perspective, the core customers for any organization are the lifeblood of brand, revenue, profit, and growth. The NHL has a long-standing set of core fans who are loyal customers and who have built that loyalty to a product that includes fighting. Why mess with that?

Simply stated, the decision to deal with fighting is very complicated and even more complicated when you consider the implications beyond hard-core fans and loyal customers. There are business and social outcomes at play. Is the hockey parent who covers their kids' eyes during a fight more or less important than the fan jumping out of their seat and mimicking every punch taking place on the ice?

We can address the issue and analyze the decisions tied to keeping fighting (or removing it) in the NHL by contrasting the benefits of fighting with its drawbacks and then by extending the issues and learning to other contexts. Thus, we might ask you how you look at this subject from a variety of perspectives: sport, business, society, athlete health, and fan marketing.

The Sport Perspective on Fighting in the NHL

Fighting in the NHL is a long-held tradition and a bedrock element of the sport. In fact, during the August 2020 playoffs fighting increased, with eight punch-ups taking place during the first week alone. The reason? Months of inactivity, empty seats, and a unique best-of-five knock-out round made it seem like every shift and every chip (or cheap) shot mattered. Once the surviving teams reached the Conference Finals that September, the intensity elevated even further. Case in point: during Game 4 of the Lightning-Islanders series, New York's Matt Martin launched a long shot on Tampa Bay goalie Andrei Vasilevskiy a fraction of a second after the first-period horn sounded.

The shot was meaningless, breaking unwritten NHL rules, but Lightning defenseman Kevin Shattenkirk immediately took off after Martin and the gloves came off. So incensed were the Tampa Bay players, they were willing to wear, with the Islanders, a roughing penalty (after the horn!) to start the second period.

From a codification perspective, fighting has been a key element of the game from its earliest days. As a result, clubs (coaches and players) have used fighting to change momentum, intimidate an opponent, or get a key player off the ice (via penalty time). The

enforcer or goon (a player who specializes in fighting and protecting the club's star players) was once a requirement on each team and
remains something that most teams still draft or recruit for today.

By traditional definition, this player often is not as skilled at
passing or shooting, plays limited minutes on the ice, but is available when needed to fight. Dave Semenko, one of the early en-
forcers, found that his primary job was to protect rising young star
Wayne Gretzky and create room for him on the ice.

From a control perspective, fighting is penalized by League
rules but not in a strong way. Since 1922, when the rule was put
in place by the NHL, each player who fights receives a five-minute
misconduct penalty, which means that player is lost to their team
for five minutes of game time (i.e., they must sit out the next five
minutes of the 60-minute game). However, the team of the penalized player does not have to play shorthanded (i.e., they do not
need to reduce the number of players on the ice, like they do for
other penalty types, such as tripping or slashing).

In 1992, an "instigator" penalty was added by the League, which
gives officials the ability to penalize a player – with a minor two-
minute penalty (which does lead to the team being down a player) –
who clearly started the fight. Many argue that this rule has decreased
the number of fights, as a player does not want to put their team in a
shorthanded position if they expressly start something.

When a fight happens on the ice, the two line officials will let
the players go at it until the fight stalls or one player goes to the
ice in a compromised position. This is the point when the lines-
men jump in and stop the bout. This practice allows the fight to
continue to a conclusion and for it to continue long enough to be
a spectacle for fan consumption.

A player can also fight more than once per game, without extra
penalty and without threat of future suspension. As noted, after
a third fight, a player will be ejected from a game, but with no

negative consequences to his team on the ice. A variation of this rule exists in other countries, such as Australia and its Australian Rules Football where AFL players may fight and stay in the game. The difference is that upon completion of the contest (usually early the next week), a tribunal will determine whether a player is required to miss any upcoming games.

Interestingly, in European, collegiate, and junior hockey leagues, fighting results in an automatic ejection from the game. An argument can be put forward by some that fighting reduces more violent activities on the ice, such as spearing, injurious slashing, or cross-checking. This argument is based on the reality a player or one of his teammates can respond with a fight. The enforcer's role (such as a player like Semenko) is based on this paradigm because the threat of the enforcer coming after a dirty player deters many players from harassing or becoming overly aggressive against a star (or key) player on the enforcer's team.

In comparing these two possible benefits of fighting, the argument considered to have more weight is when discussing a star player who could otherwise be the target of violent play, save for threat of a fighting response by his enforcer teammate. Like many pro sports leagues, the NHL realizes that star players sell tickets and having fans miss out on seeing a Crosby, McDavid, or Ovechkin is bad for the game.

An assessment of the on-ice performance involving teams that fight during the last 40 years finds that teams who fight more than average perform less than average (i.e., win fewer Stanley Cups and President's Trophies). However, we take this with a grain of salt, as the number of fights may not be indicative of fighting's role or use by any high-performing team.

Chara, as noted in the introduction, is the classic example. Throughout his more than 20-year career, he has only fought a few times per season, likely due to the fact that most players have no interest in fighting him. However, the impact of the fear of fighting him and his presence undoubtedly influences the success of the teams he has been on, having won a Stanley Cup and been on a winning team most years of his career.

The Business View of Fighting in the NHL

Lest anyone forget, the NHL is a business. And although the League is structured as a not-for-profit, each club is a for-profit organization. The League, even as a not-for-profit, has a high priority on revenue generation and the ability to share as much revenue as possible with the clubs, particularly those in small markets or in markets where hockey is well-established.

The NHL manages brands (League, 32 clubs, and more than 750 players) all requiring clear attention to detail and insight on where acceptable future revenues will come from. In addition to ticket sales and media rights, revenue is drawn from merchandise sales, sponsorship, and digital marketing.

These elements require the devotion of fans (consumers) who are willing to part with their time and money. What role does fighting hold in the decisions of fans? Of sponsors?

At the brand level, fighting matters. Probert, Domi, Chara, and Boogard were important brands for the NHL and fighting was a core element of their identities. It helped them sustain long careers and benefit their families financially but at a very real physical cost.

Teams have also successfully branded around fighting, including the famous "Broad Street Bullies," the nickname of the Philadelphia Flyers Stanley Cup winning teams in the 1970s. Examples can be drawn from other sports as well.

In basketball, for instance, the Detroit Pistons were known as the Motor City Bad Boys and their fierce style of play helped them win two NBA championships. Similarly, in the NFL, nicknames (brand monikers) were created for units with names such as the Fearsome Foursome, Legion of Doom, and Steel Curtain.

Setting aside old nicknames, contemporary sports involving fighting are part of this discussion as well. Yes, prize fights in boxing declined but, in a contradictory manner, mixed martial arts (MMA) rose dramatically, and the UFC was valued (in 2021) at more than US$9 billion.

Additionally, MMA regularly features not just men but also women fighting for championships. And, unlike hockey where there are goals and fantastic saves, in the UFC world, there is nothing else. It's all fighting, all the time. This form of fighting has a core fan base and growing appeal with younger audiences.

The Societal Perspective on Fighting in the NHL

There is really no questioning that "violence breeds violence" and there is a litany of research in many fields to support this as fact. However, we also acknowledge that despite the numerous issues associated with conflict and injury, violence is entertainment.

In the same way that fighting may attract fans to the NHL, Formula I, Indy Car, and NASCAR all recognize that defined percentages of their fan base hope there will be a crash during a race they are watching or attending.

In general, the two statements above about violence are true. On one hand, violence can generate more violence, yet observation shows that violence might be appropriate in some situations (e.g., self-defense, emergency conditions of entrapment).

On the other hand, we acknowledge a competitive battle between two humans (in the time-tested form of fighting or wrestling) is something many readers enjoy and watch with interest.

Indeed, many sport purists are drawn to raw sports (i.e., without technology and sophisticated equipment), such as fighting sports, running, and swimming.

This idea captures the dichotomy of fighting in the NHL. It is part of the game, something some fans love and something many people enjoy watching. However, it is also violence where a player may sustain injuries, where a young fan is exposed to bad behavior, and where it may encourage an adult fan to copy this behavior at home or in a public setting.

As noted, fighting is not new. In fact, a quick history lesson tells us it has been part of the game since the late 1800s when elite ice hockey took shape in Canada and along the northern US border. Some believe it became part of the young sport due to the "natural" in-game elements (e.g., body checking, neutral zone play), which led to elements such as "intimidation," "momentum," and "need for space on the ice for skill players," which in turn led to fighting becoming part of the game.

Alternatively, some sociologists argue the fighting grew out of the culture of Canada in the 1800s that included high poverty levels, crime, and hardscrabble lives. In recent years, medical associations, celebrities, politicians, and groups have publicly suggested that fighting should be removed from hockey, including influential people such as Mary Simon (Governor General of Canada), Gretzky, and Luc Tardif (IIHF president).

The Athlete Health Perspective on Fighting in the NHL

Perhaps the most challenging issue facing team sports today is the health of athletes, with particular emphasis on head injury (concussions) and neck/back injury (spinal cords). Whether American football, rugby, soccer, lacrosse, or ice hockey, the short-term (i.e., ability to play) and long-term (i.e., post-career) health of players has become a very important issue. In the NHL, like in the NFL, this is of concern to players and owners alike, not to mention families and friends of players and the financial advisors to various parties for investments of differing levels.

The NHL, like many pro leagues, has been working to protect the health of its players. This has been happening for a while. For instance, in 1971, the NHL added its "third man in" rule, which meant that a third player who joined a fight between two players already underway would be ejected from the game (and possibly more). This has reduced the number of multiplayer (i.e., three or more) fights or brawls in hockey where a punch from behind was more likely. In fact, the number of bench-clearing brawls has been reduced to zero in the NHL (in recent years) with this rule and others.

More recently, new rules to reduce hitting from behind, stick work to the head, hits to the head, and hits to unaware players have been put in place by the NHL to further protect athlete health. Although not directly about fighting, these rules have made the game safer for players but also reduced instances that traditionally led to a fight.

The Fan Marketing Perspective on Fighting in the NHL

It is widely argued by hockey administrators that most fans and players prefer to keep fighting as part of the NHL. However, as any marketer understands, consumers (or fans, in this case) are not homogeneous; they are segmented groups with different backgrounds, needs, wants, and characteristics. Niche markets exist in hockey as they do in any professional sport.

Thus, we clearly know there are groups of fans (or potential fans) who are turned off (either partially or fully) by fighting. So, while the reduction (or removal) of fighting from the NHL risks losing some hard-core loyalists, it can also attract new fans and make current fans ambassadors to potential new fans.

Want an illustration? Picture the mother covering her young child's eyes during a second-period fight while a hardened fan stands, shadow boxes, and cheers during that same fight. They are from two different segments with two different views.

The big question, then, is which segment is larger and how much of a deterrent to fighting is appropriate for each? For instance, would the diehard fan who loves fighting stop consuming NHL games if fighting were entirely removed?

Evidence from other settings where fighting was removed (NCAA, Olympics) suggests the game still thrived. Would the (potential) fan who dislikes fighting consume more NHL hockey if this element was officially removed? There would undoubtedly be movement in either direction, but the magnitude of such decision making might be irreversible.

Next, consider the significance of the need for revenue growth or brand awareness on the decision. Does the discussion change if we are talking about youth participation or player safety? The reader should quickly see that there is no easy answer but the NHL's stewards, acting in the best interests of the game, must walk a tightrope featuring tradition on one side (and fans who enjoy fighting) versus societal evolution on the other (where one head injury is one head injury too many).

This is not unlike the matter of placing nets around rinks to protect fans from getting hit by errant pucks. Purists believe individuals should always watch the puck and nets interfere with their view of the game. But when a young person is hit, which happened in Columbus in 2002 when 13-year-old Brittanie Cecil was struck by a puck leading to her death, the impetus for the NHL to protect its fans led to nets as an NHL regulation.

Rick's Recall: Famous Hockey Lines

This Recall doesn't involve fighters (by name). Instead, it identifies famous front lines that benefitted from the collective protection provided to them, protection that often facilitated their goal-scoring efficiency.

Where to start? First off, it's not possible to write about every famous NHL hockey line (i.e., the group of three – center and two wingers who play together shift after shift) that ever-thrilled NHL fans.

My favorite is Buffalo's **French Connection Line** with Gilbert Perreault, Rick Martin, and René Robert, a trio from Quebec that clicked impressively for the Sabres from 1972–9.

In short, hockey lines are important and recognizing the mid-1990s Flyers' **Legion of Doom Line** (Lindros, LeClaire, and Renberg) and Colorado's **AMP Line** (Alex, Milan, and Peter) quickly come to mind. If you live and breathe hockey, you have a few of your own.

What's important is reminding readers to think about aligning workers who work well together and rarely fight. Employees who anticipate needs before problems hit. Or finish sentences for others to make sure a key point is communicated and understood.

We appreciate great lines in hockey because they score goals and tire out the best defenses. They make opposing goalies nervous and cause fans to get a little more excited. They sell tickets.

Businesses can benefit from that same kind of thinking. One boss may only see a maze of cubicles filled with faceless drone-like workers. But another, an opportunist, may realize that seat assignment and group project assignments matter.

Many people have worked in large offices (before COVID-19) and know employees talk over and through the foamboard. They time coffee breaks and lunches to fit into the schedules of people they like. They stay late, working extra hours, because someone nearby is inspirational.

So, why talk about great hockey lines here? Do they matter?

Most journalists have written about a "line" developing an innate sense of cohesion. Having spent months and years working together, each player knows microscopic elements about their line mates. Things like where (on the stick) they like to receive the puck, which skating leg is dominant, how much space a player needs in traffic, how much ice a player can cover on a breakout.

One way of thinking about hockey units is by drawing from Malcolm Gladwell's famed 10,000-hour rule in his 2008 book *Outliers*. In that seminal text, Gladwell suggested practicing something repetitiously for 20 hours a week for 10 years would enable the worker to enjoy a higher level of proficiency and success.

When we look at hockey lines and combine the number of hours practiced and games played in school, juniors, the minors, and NHL, we see how each player moved toward Gladwellian success. Taking three players and linking them (that is, making them play together for years), is like the 10,000-hour rule on steroids.

Can that efficiency be modeled in the workplace? Yes, but it involves managers and directors showing a willingness to explore combinations. NHL coaches do this all the time trying to reach states of perfection they mysteriously refer to with words such as "flow," "rhythm," "awareness," and "clicking."

Readers must understand good coaches are always observing players. A coach tinkers. The modern ones look at data covering plus/minus or hundreds of other metrics. The older ones believe they "know" intuitively what generates wins and achieve team goals. They worry whether they have pushed players to reach their full potential.

Bosses have the same obligation but may not look at daily, weekly, monthly, or annual results in the same way as a hockey coach. They may see only the blur of the business and not the way the workers interact and cohesively bond.

Are they fluid? How do they handle pressure? Do they continually outperform other combinations? Do they like each other and look forward to making others around them better? These kinds of questions matter when bosses are analyzing cohesion, efficiency, productivity, turnover, profitability, and performance.

Just as coaches can lose their jobs when they lose their teams (and lose too many games), bosses are not immune from getting fired.

Thus, it falls to bosses to think about such things and even to imagine giving great office combinations nicknames the way journalists do. If the NHL could produce the **Bread Line**, **Punch Line**, **Sky Line**, **Production Line**, or **Party Line**, maybe you can devise a creative way to acknowledge the greats in your office.

What Do We Think? What Can Businesses Learn from Hockey Fights?

This chapter suggests there are numerous points of views and ideas around fighting in hockey. The old adage "it depends" is easy to invoke but we wanted to take a stand, share our viewpoint, and then link that viewpoint to other business contexts.

First, we'd say the NHL has done a very good job in removing the most violent episodes from hockey, such as bench-clearing brawls, fighting with fans, two-on-one battles (third man in), sucker punches, hits from behind, and stick-swinging incidents. The instigator penalty and related rule changes have rendered the fighting specialist irrelevant in hockey, so a player who fights must have it as part of their entire package (à la Chara).

Secondly, our opinion should not shape the reader's real-world intuition but rather make the reader more informed and better able to extend new learning (or ways of thinking) to their own contexts and areas of interest. The physicality of the NHL and the existence of fighting during the game is something we grew up with and something we would hate to see go in its entirety. We believe that fighting – in the form of an honest, one-on-one battle that is integrated in the game – is a part of the NHL's tradition, brand, and appeal. We are aligned with the NHL to rid the game of bench-clearing brawls, hits from behind, and knockouts that lead to permanent health issues for a player.

We also know research consistently reveals there exists a segment of NHL fans who attend games because of the possibility they will witness a fight. We also think individuals who are offended by fighting, violence, or conflict have already chosen to avoid attending or watching NHL games. In other words, that audience has been lost already.

As well, we know that there is much more to a market than two homogeneous segments. Thus, there are fans who fall between these two solitudes who certainly would find a faster, higher-scoring, and less violent version of the game more attractive.

Third, there is no better source of evidence to inform an issue like this than performance data. So, let's marry the fact that the NHL enjoyed its highest Stanley Cup ratings ever in the United States in 2019 and one can make a case for not changing the game further as relates to the rules governing fighting. The old saying "if it ain't broke, don't fix it" still works. But let's always be open to modifications. Things (people, eras, leadership, values) change.

But note also, in a world where a share point (often discussed as a slice of a 100 percent marketing or revenue pie) is worth tens of millions of dollars, losing market share to sports that adapt more quickly to societal needs is unacceptable to the bean counters. The NHL, therefore, always aggressively guards how its game content (its brand) is consumed and leveraged. And it is always aware that a fight on the ice will draw media scrutiny.

Fourth and finally, does fighting (as it relates to the corporate organization or small business operator) matter? Most readers will agree there is no place in the workplace for any kind of bullying, fisticuffs, or physical contact. And we completely agree. Without exception.

But what about disagreements or conflicts that are positive? It's well-documented in psychology that the best performances (sport, business, or otherwise) come when we are focused, stressed, pushed, motivated, and faced with a fierce competitor. Although not fisticuffs, this is a form of fighting. Crosby plays his best against Ovechkin, and Coke brings its innovative A-game when Pepsi pushes them. Apple and Samsung have often fought in courtrooms and markets around the world, but the resulting innovations in technology and products are easily observed. The list of business competitors is endless.

Practically, can we look at every issue that a business faces and suggest that finding peaceful consensus on every operational issue is the best path forward? Clearly not. Is a verbal disagreement that leads to constructive criticism and pressure to perform capable of serving the same purpose as a hockey fight? Absolutely.

Thus, the learning we'd emphasize is the creation of a culture where conflict – within reason – is turned into high performance and competitive drive. Yes, we would suggest that fighting in hockey represents a value that managers can extrapolate. Indeed, office managers need to understand that occasionally, people must disagree or stand up for themselves. Not in a fighting way but in a constructive way pushing toward innovation and competitive flare.

Like the NHL, fighting in public is virtually non-existent. But in an age of mass shootings, terrorism, and uncertainty, we must understand that frustrations in the workplace are causing situations never imagined in the past. That was a time when a less civilized society used fist fights and duels to resolve issues.

Today, conflict resolution is an integral part of day-to-day leadership and management. So, think about fighting in the NHL as an abstract construct. It may serve as a metaphor or device for talking with employees about their real or imagined conflicts.

CHANGING THE LINES

11

Veterans Matter

Hockey, like any physical, high-speed sport, is a young person's game, at least at the high-performance level (e.g., KHL, NHL, Olympic, Paralympic). For example, at the 2018 Olympic Winter Games, the women's hockey teams from Canada and US featured average ages of 27 and 24, respectively, with no woman over the age of 33 (it was 30 for the US).

Like we said, it is a young person's game.

So, when a player competes in the NHL or at the Olympics well into their 30s, 40s, or even 50s (shout out to NHL legend Gordie Howe), it is exceptional. To draw comparisons to the regular business world, we'll compare 35 and 40 in hockey to 65 and 70, respectively, in most business contexts.

Although mandatory retirement was common in the global workplace, it was never a formal thing in the NHL. Informally, however, many clubs, coaches, and even national governing bodies for Olympic teams put measures in place to move away from older athletes in favor of younger ones.

For instance, Sport Canada, which financially supports Canadian athletes focused on Olympic Games competition, allows sports – the National Sport Organization (e.g., Hockey Canada) – to put age limits on Sport Canada funding (at their own discretion). Not surprisingly, coaches and general managers have also informally been known to phase out older players for younger talent.

For the regular working world, beginning with a US Congressional decision in 1986, many governments and public sector organizations around the world have eliminated mandatory retirement at 65, changing the career trajectories of Baby Boomers and complicating the retirement decision for many.

Of course, working past 65 has long existed in many fields, but historically it was not an option for most. For example, in 2020, the late actress Betty White was still making movies and TV shows at 98 and Warren Buffet, who turned 90 that same year, was the working chair and CEO of Berkshire Hathaway, one of the leading investment firms in the world.

While some people in particular careers (e.g., small business owners, rock musicians, consultants) thrive after 65, it was very rare and was frequently prohibited in any highly formalized work environment – such as manufacturing, government, retail, or education – where employees worked under very specific conditions and/or negotiated agreements that broadly adhered to employment laws or government policies.

In the NHL, the highly detailed collective bargaining agreement (CBA) is much more complex and outlines working conditions that are much more specific and directive than what most managers or employees deal with on the job.

Our respective places of employment – universities (a public and a private) – were among the first to make this important decision allowing workers older than 65 years. In fact, the first evidence of this decision is linked to the Hoover Institution at Stanford University, which decided to engage retired Nobel Laureates. That decision reportedly led to success and positive outcomes for the institution and the university due to the credibility and prestige these new hires (or existing staff who were encouraged to keep working) generated.

The Pros and Cons of Retirement

But decisions surrounding retirement are not all roses. It is not easy for the governments or firms who make them, and yet it's an important one with a notable list of pros and cons. Let's start on the "pro" side.

First, as evidenced by the Hoover Institution's decision, at 65, people do not suddenly become outdated or irrelevant. In fact, in some fields – particularly those grounded in knowledge – individuals over 65 can be the most important people for an organization on a particular topic.

Imagine NASA having to release one of its most accomplished engineers because she turned 65? Or a university pushing subject-matter experts (who have spent 40+ years building expertise and are on the edge of a research breakthrough) out the door because of a specific birthday. It would make no sense.

Second, a point very similar to the first pro, but at an industry level, is that an exodus of large numbers of industry experts who hit retirement age concurrently can arguably damage an industry (or industry sector) with considerable loss of institutional knowledge and experience. In hockey terms, this might be like an organization trading or pushing out all of its veterans and announcing they were only using rookies and first-year players.

Third, removing these limits responds to the argument that "forcing out" or firing an older worker because of their age and not their ability is discriminatory.

There is also the issue of soft skills. Often senior people bring important leadership, team chemistry, and cohesive group dynamics to an organization. These traits go beyond job description contributions and often play significant roles in the tacit outcomes of specific positions. Sometimes older employees are the best mentors, coaches, or role models. They set the tone in the "locker room."

Finally, from a financial perspective, an individual who works longer makes more salary, increases their pension, and extends their benefits (if applicable). This can be good for the employee but costly for the organization. So, this point is both a pro and a con.

Now, let's flip to the negative aspects. The cons. To begin, one of the most discussed negatives of not having mandatory retirement (or even limits on terms in leadership positions) is that a person in a position of power (often for too long a period) can become overly used to their influence and possibly ineffective (i.e., stagnant) in this "untouchable" position. Here, their reputation (of past glories) allows them to believe they are good as they once were. The truth is a discussion of erosion.

In the Olympic Games, the 100-meter sprint is won by the athlete who slows down the least at the end of the race. Thus, much may be made about final times, wind conditions, and the explosion "out of the blocks," but sprints are won at the end. Not the beginning or mid-race.

Second, it is well-known that new blood, those employees with youthful energy, up-to-date technology skills, unique curiosity, and modern views on leadership, can bring significant value to an organization. But without a mandatory retirement policy, the number of new employees entering the organization will decline because there are fewer annual openings.

Next, there could be a series of individual-level negative outcomes for people who continue to work well beyond 65. We'll list a few here:

1 Working after 65 in a stressful environment can bring on subtle or highly evident health challenges as the worker ages. Of course, there is a counter argument that, for some people, retiring early from a job they love and one that is a major part of their identity is detrimental to their overall health as soon as they retire. We all know stories of people who do not retire well (as well as tales of those who flourished).
2 Older workers generally realize that the longer they work, the more they forgo opportunities to enjoy retirement age, including travel and time relaxing with family/friends, and opportunities to try new things.

So, clearly, there are two sides to this retirement discussion. We would suggest the pros generally outweigh the cons, but our opinion matters only if you and your staff discuss these issues collaboratively and design policies for employees approaching retirement age.

Retirement and the NHL

The same issue exists every year in the NHL. GMs hold private meetings with aging stars, many coming off injuries or less-than-sterling seasonal stats. Those GMs almost always ask questions like "How much do you have left in the tank?" or "You got another one in you?"

As everyone in the organization knows, from the owner down to the junior communications assistant, a debate is raging in the GM's head about whether the time has come to cut ties. Where is this player in their contract? Will they commit to off-season workouts? Have they lost a step? What do they give us that we can't find in someone else?

This is never a topic to ignore because employees talk about turnover (more often than many bosses realize) and employees who reach the age of 60 often spend a great deal of time planning for or thinking about retirement. Some believe they cannot afford to stop working while others become convinced retiring will make them happier (increased free time!). Others fear retirement (too much free time!) or believe they still have much they want to achieve in their careers.

Norm's Nostalgia: Hockey and Veterans

Rick and I, and certainly many readers, especially anyone over 35, will immediately relate to this nugget. Quite simply, "life gets in the way of friendships." A lot.

Think back to your core group of friends during childhood, high school, and/or university/college. What about that great group of colleagues from one of your first jobs? They had a huge impact on your life. A massive and undeniable one.

But, if you are like us, it gets harder and harder to keep in touch as time goes on. Interests change. People enter long-term relationships. End relationships. Build careers. Move. Get married. Have children or adopt. Develop health issues. Assist elderly parents. Economies crash. Dreams are chased. Pandemics explode. People lose jobs or take new ones.

We all earn our "veteran status" sooner than many of us would like.

We believe, though, that sport – and more specifically a team sport, like hockey – is one of the great ways to keep these friendships alive.

In my case, these friendships are the Lindsay Crown Royals.

Yes, a hockey team named after the town I grew up in and the favorite rye whiskey of many on the club. Sure, it is rare any of us would have that drink anymore, but occasionally we do. And the flood of nostalgia it delivers is palpable.

Here's how it happens. Every year (except when we are dealing with a pandemic), we – a group of friends all from the small town, plus a few additions (brothers, friends, etc.) – pick a tournament location (it's amazing how massive the tournament industry is across North America). Think Chicago, Las Vegas, Montreal, Mont Tremblant, Nashville, Niagara Falls, Quebec City, and so on. We pick the event well in advance so we can work out and coordinate family and work schedules.

Then, we travel. Some drive. Some fly. Some even end up canceling when life gets in the way.

Eventually, a rag-tag team hits the ice. Sometimes we get our butts kicked and every now and then we win (including 2019!). Sometimes it is amicable. Sometimes it gets nasty (but, hey, that's hockey – see chapter 10!).

Win or lose, it's irrelevant.

What I love, even crave, is the feeling of walking into the dressing room, a year removed from last playing with this group, and a huge wave of nostalgia washes over us. Admittedly, I find myself holding back tears as I walk around the room giving everyone a hug.

Then, within minutes, as if nothing ever changed, it's 1986 again. The past made present like some improbable movie involving ghosts or phantoms.

The hockey performance really doesn't matter. It's the essence of the sport and our feeling of interpersonal commitment that makes these annual reunions so much more than important. It's the experiences of a set of veterans, together again, sliding right back into their comfort zones, contributing and enjoying every minute. Something many a rookie cannot possibly grasp.

From left to right, back row: Ian Clarke, Kevin McCarthy, Andrew Suggitt, Sean McColl, Matt Holloway, Doug West, Matt Noel; *front row:* Norm O'Reilly, Matt Suggitt, Dan Gardiner, Brian Reeds, Chris Walling.

To highlight the importance of veterans and bring this discussion back to the ice, let's draw on a few stories about veterans who played well past the expected retirement age for traditional NHL players.

Think of Jaromir Jagr, the NHL's second all-time leading scorer, who played his last NHL game at 45 years of age and, at the time of writing, as a 50-year-old, had 19 points in his first 43 games of the 2021–2 season for the Kladno Knights in the Elite Czech

League. Or how about Chris Chelios, one of the NHL's great defensemen, who, over the course of 26 seasons, played until he was 48. Think that's old? What about the legendary Gordie Howe? Mr. Hockey played 26 NHL seasons and six WHA seasons, retiring at 52. Most notably, Howe played at a very high level in his 40s, winning a WHA scoring championship while playing alongside his two sons. Howe's record of most NHL games played was broken in the 2020–1 season by Patrick Marleau of the San Jose Sharks.

There is also Tim Horton, the co-founder of one of North America's leading coffee chains, who was still playing (and playing well) at 44 when he died in a tragic car accident. One could say Horton was extremely skilled at multitasking since he launched his business at age 34 while maintaining an NHL playing career. One wonders what his final statistics and his namesake company would look like had he avoided the tragedy that took his life.

As for goaltenders, there is no leaving out Dominik Hašek, who retired from the NHL at 43 and then played in the KHL until he was 47. Hašek was the only goalie to be named the League MVP on more than one occasion and won the award for most valuable goaltender six times in his 16-year career. Any member of this legendary and enduring set of stars could have been the focus of this chapter; however, we selected the oldest active NHL player when we started writing this book to embellish this "playing old" story.

The Zdeno Chara Story

His name is Zdeno Chara. As we were finishing our writing, he was 45 years old and his newest team, the Islanders, had finished its 2021–2 NHL campaign. Notably, at an impressive 6-foot-9, this brawny defenseman is the tallest player to have ever played in the NHL. In addition to his height, he is a fearsome fighter (when called upon), holds the hardest recorded shot in NHL history (nearly 109 mph at the 2012 NHL All-Star Game), and had appeared (as of late 2021) in an amazing 14 Game 7s (i.e., the deciding game of a playoff series) during his long history in the Stanley Cup playoffs (the most in NHL history).

2021–2 was Chara's 24th NHL season, and his first back with the New York Islanders where he started his career in 1997. Prior, he spent a season with the Washington Capitals. He spent 14 years with the Boston Bruins, a team with which he won his only Stanley Cup (2011) and made his mark as one of the greatest NHL defensemen ever (including winning the 2009 Norris Trophy as the League's best defenseman).

In providing a bit on Zdeno's background, we note his Slovakian heritage, his two silver medal–winning teams at the IIHF World Men's Hockey Championships (2000, 2012), a bronze (2004), and his service as Slovakia's flagbearer at the 2014 Sochi Olympic Games. He was drafted by the New York Islanders, playing there from 1997 to 2001, then traded to the Ottawa Senators (2001 to 2006) before moving to the Bruins.

Why tell Chara's story? There are numerous good reasons. First, if you identify yourself as a manager or leader, how good are you at identifying the value of a Chara, Chelios, Hašek, Horton, Howe, or Jagr when they are 25 years old (and not 40)? Think you can spot talent that will age like a fine wine and produce at high levels for the next two decades? What signs should you be looking for?

We'll grant you that each of the above players was good at 25 or even 30, but few could match them over the long haul. Which brings us to our key takeaway: all of us need to work at identifying talent early and ensuring that the great ones remain with an organization (unlike the Islanders and Senators who both lost Chara).

Second, managers and leaders should recognize the importance of a leader whose specific individual performance (perhaps based on only one metric) may be declining but whose overall value to the firm, division, or department remains high. In Chara's case, his TOI (time on ice) went from nearly 28 minutes/game in 2006–7 to 18 minutes/game in 2021–2. Meanwhile, his points total drifted from a high of 52 in 2011–12 down to 10 in 2020–1, yet his position as the captain of a continually successful club remained, including helping the Bruins reach the Stanley Cup finals in 2018–19 and the second round of the playoffs in 2019–20.

In addition to his height, fighting prowess, rocket shot, and winning ways, Chara also became known for a famous sport marketing moment of inadvertent ambush marketing. We mention it here because we think it is another example of an old guy getting more attention than others and the story provides evidence of the risk/reward nature of aging veterans.

This holds for most industries where a veteran performer is more expensive (i.e., higher pay) but has a shorter runway (i.e., the veteran is closer to retirement and possibly declining in some performance areas). A good veteran consistently holds corporate value in terms of institutional knowledge, mentoring, political (or bureaucratic) know-how, getting-things-done management, and so on.

They are also probably a much lower "flight risk" (to leave for a competitor) than a young high performer seeking opportunity, although we acknowledge that Chara did depart Boston at the end of 2020 and legendary quarterback Tom Brady also left New England's Patriots before winning the 2021 Super Bowl for the Tampa Bay Buccaneers. A debate, yes, but sometimes the old pros bring more value than we think at first glance.

Let us close with the infamous Chara "ambush marketing" example. It happened in late April 2011 during a deciding Stanley Cup playoff game (Game 7 of the Eastern Conference Quarterfinal) between the Bruins and Montreal Canadiens. During the game, Chara was caught on camera drinking a Coke out of the bottle (on the bench) during an intense game, where he had played nearly half of the on-ice minutes and was facing physical challenges caused by dehydration, which he had suffered from during a previous game in the series.

Colas are known as a drink of choice for pushing the body late in taxing sporting events. For instance, Ironman triathlons have cola available at aid stations during the run segment to provide a sugar and caffeine boost when competitors' energy stores are depleted.

So, what was the issue for Chara? Well, Pepsi was the NHL's sponsor and, by contractual right, was the only soft drink brand that could be displayed in NHL venues. Yet, here was one of the League's stars, known for his strength, endurance, and powerful presence, drinking a Coke – out of the bottle – on the bench! – in a vitally important playoff game.

Okay, that was good for Coke and horrific for Pepsi. It certainly was a problem for the NHL. As a result, Chara reportedly received a stern memo from the NHL and much social media chatter ensued about Pepsi versus Coke, whether carbonated soda is a good energy choice in such a situation, and whether Chara should have been fined or not.

But back to the topic of a veteran. Did Chara get more attention from this due to his stature? We think so. Did he get a lower penalty than a young player due to his history, image, and following? We'd bet on it.

Chapter Learning

So, where does this leave us? If you are managing people – which we assume many readers are (or will one day) – there are some *very* important takeaways to acknowledge.

First, age should be viewed as a potential asset in an employee. If they are productive, keep these inspiring, experienced vets on hand. Give them chances to mentor and coach others. And make sure they pass their know-how and experience on before leaving.

Second, communicate honestly and openly with older workers and make sure to identify who wants to keep working. Note those who have exceptional talent or experience. Build individual plans for each with retirement timelines that make strategic, not chronological, sense.

Third, put in place formal mechanisms for knowledge sharing/retention between old employees and young ones. This could be formal mentorship/coaching, digital information sharing/transfer, or job-shadowing programs.

Finally, think about the Robert DeNiro movie *The Intern*, and remember that in a world where people are healthier, living longer, seem more driven, and, in many cases, do not want to retire, you need to change your perception of who an intern might be.

You might have a frontline group that includes Chara, Chelios, Hašek, Howe, Jagr, and Selänne on your team. And even if you don't have the equivalent of those six on your office roster, just finding one of them to help mentor the rookies is worth the scouting report and incremental investment of time and managerial support.

12

The Don Cherry Story

In this chapter, we'd like to share a cautionary tale and offer some advice on matters of inclusion going forward. We'll do this by visiting the difficult topics of discrimination, exclusion, bias, and xenophobia (essentially a fear of different cultures or strangers).

In 2020, the long-standing history and significant prevalence of these topics was realized in violent, shocking, and traumatizing ways, such as the death of George Floyd; the January 6, 2021, insurrection at the US Capitol; and the mass shootings in Nova Scotia. All with COVID-19 looming.

Against that backdrop, we want to share the story of Don Cherry, a coach who rose to the height of celebrity as a controversial, passionate, tell-it-like-it-is NHL commentator.

Cherry's storied career in hockey spanned more than 50 years, decades characterized by the rise of the NHL and a vastly changing social landscape characterized by the events of 2020. Perhaps his termination in 2019 was a foreshadowing of things to come.

In discussing Cherry, we will land on an impactful lesson that involves a major Canadian television hockey personality, fired from his high-profile job as an NHL TV commentator, for stating his views on society but also because of his influence on Canada's understanding of the NHL, hockey, and society. This chapter about Cherry provides an opportunity to comment on the polarizing nature of "free speech," political correctness, and prevailing narratives in sport and in society.

The Cherry Dismissal

November 9, 2019, is the best date to start with because it's the date Cherry's career as a television sports personality started to end. On that Saturday evening, close to the annual November 11 Remembrance Day holiday in Canada (a day when many Canadians remember veterans of past wars), Cherry made statements that offended thousands.

As background for non-Canadians, we note that a common Canadian way of expressing support for military veterans is to wear a poppy (a red flower found in the fields of Belgium, a country where numerous World War I battles were waged and many Canadians died). Plastic versions of poppies, pinned on shirts, are a symbol of remembrance and worn each year in early November leading up to and around the official holiday (November 11). It is recognized as a statutory holiday by the Government of Canada.

Most Canadians and hockey fans will remember what happened that November 9, but before we spell it out, let us provide a brief Cherry biography. A former professional hockey player (mostly in the minor leagues, taking the ice in just one NHL playoff game), Cherry was a successful NHL coach with the Boston Bruins and Colorado Rockies before emerging as a very successful television commentator on "Coach's Corner."

This segment aired each Saturday night during *Hockey Night in Canada*. By some accounts, at his peak, Cherry was seen as the most popular television personality in Canada.

Cherry co-hosted "Coach's Corner" from 1986 until November 2019 with Ron MacLean, and the duo was widely celebrated across Canada and in nearly every corner of the NHL. MacLean was generally known for his quick wit while Cherry was recognized for a flamboyant style, fashionable suits, and a highly outspoken outlook on every aspect of hockey and broader society. Both men were recognized as having deep knowledge of the NHL and the game.

Cherry was also co-host of a long-running radio show (Grapeline), a key personality behind a video series known as "Rock'em Sock'em Hockey," and a frequent interviewee about his strong support of police, the military, Canada, and Canadian-born hockey players.

His outspoken nature often caused him to take aim at Europeans in the NHL, French Canadian hockey players, players who wore face guards, and political stances he disagreed with (such as Canada's decision to not participate in the 2003 Iraq War).

He would offer advice to young hockey players at home and his distinct style was highly popular (at least in terms of ratings). It was often reported that viewers of the French language *La Soirée du hockey* would instantly switch channels at intermission just to watch Cherry in English. Further, when Cherry made public appearances at events and arenas across the country, people came out in droves.

A Canadian Legend

To emphasize just how popular Cherry was in Canada requires acknowledging a 2004 CBC television series called "The Greatest Canadian," where more than 1.2 million Canadians voted on who they felt was the country's greatest citizen ever.[1] That year, Cherry came in seventh.

Not only did a hockey broadcaster poll seventh, but even more unbelievable, he was the top hockey person! Ahead of the legendary Wayne Gretzky, who was tenth (and who had retired only a few years prior), and other stars of the game.

The only Canadians who ranked ahead of Cherry were three politicians (Tommy Douglas [first], Pierre Trudeau [third], and Lester Pearson [sixth]); an environmental advocate, David Suzuki (fifth); a scientist, Frederick Banting (fourth); and Terry Fox (second), a one-legged young man who died during his run across Canada to raise funds for cancer research.

The man who invented the telephone, Alexander Graham Bell, ranked ninth, two slots behind Cherry. He was loved by many despite his frequently controversial commentary.

Norm's Nostalgia: *Hockey Night in Canada*

Don Cherry's passion for hockey and Canada, as well as his unwavering stances on the causes he believed in, attracted viewers whether they agreed with or disagreed with him. And it is unlikely few Canadian hockey fans disagreed with or were offended by his love of Canada and hockey. This passion drew people to watch him.

An interesting story that few remember today involves the St. Louis Blues – 2019 Stanley Cup champions and a regular playoff participant (having missed the playoffs in only nine of their 52 seasons). Turns out, the Blues were very close to becoming the Saskatoon Blues in 1983, with Cherry announced as their next head coach. The NHL intervened to stop the sale of the club, finding a new ownership group to keep the team in St. Louis.

From the early 1990s until the mid-2000s, small-market NHL clubs in Canada struggled financially for numerous reasons, including a very low Canadian exchange rate (relative to the US dollar), higher tax rates (relative to many US states), and a lack of media/marketing revenues (compared to similarly sized markets in the US).

The Ottawa Senators from 2001 to 2006 are a good example of this reality. This was a time when the "Sens" were among the best clubs in the NHL. In 2002–3, they won the President's Trophy for the best regular season results and, in 2005–6, after equaling their regular season total points from 2002–3, sent a total of nine players to the Winter Olympic Games. However, at those Games, Ottawa's Dominik Hašek, on a goaltending tear that year and known as one of the greatest goalies in NHL history, was lost to an injury and didn't finish the season. Many felt Hašek's injury cost the Senators the Stanley Cup, especially when they reached the finals the following year (ultimately losing in five games to the Anaheim Ducks).

Following the 2005–6 season, star defender Zdeno Chara (highlighted in chapter 11) left the club following his best season to sign a lucrative free-agent contract with the Boston Bruins. Public reports noted Chara wanted to return to Ottawa, but the club chose to sign its other star defenseman, Wade Redden (also a free agent). This was due to financial constraints, which dictated they could only afford one of the two players.[2] Although the club reached the Cup finals in 2007, Redden's career did not match Chara's.

One January day in 2010 while at my office at Stanford University, I received a call from Dave Naylor, a well-known Canadian sportswriter who was making the move from newspaper (*Globe and Mail*) to a sports network (TSN). Naylor was planning a major piece on the NHL and whether an American or expansion club or two might come back to Canada, after the Winnipeg Jets and Quebec Nordiques had left for Phoenix and Colorado about 15 years earlier.

The interest expressed by Naylor stemmed from a few factors, including (i) the Canadian dollar was now much stronger, and (ii) the NHL (as described in chapter 5) had signed a new collective bargaining agreement (CBA) following intense negotiations. The loss of the 2004–5 season meant there were new provisions to support small market clubs, including a salary cap to restrain spending, and revenue sharing to distribute resources more evenly. There were also rumors abounding of individuals and syndicates interested in owning clubs in Hamilton, Quebec, Toronto, or Winnipeg. There were even discussions of Saskatoon surfacing again, even with a metro population of only 335,000 people.

Naylor tasked me with undertaking an analysis of the market attractiveness and franchise viability for a return of an NHL club – either relocation or expansion – to each of Hamilton, Quebec, Toronto, and Winnipeg (sorry, Saskatoon).

I was provided with all the data I needed and set out to build a model to analyze each of the four markets. Fortunately, I had previously done work on NHL club profitability with my close colleague Dr. John Nadeau, so I was well versed in the topic.[3]

Armed with data, I set off to build a model that accounted for demographic factors, ownership potential, support of the League (and other owners), marketing potential, corporate presence, player investment potential, and other variables that could make a city attractive for a new owner or ownership syndicate.

Although complicated, we boiled the model down to two scores (ranked on the classic A-B-C scale that many schools use) for each market. Although Toronto (A+) and Hamilton (A–) scored very high on market attractiveness, both scored quite low (Toronto D– and Hamilton D+) on franchise viability, as both would face existing teams in the Maple Leafs and Buffalo Sabres. Further, they were unlikely to get NHL approval (much like Saskatoon Blues in 1983).

Quebec and Winnipeg scored equally on market attractiveness with a modest C+ largely because their location in cities where hockey is the number one sport was offset by their small market size (both under 1 million people), a limited corporate sector, and restricted potential for media/marketing revenues.

In both cases, new arenas, interested ownership groups, and very supportive fan bases were reportedly in place. Due to the expression of interest from the Government of Quebec in fully supporting a new arena for the Quebec club, its franchise viability (B+) was placed slightly higher than Winnipeg (B).

Due to the high interest in the topic, a six-part series was developed and shown on Canadian sport network TSN each night for six nights and printed in the *Globe and Mail* during those same six days. In short, there was a lot of media coverage for this story. I was also interviewed on *Hockey Night in Canada* by Cherry's partner Ron MacLean later that year about the research.

The six days of coverage garnered a lot of attention.

The first day described the model, with four days then provided for analysis of each city, and a final day for a summary. In my mind, all four cities were equally represented.

Looking back, I can say I was fortunate to be included in this media coverage as an interviewee and to have my analysis featured. Other interviewees included NHL Commissioner Gary Bettman, potential owners in each market, and local experts. Perhaps the research played a small role in helping the Jets return to Winnipeg.

Returning to the Cherry case, the facts seem indisputable. In a discussion with Ron MacLean about Remembrance Day, Cherry was quoted as saying, "You people that come here, you love our way of life, you love our milk and honey, at least you can pay a couple bucks for a poppy or something like that. These guys paid for your way of life that you enjoy in Canada. These guys paid the biggest price."[4]

After the game ended there was social media outrage that Cherry's comments were, if not racist, offensive to immigrants slighted by Cherry's suggestion that "you people" were not toeing the official Canadian line. Sportsnet, the NHL, and MacLean all expressed publicly (and immediately) that they didn't support Cherry's comments or the views he expressed. But the media heat was about to get turned up.

With Cherry refusing to back down, MacLean began apologizing for a failure to respond on-air and aggressively rebut Cherry's comments. Not surprisingly, the incident was the topic of extensive discussion and public discourse and, on November 11, Cherry was fired by Sportsnet.

It surprised few.

Following his dismissal from the network, Cherry said: "I know what I said, and I meant it. Everybody in Canada should wear a poppy to honor our fallen soldiers. I would have liked to continue doing 'Coach's Corner.' The problem is, if I have to watch everything I say, it isn't 'Coach's Corner.'"[5]

In later interviews, he remained strong in his words, continuing to suggest he still meant that everyone should wear a poppy on Remembrance Day. Following his termination, reports surfaced suggesting Cherry's firing hurt *Hockey Night in Canada*'s ratings.[6] Most, however, felt it was the right decision at the right time.

Free Speech versus Hate Speech

Regardless of your position on Cherry, much can be learned from this situation and the wider ramifications that organizations must think about when free speech is confused with hurtful or hateful words. In an age when a single social media comment can spread virally around the globe, corporations, limited liability companies (LLCs), not-for-profit organizations, and sole proprietors must ensure their leaders, representatives, advocates, and employees are aware of contemporary social norms and adhere to acceptable behavior as representatives of the organization.

This is a difficult concept for many who feel that a first amendment right exists (at least in the US) and gives individuals permission to say anything (or wear anything) regardless of how their language or symbols may offend. At the heart of this discussion is the conditionality of employment. In many US states, organizations can terminate employees without cause. In other states and provinces, most organizations must show cause or risk a lawsuit that a firing was unjust or unwarranted.

How then do we think about an employee making an extremely hateful, hurtful, deceitful, or discriminatory statement? This is no easy question because, as was witnessed during the four-year term of American President Donald Trump (2017–21), some individuals can Tweet insults and falsehood (frequently) without, at least in Trump's case, reprimand from their bosses (i.e., Trump's own political party).

The same reality is unlikely to exist at most companies and particularly in high-profile sports or entertainment firms where administrators, athletes, actors, and agents are regularly quoted or observed under a media microscope. But what of a small business in a small town? If an hourly worker is observed saying or conveying something that is racist, sexist, homophobic, religionist, or in any other way discriminatory or hurtful, should a firm take steps to fire the employee?

We feel, in 2022, an era when systemic oppression is widely discussed on multiple platforms, that managers, directors, vice presidents, CEOs, and founders must act or risk the suggestion that senior leadership (and the firm as a whole) condones the actions (words, symbols, images) of the individual. Again, this is a difficult position for many because there are leaders who do not want to believe the individual employee represents the whole or who believe the individual is entitled to their opinion or "free speech." In most places, this is an unsustainable position, and such a stance will leave the boss or leader on the wrong side of the history.

Often, the organization will not see the issue coming. Case in point: for years, the NHL's Philadelphia Flyers played a recording of Kate Smith singing *God Bless America*. In fact, after Smith sang the song in person prior to Game 6 of the 1974 Stanley Cup (which the Flyers won), the Flyers ownership group was so moved that in 1987 they erected a statue in front of the Spectrum (later it was moved to the front of Xfinity Live) honoring Smith's American patriotism.

But in 2019, it was discovered that nearly 90 years earlier (in 1931 and 1933), Smith had recorded songs with racist lyrics. Immediately, the Flyers were under attack and quickly made the decision to halt the use of the pre-game Smith recording and to remove her statue.

In Cherry's case, commentary that might have been considered entertaining, racy, or edgy in 1985, 1995, 2005, and 2015 was grounds for immediate firing in 2019. In fact, one could easily argue Cherry had uttered far more provocative and hurtful comments previously that never led to dismissal. This leaves us with four takeaways to stress:

1 Be aware of the changing world around you (your organization) and adapt to it. The fact that in 2019, the NHL, Sportsnet, and many other entities immediately responded against Cherry's comments reveals that social values evolve. The actions of those institutions represented what was required

of that enlightened era. In many ways, this concept has been discussed (circa 2020) as a calling for leaders to better understand *behavioral economics*,[7] a concept best explained by this calculus: if the downside risk of a decision (i.e., human judgment) can lead to scandal, corporate embarrassment, or the threat of career termination, then there is little to be gained by fighting for free speech or, in some cases, historic precedent. In other words, if the risk outweighs the upside benefit of free speech, most decision makers will err on the side of prevailing social norms. They simply can't wear the "heat" or public shaming that is now easily levied by outraged parties. Further, the concept of "evolving social norms" is difficult for many employees who are fixed in their ways or believe their rights "trump" the interests of the larger community or greater good. As an example, in 2020 during the COVID-19 pandemic, many Americans refused to wear face masks because they believed their individual rights were more important than the possibility of killing their neighbors. Frequently, Americans were heard saying, "No one is going to tell me to wear a mask" or "It's a violation of my Constitutional rights to require a mask." It wasn't, but explaining seat-belt laws or not yelling "fire" in a crowded movie theater was virtually impossible.

2 Identify (as early as possible) potential sources of negative outcomes and who may share in or receive the blame. Clearly, Cherry was a risk to others when he made offensive comments. Still, risk management is tricky business. If Cherry made inappropriate comments, who else was responsible? It wasn't just Cherry. It quickly became network executives (for employing Cherry), League administrators (for allowing him to continue), and sponsors (for endorsing) who would face withering criticism for employing or endorsing someone simply because he could deliver ratings.

3 In many cases, and this is seen frequently, only one employee
or a single customer needs to state they are offended and demand immediate change (often someone's resignation), an
apology, or a financial retribution. When the one is joined in
outrage by the many, the risk to the organization multiplies
exponentially. What to do? Get out ahead of the crisis because
the last thing a league, team, network, advertiser, or sponsor
wants (or can afford to "wear") is lost ratings, upset fans/
viewers, or a globally viral public relations nightmare. This explains why so many individuals are now terminated so quickly.
And don't believe that these issues only happen to other firms.
This can happen in the smallest village or at the smallest company. In an ideal world, Cherry would have been counseled
as he entered the last few years of his celebrated career and
advised that Canada was a different place. That any ranting
he generated could be perceived as "out of touch" with the
prevailing winds. Why wasn't he? Perhaps he was and perhaps
he did not care. The hard truth is that no institution should
go "soft" on matters involving racism, sexism, homophobia,
or a host of other discriminations that target a marginalized
community.

4 Understand that the past no longer matters. As Rebecca Solnit
noted in her book *A Field Guide to Getting Lost,* "Perhaps, it's
true that you can't go back in time, but you can return to the
scene of a love, of a crime, of happiness, and of a fateful decision; the places are what remain, are what you can possess,
are what is immortal."[8] What this suggests is that the choices
and actions of the past will always remain in those mentally
composed places. But they can also, for the hungry researcher,
provide damning evidence. The world of 2022 and beyond
is far different from the past and it explains why orientation
for every newly hired employee must reflect society's present

values. Your subordinates may revere the past ("how things used to be") and they may wish things hadn't changed. But they have. For many of your employees, you are obligated to help them transition to the conditions of a new place, this new age. If you don't, you and your firm are at risk.

Don Cherry entertained millions of Canadians and made discussions of hockey's greatest players water-cooler fodder for years. He wore his red maple leaf proudly and entertained almost weekly with his insight and candor. But like others before him, he eventually failed to understand the power of his words or the pain they created. Or how one day they might reverberate in ways he didn't (or couldn't) fully comprehend.

We would suggest that whether you are an employee or a boss, you recognize the two major challenges of communicating in contemporary society. First, we have rights as individuals but, as social media has shown, we now play with a very large group of teammates. Second, social media allows for direct and immediate interactions with wide, even global, reach.

13

Talent Is Everywhere: The Manon Rhéaume Story

Changing lines from a male-centric focus to a chapter dedicated to female empowerment and opportunity, and from extrovert to introvert, this section moves from the in-your-face, blunt, direct approach of Don Cherry to the often-discussed story of goal-tender Manon Rhéaume, the only woman ever to play (to date) in an NHL-sanctioned game.

She was also the first woman to play in the CHL, the junior elite league that serves as one of the leading sources of NHL talent. Manon's tale is a classic 1990s example of a group wanting to break a gender barrier while also typifying ongoing bias and perhaps the wrong approach to developing talent.

In our opinion, Manon had the ability to play and got her chance, but she did not really get a fair shot. Various reports (years later) suggested coaches (who felt she had the talent) and owners (who were interested in the attention she was bringing) may have held differing views. The fact she was female and attractive influences how this story is told and helps shape the future.

The Manon Rhéaume Story

In both 1992 and 1993, Rhéaume was invited to try out for the NHL's Tampa Bay Lightning, playing in a pre-season game each year. This gave her celebrity status in hockey, across Canada, and in her home province of Quebec. Even south of the border, she achieved much notoriety, including, much later, an appearance on the *David Letterman* late-night talk show in 2012 and a cameo appearance on a Canadian television sitcom, *The Beachcombers*.

But could she play? By most accounts, the coaching staff felt she had the ability to reach the NHL. And, based on her quotes to the media, she certainly felt the same.

Her NHL experience followed a few previous historical firsts that Manon accomplished as a female playing in male-only hockey leagues. She was the first female to play at the highest level of youth hockey in Quebec, and when Rhéaume joined the now defunct Trois-Rivières Draveurs in the Quebec Major Junior Hockey League during the 1991–2 season (where she played one game), Manon was the first to play major junior hockey.

Following her breakthroughs at the AAA (highest level of boys minor hockey), CHL, and NHL levels, during a five-year period (1992–7) she played more than 20 regular season games for seven clubs in the IHL, an all-male minor professional hockey league that existed from 1945 until 2001. She made a comeback in 2008–9 playing again in a new version of the IHL (that existed from 2007 to 2021) and then joined the Western Women's Hockey League.

In women's hockey, Rhéaume was highly accomplished, winning an Olympic silver medal in 1998 and being named to All-Star teams for both the 1992 and 1994 Women's World Championships, where she won gold medals with Team Canada.

Rick's Recall: Advocating for Out-of-the-Box Talent

As the story of Manon Rhéaume reveals, talent is found in many places, but it can also be squandered for the wrong reasons, including bias.

I recently guest lectured in a sport management class intended for high school juniors and seniors. In talking about skills young people might consider developing if they wanted to work in the sports industry, a young woman engaged me with a question about working in professional hockey.

As I later learned, Alexa Potack was already (while still in high school!) serving as the director of a New York Rangers blog and frequently contributing stories to that website. She was managing the Twitter feed for *Rangers Nation* while building a passion for international leagues, particularly the Swedish league.

A few years previously, Alexa became a Frölunda HC fan because it was the organization where Henrik Lundqvist started playing professionally prior to his NHL and gold-medal-winning Olympics career. Armed with that knowledge, Alexa indicated she went so far as to secure a Lundqvist Frölunda jersey from the early 2000s and started wearing it to Rangers games beginning in 2016.

Suddenly, Swedes were approaching her at Madison Square Garden because of the jersey and those interactions inspired her to watch more of the Swedish Hockey League (SHL). At first, the style of play, the fans, and the language confused her, but it fueled her curiosity to the point she found herself watching as much Swedish hockey as the NHL.

She even started learning Swedish with a goal of someday working in Sweden for the SHL or for the NHL. As any reader might imagine, I was blown away by Alexa's maturity, vision, commitment to professional development, and unique engagement, by a North American, of a global property like the SHL and Frölunda HC.

It showed just how important young thinkers are for any organization. Reflecting on it, I know if I were NHL commissioner, I would have hired her immediately to work from home. I liked her gumption, initiative-taking, and smarts.

But note the following: in past decades, employers have tended to look for individuals with university degrees who often fit the singular profile of mature-acting white males. That bias or systemic racism and sexism has held back millions of qualified candidates.

Today, nearly every contemporary organization realizes talent identification must avoid historic limitations (call them blinders) such as gender (or gender identification), race, sexual orientation, age, country of origin, religion, and perceived physical or mental abilities.

Alexa's story makes clear that a company's youngest nontraditional employees may feature an upbringing and knowledge base completely different from those familiar to the boss. And think how exciting that is for a leader to imagine leveraging.

Said another way, if good leaders look for people with skills that complement their own, what better way to deal with 2022 and beyond than to hire someone born after 2002?

Hiring young people was traditionally frowned on because of perceptions an individual had not learned enough and because of child-labor laws dating back to earlier centuries. Young people were off-limits.

Somehow, though, COVID-19 and the rapid rate of technological advancement has meant many young people are mastering skills such as social media distribution, writing computer code, programming, statistical analysis, second and third languages, and complex problem solving. This seemed to happen overnight during the pandemic.

I may never be able to hire Alexa but after one Zoom class-room and a few emails, I'd endorse her for any hockey opening I encountered. For the cynics, that will seem foolish because the thought of hiring a high school senior would seem short-sighted or undisciplined. I know with certainty the cynics would be wrong.

Trailblazer

As this book went to press in 2022, we noted how more than a dozen women have followed in Manon's blade lines and played profession-ally in traditionally male hockey leagues in North America and Eu-rope. Not surprisingly, the quality and level of the women's game continues to rise. Additionally, more and more women have entered hockey's workforce as administrators and coaches, filling key roles with the NHL, its member teams, various Olympic Committees, and national governing bodies such as USA Hockey and Hockey Canada

Looking back, we wonder whether Manon Rhéaume has been sufficiently recognized as a trailblazer. When she tried out for the Lightning in 1992, she was just 20 years old and much of the media coverage or public attention was focused on her perceived good looks. That sexism played a huge role in preventing a woman from making a much-needed breakthrough in professional hockey.

Many today might ask what if her play had earned her another "shot" to play more games? She never played again for Tampa. Why was that? Was there zero upside to further developing her skills? If the team had calculated behavioral economics, they might have emerged as the team known for empowering women and forever received rec-ognition in the same way Brooklyn's Dodgers did for breaking the MLB color barrier in 1947 by signing baseball's Jack Robinson.

Rhéaume should now be seen as an ongoing inspiration to young girls. Here was a woman who took the opportunity to improve her skills and reportedly turned down offers to pose in magazines,[1] further supporting her role model status. Here are four takeaways we like about Rhéaume's story:

1 Find and celebrate opportunities to showcase and celebrate trailblazers, no matter what form they take. Your voice matters in making a difference. Case in point: should the great Hayley Wickenheiser, now assistant general manager with MLSE in Toronto, have been given a chance to play in the NHL? The presumption would be that her speed and physicality would not match that of any male in the League. But do we know that for certain without exploring a test of the premise?

2 Encourage and support trailblazers to stay the course; avoid situations where your organization opts for the status quo and ultimately undermines diversity, equity, inclusion, and accessibility. Case in point: *Sports Business Journal* recognizing NHL social media manager Rebecca Friedman as a New Voice under 30 in 2021.

3 Recognize the mistakes of the past and embrace the bold choices of the future. The Baby Boomers (those born between 1946–64) have finished their "run." They are retiring in massive numbers each year, replaced by members of Generation X, the Millennials, and Gen Z. This is creating dynamic thinking and new approaches to problem-solving. Make sure your organization does right by the trailblazer right in front of you.

4 Talent identification is treasured in sport. Stories abound about the scout or GM who saw something in a young player and fought for a tryout, training camp invitation, playing time, or starting role. Many businesses resist "gambles" of this nature because of onboarding costs and legal liabilities. But they also resist due to bias and historic (systemic) blinders.

Team Chemistry

Reviewing the many public reports about the story of Manon, particularly those written in recent years, creates the opportunity to discuss group, or team, dynamics. Was Rhéaume accepted by her teammates? What about her opponents? Did having "a girl" in the locker room or on the ice change things? For better or for worse?

Reports were that she demanded – when a sponsor offered her something – that the same be provided to everyone on her team. Others said that her male teammates were sometimes skeptical at first, but her work ethic (reportedly she was first on the ice and last off) and talent (she was a very good goalie) won them over.

Still, she required a separate locker room. How big an issue was that? We tried to imagine what it would be like being Manon or playing as one of her teammates. Was it out of the question to construct co-ed dressing rooms where every team member felt comfortable?

How could the Lightning have structured team-building exercises to remove gender as an issue? Was there a gay player on that year's roster? A person afraid to reveal their sexual orientation for fear of ostracization? What if the gay player was the best player? What if Manon was the next Ken Dryden? What if she became the greatest NHLer ever to wear #33 on her back, much like *Sports Illustrated* (2014) said about Dryden and the #29 on his back?[2] Imagine if instead of one woman on the team, there were three, then seven, then half the team? This discussion lends itself notably to the notion of team chemistry and how it is built.

In her marvelous 2020 book *Intangibles*, author Joan Ryan started her introduction with a quote from one of baseball's greatest managers (third most wins in MLB history), Tony LaRussa, who once said, "Every once in a while, you hear an expert that says team chemistry is overrated. You just write that person off."

214 Changing the Lines

That got us thinking about Manon and the best NHL teams when it came to tangible cohesion. We asked ourselves, "Best NHL team chemistry ever. Go."

One of us said, "Has to be the Edmonton Oilers of the mid-1980s. They all cried when Gretzky was traded." And strangely enough, many of the key players from that squad ended up playing together again in other cities.

They were a tight-knit clan that created an official dynasty and they were the highest-scoring hockey team ever. By a lot. It was hard denying that Oilers team had chemistry. They won Stanley Cups in 1984, 1985, 1987, 1988, and 1990. Five in seven years. Even now, the surnames roll off the tongue and their exploits amaze: Anderson, Coffey, Fuhr, Gregg, Gretzky, Huddy, Kurri, Lowe, and Messier. Of the nine, all but Wayne Gretzky and Paul Coffey held the trophy aloft five times. (Gretzky's team won four Cups and Coffey's won three.) Most of them are honored in the Hockey Hall of Fame.

Cynical readers will believe Edmonton won five times because they had amassed superior talent. The same comment is often made about the four straight championships won by the New York Islanders with Mike Bossy, Denis Potvin, Billy Smith, and Bryan Trottier; or the more recent three Cups won by the Pittsburgh Penguins with Sidney Crosby and Evgeni Malkin.

But setting aside cynicism, the Cups won by the Oilers, Islanders, and Penguins drew much from the coaches (primarily Glenn Sather, Al Arbour, and Mike Sullivan) who carefully built highly functional and interdependent teams. The players needed each other.

Many clubs with great players have consistently lost and authors like Sam Walker (*The Captain Class*) and Ryan (*Intangibles*) invested years researching what makes some teams special. They asked what magic glue made one team cohesive while other units flew apart.

Ryan believes team chemistry is "actually a dynamic combination of biological and social forces that continually encourages players to be the best versions of themselves." She emphasizes that in situations where there is a "failure to thrive," observed and researched subjects (human and animal) died.

How often have sportswriters used clichés to describe the actions of a selfless player who conceded more playing time to a teammate so the club might win. Or a player made a statement after the game that ran along the lines of "He's always the first person on the bench to congratulate me. And it always tells me we're a lot more about the team and not the individual stats or person scoring the goal."

Where does that selflessness come from? What makes these super-achievers put team and teammates ahead of personal accolades?

"We had a love for the game," Gretzky told NHL.com when asked about the secret to the Oilers' 1980s chemistry and his relationship with Paul Coffey and Jari Kurri. "The three of us [who had been named to the NHL's list of greatest players][3] loved being at the rink. We loved playing and we loved practicing. I think from [Mark] Messier, to [Glenn] Anderson, to Paul [Coffey], to Kevin Lowe, to [Jari] Kurri, we showed up for practice. We practiced hard."

So many uses of the word "we." Wanting to win is one thing but, as we observed with COVID-19 stopping play mid-season, re-establishing team cohesion was one of the most discussed topics.

In a story about the return of the NHL in June 2020, the Associated Press noted, "Among the unknowns about the NHL returning amid the coronavirus pandemic is what the on-ice product might look like. In a team sport that demands rhythm and chemistry, players will have to quickly adapt after so much time apart to recapture what it takes to jump right into the playoffs and compete for the Stanley Cup."[4] Funny to imagine that of all the traits we could discuss, like conditioning, game legs, and mental focus, a key one is chemistry.

Extending Team Chemistry in the NHL to You

So, let's ask this: who is responsible for how your team – your employees – engage one another? Does your organization acknowledge the importance of chemistry? Does anyone take the time to prioritize it? Do you have a culture that allows, if not encourages, "we" chemistry to take root and grow?

Such situational awareness informs how we look backward and how we alter group behaviors going forward. What could have been done when a different kind of player – like Rhéaume – was parachuted into the Tampa Bay Lightning training camp in 1992 with legions of media following her every move, and a set of teammates (all males) wondering what coaches and owners were planning?

In *Intangibles*, Ryan notes "male athletes are so much more physically affectionate with one another than men in general [at least American men]. They *always* seem to be touching each other – hugging, high-fiving, slinging their arms around one another, holding hands at courtside as the final seconds tick down in a close basketball game. Teammates embrace with full-bodied gusto, not with the shoulder bump that passes for a hug in the outside male world."

Ryan's conclusion? Oxytocin (the "love hormone") aids in bonding and operating "as a close-knit tribe." She suggests (and we feel bonding also happens in female sport; cohesion is not just a male-centric benefit) all of us need "a trustworthy pack with whom to hunt, gather food, and fend off enemies." Prehistorically, that meant the "human brain had to figure out a way to create bonds so strong that members would sacrifice themselves for the survival of the group."[5]

How is this influenced when a female is brought into the mix? Asking this or extending Manon's case may sound a little too heavy in a world where few will sacrifice anything. But here again, the actions of NHL players may well benefit how any leader thinks about their department or division.

Do the team members in a corporate setting (think office cubicles or working from home) or a small machine shop feel they are obligated to the others around them? If your answer is no, you may want to think about ways to improve this facet for your employees.

All of us see the world autobiographically and thus believe we understand our own motivations and needs. While contemporary research is beginning to suggest we may not even know ourselves (as well as we think we do), how we view others shapes our ability to fit with others who look, sound, or think differently than our "accepted" view of self.

Most sport coaches today desire team unity and while there is room for individuality, fitting into "La Familia" or what Syracuse football coach Dino Babers calls (from his time in Hawaii) "The Ohana." If we can see ourselves as "Family" we can be different but still ourselves as bonded by a single purpose.

Talent Management Takeaway

Thinking back to how it must have been for Manon Rhéaume in the dressing room, appearing on the Letterman show in the early 1990s, dealing with jokes and flirtation from Letterman and others, or trying to play after getting inserted into a 5–5 game late in the match, we must revisit those leaders in team management who first made the decision to invite Rhéaume to camp but found themselves instantly struggling to offer her a legitimate chance to make the team.

As anyone versed in diversity, equity, inclusion, and accessibility knows, it is one thing to have a quota and hire/recruit people of various backgrounds, but it is another entirely to create a culture where the beneficiary feels welcomed, motivated, and inspired to stay. Researching this topic, we drew upon our collective experiences. As one might expect, the literature on talent identification, recruitment, retention, and motivation is vast, practical, and empirically supported. In a few words, it consistently offers relevance linked to Manon and talent identification.

First, to be successful, a talent manager needs to build an environment and create a culture of "curiosity." By that, researchers mean a place where talent can thrive in a today's complex and volatile world. Where the subject can comfortably explore and enjoy the ability to navigate their job and work environment.

We doubt Manon felt curious. Fear and pressure likely characterized her experience during a decade of breaking through ceilings at the youth, junior, and pro levels in men's hockey. What all of us can take away (and this is supported by research) is that most people will thrive in an environment where curiosity is allowed, and opportunistic success is a shared goal.

In a related way, the opposite of curiosity is conformity. Something we don't want, but often support for fear of "rocking the boat." For a woman to fit into a male-only culture was no doubt daunting. And reading the coverage of Rhéaume's NHL experience, the rhetoric is not about curiosity. It is about conformity and not disrupting the "steady state."

Don't get us wrong; we're not saying the management of the Lightning did anything wrong. In fact, we might argue the opposite. They took a vital and important step – in the early 1990s – that unquestionably helped women in hockey.

Now, we're well into 2022 and witnessing an ever-adapting, ever-changing environment where leaders need to embrace diversity, equity, inclusion, and accessibility. They need to foster curiosity, work at developing young talent, and avoid the trap of not seeing the emerging picture. Increased profitability, sales growth, new customers, larger purchase orders, and more billable hours are always our goal. Getting there with the best possible team is an ongoing obligation.

14

Emerging Trends: Appreciating History and Video Games

Like any industry or any "traditional" organization today, digital competitors, products, and opportunities boldly characterize new realities. Perhaps the best example is the EA Sport video game *NHL 22*. Developed by EA Vancouver, *NHL 22* is the 31st version of the popular video game and its cover shows Toronto Maple Leaf star Auston Matthews. The prior version, *NHL 21*, used the ageless veteran Alexander Ovechkin.

Strangely, many fans will recall playing the original version and owning most of the next 30 installations. So, why start this chapter writing about the newest edition of a video game?

The answer? Because history (written or presented as video game narrative) is often the device that helps explain an entity's past trajectory. In short, recording and celebrating performance (keeping achievement stats) is important for every business. Even if those achievements are often fleeting.

An Old-Fashioned Example

Let's show that by using a quirky, old-school, hockey example. During the recent COVID-19 pandemic, Rick's wife, Barb, decided things from his past could be thrown out. It would give the

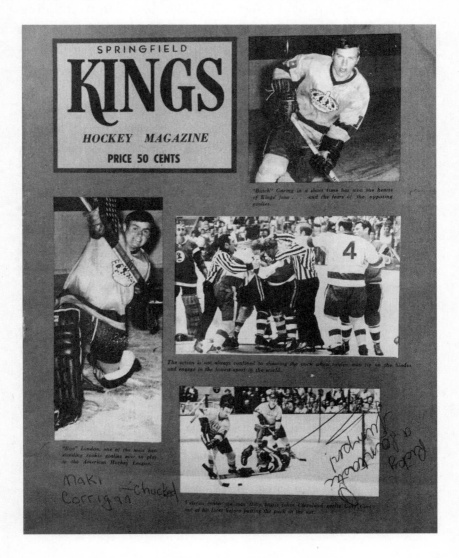

Burtons more space in the basement. Digging around, Rick found an AHL game program his late parents had saved for him during his time growing up in Springfield, Massachusetts. What a find!

Memory suggested he bought the *Springfield Kings Hockey Magazine* for 50 cents during a Saturday, March 21, 1970, home game between the Springfield Kings and Buffalo Bisons in West Springfield's Eastern States Coliseum. By historic standards, that one game was meaningless and yet, looking back, we can argue how even a single game sat on the cusp of quiet immortality ... as perhaps all games and businesses do.

It was Buffalo's last year in the AHL (the city of Buffalo had received an NHL franchise for the 1970–1 season) but with the stellar play of goalie Gilles Villemure and future NHL notables Guy Trottier and Wayne Maki, the Bisons were on their way to winning Buffalo's fifth and final Calder Cup.

Buffalo's championship (a 4–0 sweep less than two months later) would come at the expense of the Kings, a team that dominated the AHL's top 10 scoring leaders that year, with Marc Dufour, Billy Inglis, Gordie Labossiere, and Doug Robinson making that list.

At the time, the Kings were owned by one of the NHL's greatest former players (Eddie Shore) who had leased the team to the LA Kings and their legendary owner Jack Kent Cooke. One year later, the Kings would hoist the Calder Cup behind the heroics of Butch Goring, Jean Potvin, and a stunning young goalkeeper named Billy Smith, who would go on to star with the dynastic New York Islanders teams of the early 1980s.

Shore's ownership of the Kings (once known as the Springfield Indians and only shortly removed from being known as the Indians again) would end within five years and the team would leave The Big E arena for the newly built Springfield Civic Center at the start of the 1972–3 season.

As we leafed through the 50-year-old program, some interesting observations took flight. On the program's cover, Rick had scrawled ("Maki & Corrigan chucked") to describe a fight between the two players. Inside, he had made a diligent attempt to keep score during a 7–5 Kings win (with two goals coming from left wing Robinson).

It's not as important to take anyone through the details of the game as it is to note that, like many things in life, keeping score matters. Journalists create stories about victories and defeats. Statisticians track the good and bad; analysts measure and predict outcomes, probabilities, tendencies, and deficiencies.

Not surprisingly, modern businesses and not-for-profit organizations also keep track of statistics but usually in the form of revenues, profitability, inventory, and turnover. There are hundreds of other data points, but many go uncelebrated in any kind of a regular fashion.

That's understandable but creates a challenge when we think about celebrating corporate history. Older bosses are inclined to comment, "If we did a little less celebrating and a lot more selling, we'd gain market share and see bigger bonuses." Younger employees, however, raised on a great deal of affirmation and participation awards, seek evidence their hard work for the "machine" is, or will be, acknowledged. They know from playing esports with gamers all over the world that "winning" feels good.

We won't debate how your firm should honor the hardest-working or most successful employees, but it's worth noting that in one 50-year-old game program, there were no fewer than five places where historic achievement was honored.

A clothing store (Yale Genton) listed the outstanding players for each game that year as well as the Kings' player of the month. A hardware store, advertising it sold Bauer Black Panther skates and

Victoriaville sticks, presented two of the "Visiting Stars." Bishop & McCollum Appliances was so proud of the fact it sold General Electric's high-speed, flameless, electric dryers that it saluted six of the previous year's AHL All-Stars.

Finally, the only feature story in the magazine was a "puff" piece about Springfield's Noel Price. "Shiny," as he was known, was described as the type of veteran NHL defenseman "who gets the job done all the time." The previous season, Price had been "a top defender with the NHL's Pittsburgh Penguins" but suddenly found himself relegated to the AHL when the Kings "grabbed [him] in the reverse draft."

Looking at the story about Noel Price, it's clear for most workers that their achievements are temporary. Important in the moment but fleeting in the long run. Said another way, few remember who won Employee of the Month eight weeks after the award was handed out.

The same can be said for the transitory nature of commerce. Looking at the magazine's black-and-white advertising provides a glimpse of a long-ago world. During the ensuing five decades, most of the businesses featured had been acquired or gone out of business.

Some giants still exist. McDonald's still sells hamburgers but their advertising slogan, "McDonald's is your kind of place," is long gone. Dodge has long since stopped production of Monacos, Polaras, Coronets, and Darts but, as of 2021, was still producing Challengers.

And Bauer, originally started in Kitchener and known as the Bauer Canadian Skate Company, still makes skates but since 1965, when Greb Industries owned the brand, the skate giant has been sold numerous times, including to Nike. As of 2017, Bauer was owned by Peak Achievement Athletics and based in Exeter, New Hampshire.

Leveraging Memories Traditionally and Digitally

One point to ponder is simply this: consider how the NHL, AHL, and teams all over the world leverage their history, statistics, performances, and victories. Achievement always matters. Write it up. Put plaques on the wall. Hang championship banners. Retire numbers. Hold a victory parade around your office. It matters to your employees. And to your customers.

And what of EA's NHL video game? We asked one of our graduate assistants to provide a review of NHL 21 because video gaming is sweeping the planet and copying the success of NBA 2K (see our earlier chapter "Smart Copycats Can Run with the Big Dogs") is worth noting.

At a time when many individuals were required to stay home, video games played a huge role in facilitating mental health and stimulation. Not surprisingly, new game consoles sold out around the holidays of 2020 and 2021 while the NHL worked with EA Sports to upgrade its digital participatory game product.

A Gamer's Review of NHL 21

BY JOSH HAGWELL

In my opinion, the NHL series of video games is one of the most consistent sports game franchises currently in production. Despite not getting a next-generation console update for Xbox Series X and PS5 like its FIFA and Madden counterparts have, NHL 21 is an incredibly enjoyable game with the best visuals, dangles, and varieties of playable content to date in the NHL series.

As someone who plays most of my video games solo (I prefer single player to mass multiplayer online games) the artificial intelligence (AI) improvement in NHL 21 is a welcome addition. It should be noted I skipped NHL 20 last year after playing 17, 18, and 19. So, while I can't compare to it to the 2020 installment, I can confidently say the difference compared to 2019 or 2018 is almost night and day.

NHL 21 is also the most immersive entry in the franchise. Part of my reserve in skipping NHL 20 last year was how my favorite modes: Franchise mode, World of Chel, and Be a Pro mode felt somewhat underdeveloped, especially the latter. But with NHL 21 that changed. Be a Pro mode got a significant overhaul in multiple ways and the dialogue option for speaking to the coach or media has real-world applications tied to locker room chemistry, individual branding, and team management. New skill trees, career paths, and actual consequences have breathed new life into the once overlooked mode.

It's definitely a welcome addition for someone like me who plays a lot of their video games based around that narrative and the choice-based fundamentals seen in most single-player games. Franchise Mode has also added great depth in the area dedicated to trades and roster moves (around trade deadlines), making it much more immersive. It certainly gives things that feeling of being real.

On the other side of the rink, the number of interruptions and stoppages when trying to "sim" can certainly become a hassle – especially around the trade deadline.

To me, the controls in NHL 19 were great and felt very intuitive. Somehow, EA keeps making them better and better. While there haven't been any major overhauls like there was from NHL 18 to NHL 19, the controls are cleaner, smoother, and continually get more intuitive. I must say though – being able to do "The Michigan" and the patented "phantom move" (or no shot) Nikita Kucherov deke is great and added to my game immersion.

NHL 21 offers an incredible variety to suit different kinds of hockey fans. From the traditional 5v5 to the newly introduced HUT Rush PvP mode, the variety of modes helps appeal to folks wanting to play different kinds of hockey.

While the menu navigation and UI still feel clunky and over-crowded, the quality on the ice is improved with behind-the-scenes tweaks and game mode improvements, making NHL 21 another good entry into the franchise.

All in all, I love NHL 21 and feel it provides another important way in which the NHL is a part of my life and has allowed me to view hockey as a competitive business.

Rick's Recall: Toys in the Office

Speaking of games, mental health, and house-bound stimulation, have you ever wondered about toys in the workplace?

I pondered this recently during an eBay search for old mechanical table-top hockey games. I can't be certain which one I owned as a kid, but I'm guessing it was a mid-1960s Eagle Toys NHL Stanley Cup version.

Looking at the seller's pictures of the little metal players representing the Leafs and Canadiens, I wondered whether it was worth it to pay $0.99 and then nearly $50 for shipping to get something I couldn't play by myself.

But then I Googled "Workplace Toys" and was surprised to see a significant amount of literature on gadgets designed for relieving stress, facilitating team building, and maximizing creativity. There really was a great deal to consider.

Photo courtesy of Innovative Concepts in Entertainment, Inc. (ICE)

At the sports marketing agency where I worked during the mid-1990s, we had a Pop-a-Shot basketball game in one corner. It came with flashing lights, bell noises, and was off-limits during the workday. But after 6 p.m. or on weekends, the big toy in the corner was surprisingly important for morale-building.

I know it worked with potential new hires who came into our offices and immediately thought we were a fun outfit. It also worked as a social connectivity device that allowed our staff, regardless of rank, to compete at something fun. It also reinforced our thinking that working in sports was "cool."

Today's workplace is notably different, and many people find themselves working from home. Still, "toys" and gadgets find their way into corporations, small businesses, LLCs, and home offices.

Hard to believe? Just go online and look at things like the Gnome-be-Gone Decision Maker, Henry Desk Vacuum, 3D Pin Art, Snaak Construction Toys, the Penguin Bowling Set, Hanayama Padlock, Dream Cheeky USB Stress Ball, and Desktop Cornhole.

I could have also listed bigger and bolder ideas like a Super Chexx Pro air hockey table, pinball machines, arcade games, ping-pong tables, miniature golf courses, and whiffle ball arenas. Suffice it to say, if someone has imagined it, they've built it or bought it and brought it into the office.

That's because most North Americans spend more time at their place of employment than anywhere else. Think about it: an average of 8 hours a day, 40 hours a week, 50 weeks a year times 40 years equals 80,000 hours (10,000 days) worked in a lifetime. It's no surprise we look for distractions.

What we lose as adults is the joy of play. Researchers have known for decades that play is incredibly important to human psyche and wellness. Play usually has few rules yet much imagination. Interestingly, free time for playing is a relatively modern invention.

In most agrarian or industrial societies, work is life-consuming because not working means starving. In Melbourne, Australia, however, during a gold rush in Victoria (the state), a work-play-sleep concept began to emerge in the 1850s. The premise (led by a stonemason strike) suggested eight hours of work warranted eight hours for rest and eight hours for recreation and education.

For many North Americans, there is rarely enough non-work time for rest and recreation. In response, businesses are increasingly introducing ways for employees to "play" on the job (if for no other reason than to help them re-charge their spiritual and emotional batteries and increase productivity).

In an era when mental health discussions are significant, we strongly believe opportunities to rediscover the childish pleasure of toys is worthy.

Evidence of play in the workplace is perhaps best understood (post-2022) in discussions covering esports, virtual reality, and augmented reality. For many bosses, almost overnight, it seemed employees were investing time playing *League of Legends*, *Defense of the Ancients*, *Fortnite*, *Rocket League*, *Super Smash Bros.*, and *Counter-Strike*.

These digital games are sophisticated and have lifted gamers into stunning new worlds where bold graphics captivate and world-wide competition is readily available. Do bosses want to discover their subordinates playing video games online during work hours? No, they don't.

But understanding the value of words and phrases like "fun, play, stress-relief, relaxing, take-my-mind-off-work-for-a-moment, and chillin out" are valued (hugely) by a generation raised on different entertainment options than those offered to Baby Boomers. Where Boomers went outside to play (in a relatively "safe" world), Millennials and Gen Z found themselves placed in organized sport leagues or strongly encouraged to play on computers indoors.

The bottom line? Don't rule out toys in the workplace. Your firm or start-up undoubtedly features stressed-out employees worried about getting fired, making rent, or paying bills. Perhaps adding a hockey game in an unused corner of the office will create a distraction initially, but it may work wonders for morale, camaraderie, team unity, and profits.

Spotting trends is often left to the most senior executives or high-priced consultants. That traditional approach warrants close review because the trends of 2022 and beyond have been born out of the realities of a pandemic, social injustice, massive technology advances, and game-changing economies of scale (think Amazon, Netflix, and Walmart).

As you or your organization seek to keep pace in an ever-changing world, take some time to "read" your history and make some projections about how your firm's unique narrative can serve as a resource. Also, take time to observe the trends that benefit the development of yourself or your employees.

15

Race and Identity Challenges

The point is this: no business can ever afford to stand still and assume its policies and systems are ideal. Social situations, like governments, change. This was never truer than in the recent environment when social justice rightfully took its place atop the priority lists around the world. Social incidents involving George Floyd and others were common discussion points during 2020–2 and have been highlighted through the earlier chapters of this book.

Floyd's death, in particular, set off a series of protests that indelibly changed the world and by mid-June 2020, soccer teams as far away as England were taking a knee and wearing uniforms with the words Black Lives Matter on the back in place of players' names. This awareness of racial inequality forced virtually every global organization to address and "own" the likelihood they had long practiced systemic discrimination.

Kyle Beach and the Chicago Blackhawks sexual assault scandal of 2021, although not about race, further heightened attention to negative power dynamics in sport and hockey. We acknowledge there are many serious social issues for the NHL to address, but we will focus this chapter on the race element only.

To start, the cultural sea-change of 2020–2 made many in power uncomfortable, but a review of the nightly news suggested the will of the people was firm. They wanted real awareness, a commitment to change and equity.

It was also the will of many NHL players. Early that August, Minnesota Wild defenseman Matt Dumba, representing the Hockey Diversity Alliance (HDA), knelt on a bright red carpet during an Edmonton-Chicago game's national anthem while the words "End Racism" shone from the scoreboard. Not in uniform that night, Dumba, a Filipino-Canadian, was joined by the Oilers' Darnell Nurse and Blackhawks' Malcom Subban. More powerfully, he made a pledge to match up to $100,000 in donations to help rebuild sections of Minneapolis damaged by protests after the death of Floyd.

"Racism is a man-made creation," said Dumba, "and all it does is deteriorate from our collective prosperity. Racism is everywhere, and we need to fight against it. On behalf of the NHL and HAD, we vow and promise to stand up for justice and fight for what is right."[1]

Weeks later, Dumba commented that in a predominantly white league, the burden for creating change sat squarely on the shoulders of persons not of color. "You're just relying on the minority guys to step up and say it," said Dumba. "But what would really make the most impact is to have strong white leaders from teams step up and have their two cents heard. All the other white kids who grow up watching them, who might be their biggest fans, can look up and say, 'Wow, if he's seeing this and trying to stand up and to listen, then why am I not as well? Why am I continuing to hold on to this ignorance or hate that I feel towards a subject that I maybe don't know everything about?'"[2] In some organizations, fighting racism, sexism, bias, or discrimination requires rules for that challenge. Many corporations use codes and guidelines to inform employees where safety and social boundaries lie. At almost every company (circa 2022), someone is responsible for the rules and proactive engagement.

Applying Leadership Theory

The importance of codes and guidelines is illustrated by the fact that many organizations conduct meetings that follow *Robert's Rules of Order* in the hope that defined procedures will ensure a meeting is "official" or is conducted with appropriate authority. US Army General Henry Robert first published his rules in 1876. *Robert's Rules* have provided governance structure to groups big and small for nearly 150 years. So, how does formal guidance or "structure" serve your firm?

We know from leadership theory there is a notable difference between managers and leaders. The former tend to see rules as guiding their decision making and giving them their supervisory purpose. Their authority is tied to following the rules.

Leaders acknowledge protocol but also look beyond the way things "have always been." Stephen Covey's example (from his seminal book *The 7 Habits of Highly Effective People*) talks of a work crew clearing brush through tangled overgrowth. The managers, not wielding any of the machetes, are the ones behind the workers "writing policy and procedure manuals, holding muscle development programs, bringing in improved technologies and setting up working schedules and compensation programs for [the] machete wielders."[3]

Leaders, according to Covey, are the ones who climb the tallest tree and determine the group is in the wrong jungle. In the abstract, that concept may be difficult for many businesspeople. Their comfortable position could easily suggest frontline managers must preserve order. Further, not everyone can (or should) be a leader.

Logically, we can't have all of our employees climbing figurative trees and proclaiming themselves as leaders (on the simple assumption that will increase their salary). Thus, rules and hierarchies exist for good reasons.

Still, rigid systems can become oppressive and even limit an organization's potential. Likewise, while change is often good, it can make traditionalists uncomfortable and keep a firm from achieving its true potential. Without an ability to change governance or to test concepts, we fail to learn what is possible. Imagine an NHL where the goalie can't go to the ice to block a shot or where a penalty shot following a blatant defensive foul is not allowed.

Rick's Recall: Willie O'Ree

During the fall of 2002, I found myself working on a project for the NHL as the League prepared to open its 86th regular season. At the time, the NHL was promoting the upcoming eighth annual Willie O'Ree All-Star Weekend in Minneapolis. O'Ree was the NHL's director of youth development (inside the NHL's diversity department).

In the *NHL Enterprises*, a newsletter, League copywriters noted how the O'Ree weekend celebrated "the multicultural heritage of the NHL as boys and girls ages 10–12, representing NHL Diversity programs from across North America."[4] The intention? Connect young players with NHL players by attending an NHL game in Minneapolis.

Nearly 20 years later, Minneapolis was again in the news because of George Floyd's horrific death. The pain from that tragedy forced me to consider how the NHL has long attempted to deal with concepts such as inclusion, bias, prejudice, and diversity, equity, inclusion, and accessibility (DEIA).

It's safe suggesting that when we consider North America's five major sports leagues (MLB, MLS, NBA, NFL, and NHL), the NHL is the least diverse. The casual presumption has long held that there is no diversity in hockey despite the more than 60-year presence of players like Dustin Byfuglien, Matt Dumba, Angela James, Jarome Iginla, Darnell Nurse, Willie O'Ree, Wayne Simmonds, Malcolm Subban, P.K. Subban, and Hall of Fame goalie Grant Fuhr.

And if there are few BIPOC players in the NHL, it is often, erroneously, believed there are no fans of color. That thinking is flawed and groups like the The Hockey Players of Color Movement and the Black Girl Hockey Club (BGHC) (started in 2018) are proof. The BGHC had more than 30,000 Twitter followers by June 2022 and its founder, Renee Hess, was active in working with the NHL's DEIA efforts, particularly with NHL executive vice president Kim Davis, who is also Black.

O'Ree, the NHL's first man of color, played briefly with the Boston Bruins during the 1958 and 1961 seasons and while not the first Black person signed to a contract (Art Dorrington was signed by the New York Rangers in 1950), O'Ree's ability to manage the racism of the era led to his recognition as the "Jackie Robinson of ice hockey."

Interestingly, Robinson first broke baseball's color barrier in 1946 in Montreal before reaching the major leagues with the Brooklyn Dodgers in 1947. O'Ree, who was born in New Brunswick, also showed a Quebec lineage, playing his first professional (non-juniors) season for the Quebec Aces.

Despite O'Ree's breaking of a historic racial divide, prejudice and bias were well-known in pro hockey. As depicted in the powerful 2005 movie *The Rocket* (about Maurice Richard), French Canadians were often subjected to vile racism with separate, caged-in seating sections required in venues like Montreal's Forum. French-speaking players were often berated by their coaches and teammates simply for speaking a language other than English.

Leveraging O'Ree as a diversity ambassador, the former Bruin was appointed the NHL's director of youth development. In that role, he helped expose more than 40,000 boys and girls of diverse backgrounds to various forms of hockey (ice, roller, street, and sledge).

Ultimately, O'Ree crisscrossed North America helping establish more than 40 grassroots hockey programs, all geared toward serving economically disadvantaged youth. O'Ree's message featured the slogan "Hockey Is for Everyone" and stressed the "importance of essential life skills, education, and core values of hockey: commitment, perseverance, and teamwork."[5]

As every business leader or department manager should know, unique differences make us stronger, and supervisors must understand that when an employee is different from a majority, that subordinate must never feel alone, cast out, marginalized, or defeated. Dealing with difference is hard enough. Having others actively or surreptitiously attack a difference destroys unit cohesion, group effectiveness, and performance.

A perfect example may exist in the growing interest in Para Ice Hockey, traditionally called *sledge hockey*, the term we use throughout this book. Using phrases like "adaptive inclusion," able-bodied hockey players have taken up the game that places them on the same type of sled as a mobility-impaired teammate. In this sense, each player is made equal on the sled.

Canadian Tire received numerous plaudits for advertising that showed a youngster confined to a wheelchair getting invited by neighborhood kids to join in a game of basketball where each player participated on wheels.

Similarly, a Rio 2016 Summer Paralympics trailer on Canada's Channel 4 used the catchy song "Yes I Can" while showing more than 50 types of "impaired" heroes conquering sport, music, and other activities. The tagline was "We're the Superhumans" and left no doubt inclusion was a better concept than exclusion.

When Willie O'Ree started playing juniors hockey in New Brunswick, first for the Fredericton Falcons and then the Merchants, he just wanted to play hockey. His skin color was different but the game, like our businesses, should only recognize commitment, perseverance, and teamwork.

Racism and Homophobia in the Modern World

Today, actions that incorporate racism, bias, prejudice, or ignorance are not tolerated and individuals who say or do the wrong thing are quickly punished. The usual response (circa 2022) is the quick loss of a job or a place on the roster.

These punitive actions do not, of course, eliminate racism but following the death of Floyd and the shooting of Blake, actions of silence and inactivity are also no longer tolerable. Bystanders who do nothing can be blamed. Leagues not aggressively promoting equality and equal treatment are publicly accused (often via social media) of supporting inequality.

Similarly, decisions about whom to promote and who is assigned to certain sectors or given plum assignments can be filtered through a lens that traditionally did not exist in the 1990s or early 2000s. This is hard for many "old-school" managers and leaders to understand – not because they are inherently racist but because they may have grown up unaware of what is now expected of them.

Protesters walking through the streets of major global cities in 2020 and 2021 were often spotted wearing T-shirts that simply featured the word "WOKE." That concept, to "stay woke," comes from the Black vernacular and calls for everyone to practice and support racial and social awareness. To wake up.

For many who have grown up in privilege, social awareness (and social justice) is a complicated journey for which few have trained. They believe they need time to adapt and become educated. In many cases that time is an unaffordable luxury. The learning must be achieved immediately.

One illustrative example is Luke Prokop, a 2020 draft pick of the Nashville Predators, who, on July 19, 2021, came out as gay. Prokop, who is a six-foot-four, 217-pound defenceman, played for the Edmonton Oil Kings (WHL) in 2022 and was widely supported by his club, teammates, the League, and the media.

How does someone become attuned to the challenges of another race, sexual orientation, or class? Or empathize with a person's beliefs that are very different from one's own? How does someone overcome their ignorance? Looking to the NHL, we see the League has provided a wide range of clues and initiatives for the last 30 years.

In 1995, the NHL began recognizing the need to speak to players, coaches, administrators, and media members who were not white males. Admittedly, the NHL was not a first mover in this space and the NHL had traditionally featured a player pool that was about 98 percent white.

But it hasn't stopped Commissioner Gary Bettman from frequently recognizing that regardless of ratios, racial mix data, gender, physical or mental ability, sexual orientation, country of origin, religious belief, or economic class, the 21st-century NHL was obligated to do better.

For many observers, that overdue process took a step in the right direction when, in July 2022, the San Jose Sharks announced they had hired former player Mike Grier, making him the NHL's first Black general manager. Grier played in the NHL for 14 years, and while his announcement was celebrated, it was also noted by some media outlets that the NHL was the last major professional league to name a Black GM (20 years after the NFL's Ozzie Newsome broke that league's color barrier in 2002).[6]

Today, and every day, organizations and individuals must do better in all areas of inclusion because, to paraphrase the American poet Robert Frost, we all have miles to go before we sleep.

THIRD PERIOD

16

Two Birds, One Stone

In closing, we should discuss decision making, arguably the most important task any leader or manager faces. This is an ideal way to pull all the content in the book together.

Decisions, Decisions, Decisions

Numerous sources (many non-scientific) suggest the average adult makes as many as 35,000 decisions in a day. Even if it is only 5,000, the number is overwhelming when you consider we are awake about 1,000 minutes each day. Of course, most of these decisions are made without a second thought. Brush my teeth? Of course. Put on my shoes? Seems prudent. Kill the mosquito biting my neck? Done. But now, let's move beyond the minutiae of daily living and talk about decisions where money, investment, or person-power is involved.

We estimate that every business day, in countries all over the world, leaders, corporate managers, small operators, and entrepreneurs make somewhere in the range of 200 meaningful decisions tied to their business. They respond to emails, read contracts, get asked questions by direct reports, issue orders, and generally weigh in on various topics.

Consider the highest levels of management for a minute, such as the US president or Canadian prime minister, whose decisions impact millions of lives and thousands of businesses, with limited time to act (in many cases) and often without universal agreement or support. Beyond the decision itself, numerous complex components are tied to time, choice, and quality. What options do I have? Are there viable alternatives I'm not considering? How long before I must commit to a choice? If I make this choice, what are the next two to five outcomes that will develop? If I make the wrong choice, can I still recover?

Decisions in Hockey Terms

Let's use hockey terms. Imagine a goalie spotting a 3-on-2 break coming up the left side of the ice. In a split-second, the goaltender must assess the speed of the attack, the strength of two defenders slowing the breakaway, and the tendencies of the opposing skaters.

If the goalie commits to the left side of the net, how long before the wing moves the puck to the right? If the goalie goes to the ice (butterfly, flop, or knees-down), how will the attackers counter? If the goalie makes the wrong choice, is there still time to adjust and make the save? Can decisions by the defensemen compensate for the first mistake?

Thankfully, in most businesses, leaders and managers have more time than a hockey goalie, but frequently insufficient time is spent mapping out the logical consequences. There isn't enough time or resources to do so. Many bosses become certain they are always right and thus never question their own decision making.

This is dangerous, and many organizations attempt to set up logical sounding boards (or fail-safe systems) for every employee tasked with rendering a verdict. Take for instance former US President Barack Obama, who recently opened a conference with his simple three-step framework for making challenging decisions: (i) focus on probabilities and not certainties, (ii) ask dumb questions (when you are not sure), and (iii) surround yourself with smart people.[1] Obama also reportedly minimized trivial decisions in his life (such as what to wear or what to eat for lunch) in order to focus on the more important and complex ones he faced.

Decision making is fascinating to study, and we'll end this book by looking at a July 2020 decision made jointly by the NHL and (arguably) its most important stakeholder, the NHLPA. The NHLPA is the association (some would say "union") of all play-ers – past and present – who compete (or have competed) in the NHL, with provisions for future League players also included. As described earlier in this book, the relationship between the NHL and the NHLPA has often been filled with friction leading to mul-tiple work stoppages and a lost season. In other words, it has been progressively evolutionary … an entity that has needed to adapt, in the face of numerous wealthier competitors, to survive.

A Brilliant Decision in the Face of Adversity

Strangely, though, in the face of COVID-19 and with an impending collective bargaining agreement (CBA) negotiation staring them in the face (following the 10-year agreement that was set to expire following the 2021–2 NHL season), the League and the NHLPA announced on July 10, 2020, that not only would the League and its players stage the 2020 Stanley Cup Playoffs in a bubble format, but they would jointly extend the current CBA an additional four years through the conclusion of the 2025–6 NHL season.

Although the decision seems simple and perhaps even logical, we know the hundreds of major decisions needed to reach that point were not easy. These were not empty net shots from the near blue line, nor what to have for lunch.

The CBA issues that were up for negotiation held the power to direct the dispersal of millions, if not billions, of dollars, as well as decisions involving the participation of NHL players in future Olympic Games, outdoor showdowns and All-Star contests, and distinct details covering salary caps, rookie caps, free agency, and more. A lot of math and long-term projections were done by very smart and well-trained people.

Rick's Recall: Donald Fehr, A Noted Fighter

If memory serves, I met NHLPA executive director Donald Fehr once when he was the executive director of Major League Baseball's Players' Association. Probably at a sport industry conference.

Fehr has directed the NHLPA since late 2010 and not so long ago entered the history books as the only executive director of a players' union to play a major role in two work stoppages. For that reason, many sport industry administrators and fans paint Fehr as the bad guy when owner-induced lockouts or player strikes are discussed.

I found Fehr, a noted negotiator, quite pleasant (we both belonged to the same national fraternity at school), although we didn't spend much time together. We exchanged pleasantries and there is no reason he should remember we ever met. I bring Fehr up, though, because in February 2021 I found a quote from a *USA Today* story by Mike Brehm where Fehr discussed NHL players adjusting to the unusual circumstances created by COVID-19.

"They adapt to whatever the world throws at them: a new coach, an injury … a new opportunity, an illness, whatever it is," said Fehr. "So, will it be a challenge? Sure. Will it be different? Of course. Will the players, in the long run, have any difficulty handling it? No."

Both Norm and I thought it was a telling quote. Here was a statement by a union chief praising his members, explaining why NHL players are so admirable, and yet also acknowledging work situations sports fans around the world were facing.

To be honest, the NHL and its players deftly (and collectively) untied a Gordian knot of logistics. Both sides wanted players from 24 teams to relocate to Edmonton and Toronto and start the NHL playoffs August 11.

There's no need to detail how the players in the two hub cities handled concepts like quarantines, bubbles, or how much lower Canada's infection numbers and fatalities were compared to the United States. But one headline suggested the NHL was smart in retreating to Canada to complete that season.

To the extent that NHL players average only five-year careers, it was no surprise active roster players wanted to finish the season. But the COVID-19 pandemic was different. A player could infect their partner or child. Or supportive parents who drove them to all those 5 a.m. practices.

That's why Fehr's quote struck a chord. NHL players were willing to adjust their lives but also showed courage in attempting to balance the risk of earning a living with infecting loved ones. No one can suggest that was an easy choice. Any player who chose to play was subject to attack by any number of media snipers suggesting selfishness or inconsideration.

In actual fact, more than a few NHL players, including Mike Green, Travis Hamonic, and Roman Polak, stayed home, which was also a difficult choice.

I remember one time early in my career while working for a sports marketing agency about a decision I had to make. Our five-year-old son's class was supposed to go on a field trip with their fathers. I worked for a boss at the time who seemed to put business ahead of family. He felt every agency project was "must-win" and missing work for something like a child's school activity was folly. He was furious with me for choosing progeny over profitability.

I went to the dairy farm that day at the risk of my career.

For businesspeople reading this book, note that your employees face choices every day and many of them are difficult. Sometimes employees leave sick relatives at home because not earning a day's wage is too heavy a loss. Many women (in particular) have sacrificed their careers to care for children at home.

As such, I'd like to think Donald Fehr would demand we all bring compassion to our thinking when someone seems distracted or troubled. They too are making daily sacrifices to make it all work.

The fan in all of us believes the salaries NHL players earn easily offset missed family time. Who cares if an NHL player missed seeing his daughter's first steps because he was wrapped in a Toronto bubble?

Hockey players adapt (and adapted mightily across 2020–2) but they are not the only ones making big money. A lot of investment bankers and hedge fund managers made even more and comfortably worked from home bouncing children on their knees.

If you are a boss, look with empathy on your workplace and remember the NHL re-start during the summer of 2020 for guidance.

For individual clubs and players, as well as the League (all owners) and NHLPA (players' association), these topics were important with the needs and interests differing notably for each group. Tough decisions and negotiations were magnified by the realities of COVID-19 and the resulting tremendous downward pressure on club and League revenues globally.

If we dig into this topic, we can start by asking why we would dedicate a chapter to praising the NHL and NHLPA. What possible lessons are we trying to share? How can this material influence day-to-day business or employee contemplations?

Efficiency in Decisions

Our answer is drawn from an old expression: "two birds, one stone." In the Olde English version, the expression is violent since it involves hunting. By most accounts, the expression originated in Greek mythology when a particular deity threw a stone so accurately that the effort killed two birds with a single action.

Today, in general terms, the phrase is used to refer to a very efficient effort (or activity) where the active party (the "thrower'") accomplishes two notable tasks with an effort generally required for a single outcome. Other ways of saying "two birds, one stone" include "two-for-one" (sometimes shortened into "a twofer"), BOGO ("buy one, get one free"), and "have your cake and eat it too" (which essentially refers to a beneficial side-effect from a single action).

In the business world, there are many versions of this type of proficiency, and they are frequently delivered by consultants (billing at massive hourly rates) charged with improving efficiency (to justify those fees). Just like in the NHL, winning (being effective) is priority number one. But a close second priority is understanding what it takes to win and winning while expending the fewest human and financial resources possible. Physical efficiency is great but not if it is fiscally foolish or unsustainable.

Some examples of these above concepts include "synergistic side-effects" (i.e., a beneficial positive outcome outside of the primary target but one that delivers a close fit with the primary objective) and "double-dipping" (i.e., using the same asset/activity to get two sets of desirable benefits). Many years ago, "synergy" was a magic word and thrown around by those same consultants almost as much as "economies of scale," "service economy," and "360-degree feedback."

In the case of the NHL in the summer of 2020 (and again in January 2021), the "stone" was the desire to get the League playing again, completing the playoffs, and awarding the Stanley Cup, and ultimately administering 25,000 to 30,000 COVID-19 tests (at the NHL's cost). A *New York Times* article captured the complexity of this situation in its May 29, 2020, headline, the "NHL's Comeback Depends on Answers to a Few Dozen Questions."

The first bird was crowning a champion. The second bird was securing a four-year extension of the CBA. The NHL appeared to pull that off with the support of the NHLPA for four good reasons worth reviewing:

1 The previous CBA, as described in previous chapters, had proven to be an undeniable financial success for then NHL and its players. Why not extend it?
2 Playing the 2020 Stanley Cup playoffs (in the midst a global pandemic) required a League tightly aligned with its Players' Association. For that to happen, both groups needed to trust each other and engage in fully synchronized decisions to produce official games in a safe way. What better way to ensure this alignment than by extending the agreement to a time

(2026) when most believe the COVID-19 pandemic will have been eradicated?

3 The time required to meet and negotiate the 2020 season completion meant everyone was already at the table and open to collaboration. Why not add another item to the agenda?

4 The players were already feeling the very real pressure of COVID-19 and the spread of the virus in other major professional sport leagues made clear there would be no fans in the stands. Everyone would lose money. While both parties were incentivized to save the season, could a long-term business effort could benefit owners and players alike?

Investigating that "stone" shows the NHL announced on May 26, 2020, its intention to complete the 2020 season with a 24-team tournament in one or two hub cities and then successfully award the 2020 Stanley Cup. To do so, the NHL formally ended the regular season, canceling the remaining games.

The decision to include 24 teams did not include any details on dates, locations, or plans to offer future playoff games in a safe format. But it was particularly relevant for players and owners because traditionally only 16 teams qualify for the post-season. This decision meant eight additional teams made the playoffs, additional players earned playoff bonuses, and key fan bases found the albatross of an "out-of-contention and eliminated" season was miraculously salvaged.

The League's rationale made sense because those eight teams now held (mathematically at least) a very slight chance to qualify for the playoffs. Even better, those eight teams would retain an equal chance (12.5 percent) of being awarded the first overall pick in the entry draft; that is, they would make the playoffs but still hold attractive positions in the coming NHL draft.

The idea of increasing the number of clubs playing summertime hockey also meant more fans in more key markets could savor the chances of seeing or reading about their favorite players and teams. Generally, eliminated teams lose free media coverage but "in-contention" teams receive daily media updates and treatment. This too was a win-win for owners and players.

The lack of specifics around the logistics in May was due to the fact the NHL did not have all the answers yet. In late May, the virus was beginning to kill Americans at an increasing rate with growing concerns a second wave would hit during the fall. This mattered because three Tampa Bay Lightning players had become infected, as had numerous MLS players.[2]

Leaving the specifics of where (which hub city/cities to use) and when (dates/times) was smart and provided the League with some flexibility as it moved forward toward each decision. In other words, it bought itself some time. That extra month allowed the League the ability to decide it could start the Stanley Cup playoffs August 1, 2020, in two hub cities – Edmonton, Alberta, and Toronto, Ontario. The conclusion of the season, the conference championships, and Stanley Cup finals would take place in Edmonton.

The decision to locate the game hubs in two Canadian cities (Las Vegas had been the highly touted frontrunner for many weeks)[3] was likely due largely to the rising rates of COVID-19 in the United States and a more controlled management of the virus in Canada. Having both cities in the same country would virtually eliminate cross-border travel, a major concern of governments in Canada and the United States, not to mention state and provincial authorities.

For instance, in order to play baseball, the Toronto Blue Jays, the only Canadian team in MLB, was forced to play their home games for the shortened 2020 season and the first half of the 2021 season in Buffalo, New York, after the Canadian government declined their request for an exemption to host games in Toronto in an empty stadium with visiting players centralized in the stadium hotel. Starting July 30, 2021, the club was given a special exemption and returned home for the last half of the 2021 season. Ironically, the club played much better at home, narrowly missing the playoffs, leading many fans to ask, "What if they'd played at home the entire season?"

Success

In the end, the statistics supported the NHL's measured decision for the 2020 NHL playoffs. As of the end of the playoffs (September 28, 2020), Canada had reported 158,000 cases and 9,500 fatalities, while the US had endured 7.2 million cases and 205,000 deaths. Given Canada has roughly one-tenth the US population, this data shows how much more rampant the virus was in the US than in Canada for that period of time.

Additionally, where Canada (for the most part) embraced public safety, some Americans challenged any government entity requiring masks in public or social distancing. Some went so far as to suggest the pandemic was a hoax. Subsequently, the NHL's decision to restrict games to Canada looked smart and informed, especially after health issues abruptly emerged and two MLS clubs were forced to withdraw from that league's summer tournament due to virus outbreaks.

The NHL also announced it would implement a detailed set of safety protocols, including daily testing (every other day during training camp); isolation periods before, during, and after arrival at the hub city; temperature checks; and symptom screening. Rules for isolation after a positive test and policies for a return to play were also developed. The general concept of a bubble was also suggested, where players would not necessarily isolate at the rink but would stay in a rink bubble and then a home bubble, limiting interaction with anyone outside of these two bubbles as much as possible.

The biggest challenge was getting the players into the hub city's "double bubble" environment without anyone (players, family, staff, TV crews, officials, etc.) being infected. If that goal was achieved, the NHL would hold a decent chance to successfully conduct the 2020 Stanley Cup playoffs.

The result? By the end of August 2020, the NHL had conducted more than 27,000 tests and gone five straight weeks without a single positive test. By September 2020, the NHL had crowned Tampa Bay as Stanley Cup champions. The Lightning would capture the title again in 2021 and advance to the finals in 2022, losing to Colorado.

Norm's Nostalgia: Wow, Does Hockey Ever Matter (in Canada at Least)!

In early 2014, I received a call from two marketing professionals at Canadian Tire and Scotiabank, two major Canadian firms who are highly engaged in supporting ice hockey. They had reached out to me about trying to measure the impact of hockey in Canada. They didn't have much of a budget and wanted a credible third-party study (a university professor) to see what was possible.

For me it was exciting and thought provoking.

As you dig into the nature of such a project, your brain starts stretching and creaking. Hockey in Canada is vast, deep, and drives tourism plus the semi-permanent movement of players (and their families). The size of audience – through media and in person – is significant. Junior and women's hockey are well supported and there is growing support for sledge hockey.

It was a dream opportunity for me and was similarly for many of my students. In fact, more than a dozen signed up to be part of what could only be described as a "mega-project."

First, there was a lot of discussion. Impact of what? Where does it happen (country, province, region, city, town)? How do we make the report realistic, conservative, and – most importantly – defendable against critics because it was planned for release in the public sphere.

So, off we went ... and, just a few months and a few thousand hours of work later, our hypothesis that hockey REALLY matters was supported. REALLY supported.

Some of the highlights included those illustrated by figures 16.1, 16.2, and 16.3.

FIGURE 16.1 *Hockey has an impact on communities*

The direct economic impact on communities

$2.6 billion is the amount that moves directly between communities in Canada each year as a result of the sport of hockey that – should the sport disappear – could potentially be lost from the market. The underyling contributions of these impacts can be categorized and quantified as follows:

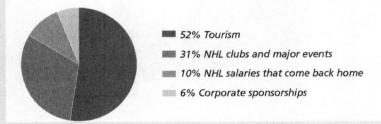

■ 52% *Tourism*

■ 31% *NHL clubs and major events*

■ 10% *NHL salaries that come back home*

■ 6% *Corporate sponsorships*

FIGURE 16.2 *Hockey has professional opportunities and inspires people to give their time*

Job creation and volunteerism

| Canada has more than 5,000 full-time jobs in hockey | While thousands more work part-time | 150,000 Canadians volunteer for hockey (coaching, administration, tournaments) at an average of 5 hours / week. |

FIGURE 16.3 *Hockey rinks are pervasive across the country*

Hockey Rinks are a part of our landscape

Hockey rinks are part of the landscape in Canada, with nearly 2,500 rinks reported in the country, led by Ontario (898), Alberta (420), Quebec (358), and Manitoba (203); British Columbia (186); Saskatchewan (165); New Brunswick (85); Nova Scotia (75); Prince Edward Island (27); Newfoundland (26); NW Territories/Nunavut (10); and the Yukon (7).

Source: O'Reilly, N. (2015). Ice Hockey in Canada: 2015 Impact Study Summary: The Economic, Social, Community and Sport Benefits of Canada's Favourite Game.

The second "bird," the side-effect with great benefit for the NHL, was the ratification of the CBA extension through the 2025–6 season, announced at the same time and in the same press releases as the return-to-play plan for the 2020 Stanley Cup playoffs. Achieving that common goal, Commissioner Bettman announced:

> Today, the NHL and the NHLPA announced a significant agreement that addresses the uncertainty everyone is dealing with, the framework for the completion of the 2019–20 season, and the foundation for the continued long-term growth of our league. I thank NHLPA Executive Director Don Fehr and Special Assistant to the Executive Director Mathieu Schneider, the more than 700 NHL players – particularly those who worked on our Return to Play Committee – and the NHL's Board of Governors for coming together under extraordinary circumstances for the good of our game. While we have all worked very hard to try to address the risks of COVID-19, we know that health and safety are and will continue to be our priorities. We know all of our fans are excited about our return to the ice next month, and that has been our goal since we paused our season on March 12.[4]

This note, showing clear collaboration between the NHL and the NHLPA, captured the essence of the NHL's plan. Bettman further clarified that the return to play combined with the CBA extension "was about maintaining, stabilizing during this time, and focusing on future of the game."

Highlights of the New CBA

Here are some highlights of the extension that both the League and the NHLPA shared publicly.

1 Six seasons of play (including 2019–20) confirmed without interruption.
2 An escrow fund larger in the early years will help deal with COVID-19 revenue implications and reduced over the following years, with a provision to add an additional year (2026–7) to the agreement if certain escrow debt thresholds are reached.
3 NHL players will play in both the 2022 and 2026 Olympic Games, to be held in China and Italy, respectively.
4 Ten percent of players' salaries for the 2020–1 season will be held back by owners and paid out in three equal installments in the 2022–3, 2023–4, and 2024–5 seasons.
5 The minimum salary rates, maximum rookie salaries, and playoff bonus pools will all increase over the life of the extension.

Much has already been written about the Lightning winning the 2020 Cup but, as authors, we were more impressed with the process attempted and achieved by two groups working in concert to generate greater sustainability for hockey and the NHL. That sustainability bodes well for the League as it would for any business.

We've mentioned consultants, somewhat glibly, and acknowledge (appropriately) that many good consultancies specialize in the concept of sustainability. For many of the big firms, sustainability servicing is a guaranteed revenue generator because so many companies fear failure. How can an organization, big or small, survive in a world where disease, technology, or competitors can upend a business in the blink of an eye?

Let us leave you with two familiar ways of thinking about that very challenge and the decisions many of us are forced to make every day. They come at us by the hundreds and all of us do our best to resolve them in an optimal fashion.

The first of our "ways," in Latin, is this: *nanos gigantum humeris insidentes*. Most know this phrase as "standing on the shoulders of the giants who went before us." It makes clear that any organization's success would not have been possible without the efforts of countless generations prior.

The second comes from Eric Weiner's 2008 book *The Geography of Bliss*. In that text, Weiner recounts a quote attributed to famed vaccine inventor Jonas Salk, the scientist generally credited with conquering polio. When asked what the main aim of his life had been, he commented, "to be a good ancestor." Weiner felt Salk enjoyed a clear understanding of his "place in the universe."

We hope in finishing this book, one that leaned heavily on ice hockey, the NHL, and the numerous stars and administrators who consistently made the game great, you were able to think about your work life and how to better serve those around you. Sustainability is an obligation for businesses but is not always attainable. Sustainability in life, our actions, the lives we touch, and the ways in which we make life better for others ... well, that is always worth attempting.

We hope you are eventually seen as a good ancestor (when all is said and done) and this book is one worth sharing. In the end, we're all teammates on a very small sheet of ice.

Or, in the words of Stompin' Tom Connors, "the puck is in. The home team wins!"

17

Give-and-Go

Commissioner Bettman kicked off this book with a foreword describing our lessons for businesses and individuals as a "business playbook." He called the combination of hockey and business "a marriage." At this stage, we want to finish with a quick give-and-go, the famous expression meaning where you pass the puck and then race to an open spot, expecting to get the puck back. The give-and-go has been used in ice hockey for more than a century and remains highly effective today. We're confident fans will see it a century from now.

The reason? Two people working together (the power of interdependence) can move faster than a single defenseman can hope to stop. Whether you frame the concept under group dynamics or teamwork, a good give-and-go generally sets up an offensive attack and often a great shot on goal. The same holds in business and we hope you never take for granted the power of a small, quick pass to a teammate or colleague who can help you out. In truth, a few give-and-gos, even in a small business, can lead to beneficial gains.

Norm's Nostalgia: Never Underestimate a Hall of Fame, No Matter How Small

As we think about give-and-go and drivers of success for both individuals and organizations, we acknowledge the outcomes must exist via long-range terms, much like the NHL's copycat of the NFL business model, which is now, more than 15 years later, still yielding rewards.

It leads me to tell a short story where a give-and-go effort led to a wonderful moment.

Let's go back to the year 2014. It's the year I was nominated as a candidate for my local Sports Hall of Fame in Lindsay, Ontario, a small town of about 15,000 people northeast of Toronto. I'm willing to bet that my dad had some part in it, but I'll never know who put me forward (although I will admit he's long been a great politician). All I know is that there were multiple nominees.

Ultimately, I received a call letting me know I was a finalist and asking me to submit some additional materials, which I did. My first thoughts were simple. Why was I nominated?

At best, I was a "reasonable" athlete. I got to represent my country a few times in triathlon at the world championships (but only as an age-grouper). I had won a few local races, had some decent results as a bike-racer, won a provincial university title in Nordic skiing (as a team, with the University of Waterloo), ran some marathons, and swam competitively at the university level. But nothing anywhere close to approaching the level of an Olympian or NHL player.

Perhaps, I thought, I was going in as a builder? That made more sense. I've taught hundreds of people now working in elite sport, have written a number of books, published articles, done wide-ranging media interviews, and attended a number of Olympic and Paralympic Games with Team Canada as an administrator. In addition, I was National Team Manager for Triathlon Canada and served on the boards of many national and international organizations. I ran events for the 2008 Toronto Olympic Bid and became a partner in a successful sport marketing.

When I got the call letting me know I'd been selected, they confirmed it was a combination of the two. Kinda cool, I thought.

But what of the award itself?

On October 28, 2015, my family and I had made the trip back to Lindsay from Athens, Ohio, where we were living. (My wife and I were professors at Ohio University.) When we arrived at the local arena for the ceremony, I could see there were about 250 people there. There were former teachers, former coaches, old friends (many of whom had traveled long distances), my wife, kids, parents, brother, sister, nieces and nephews, uncles and aunts, and numerous other family members. The list went on.

It felt like much more than a ceremony and more like a wedding.

And that's saying a lot because for everyone else it was an interruption to their day, but for me it was truly amazing. I was able to address the crowd for 10 minutes, tell my (sporting) life story and thank as many people as I could remember, including the math teacher who coached our Nordic ski team and, as I learned years later, paid for many of our training expenses. I also spoke about the cross-country running coach whose philosophy called for running triple our race distance in training before competing and the cycling coach who courageously came to a high school and recruited Grade 9 students to race for him.

Without any of those three giving ... and encouraging me to "go," I know I would likely not work in sport today. They were the early-career teammates who hit me in mid-stride with crisp, wonderful passes that stuck to my stick.

And what about my parents and my wife who supported me through all my crazy efforts? They have never stopped giving. Their support and encouragement have always been powerful. I would be nowhere without their love.

But wait, there is even a better part. For a full year (actually, 366 days since February 2016 had 29 days), there was a huge display about me in the entrance of the local arena where I'd grown up playing hockey and swimming. Every time I walked in, I was overcome with a wave of good feelings.

Below are two photos, one of my son, Kian, and one of my niece, Hannah. Kian is standing at the induction ceremony and Hannah in front of the display at the arena.

Beneficial gains are what this book has attempted to provide and looking back at the whole book, the journey you've hopefully taken, the metaphorical game you've skated with us, should bring a wide range of links together.

In building from Commissioner Bettman's foreword, our set of lessons opened by dropping the puck with the first three chapters. We borrowed from Wayne Gretzky in setting the tone by suggesting we can all skate to where the puck is going. Indeed, we took this premise to heart as we wrote these chapters.

First, we started with the NHL and its leader for the past 30 years and how the business success of hockey in North America has come from the top – with some very challenging decisions, not to mention a few ruffled feathers, to play games during COVID-19 and to thrive after COVID-19. The importance of the commissioner's "boss" (i.e., the club owners) was also described. In sum, leadership is key and a willingness to make tough decisions in the long-term interests of the organization (versus winning short-term popularity contests) goes hand-in-glove with any discussion of leadership.

The NHL's story and that of its leadership was set up in chapters 2 and 3, where we identified and supported 14 core drivers for business leaders and organizations. These drivers were taken from hockey and extrapolated to a business context. They were discussed in the context of the entire sport business ecosystem and then illustrated throughout the book with concepts and stories as we "played the game," "changed the lines," and headed to "overtime."

The first eight drivers were written specifically for the world's business leaders, all drawn from the NHL's experiences and successes. For instance, we advised readers to *innovate and expand asset value,* which was highlighted in chapter 4. That was where we outlined many of the NHL's accomplishments, such as the outdoor games and the media technologies for new fans of the sport, all driven by the four timeless influences in hockey (passion, barrier-breaking, government interest, and no borders).

Chapter 5, the copycat chapter, described in detail the business successes that accrued to the NHL after copying the tried-and-tested business model of the NFL, a classic example of the *your boss wants to make money* driver. It may not be possible to pass the market leader, but it doesn't mean an organization can't observe and emulate best practices from others.

The driver described as *brand, brand, brand* was the topic of chapter 6, which captured and described how new offerings should flow from the product or service and seek branded strategies or tactics infused with ingenuity and creativity. We would also add the word "curiosity" because creativity is always enhanced when humans, not cats, are curious.

Part 3 of the book, which we called "Changing the Lines," shared three detailed chapters on the diversity, equity, and inclusion issues facing sport and business today, with wide-ranging topics on gender, race, and culture covered in detail. Each of those chapters reinforced important drivers that we dubbed *focus on value creation for the stakeholders that matter* and *integrity matters.*

In chapter 3, we put forward an additional six drivers for the world's leading organizations that were built out and supported throughout the book. This framework set the tone for many of the chapter stories that followed.

First, *consider experiences as your product focus* was illustrated in chapter 8, which dug into the marketing efforts – past and present – of the NHL that are characterized by relevancy to the environment of the current time. We feel strongly the NHL has evolved and adapted its fan experiences over time to much success, which all organizations can learn from.

Second, the illustration of the copycat chapter and the incredible business benefits gained by the NHL from adapting the NFL's business model is a classic example of the drive how *major innovations should be prioritized over history.* Specifically, the NHL and its leadership committees were willing to ignore past practice and potentially limit the abilities of its most successful clubs, but to an end that benefitted the League and all clubs, particularly the smaller-market ones.

Third, *focus on both the numerator and the denominator of value* was highlighted multiple times in the middle chapters. For instance, the "Veterans Matter" chapter shared stories, particularly the one about Zdeno Chara and how the perceived quality of having such a player continue for the fans, the League, and younger players at a normally decreased cost (i.e., progressively lower salary as a player approaches their 40s) meant a better "value fraction" for all involved.

Next, *focus on trust with your customers* was highlighted in the fighting chapter ("Conflict Management") where we attempted to balance the reality of fans who love fighting in hockey and fans who do not want it. Given the need to prioritize player health and safety, the League has gradually moved to a situation where fights are rare, where fights with more than two players have been largely eliminated from the game, and where the role for the "one-dimensional" fighter (who does not contribute to other parts of the game) is gone.

Fifth, *create advocates for your brands* is a common theme throughout many chapters, including the chapter on women's professional ice hockey, which outlines the potential brand benefits of reaching a new customer base and fan segment through a brand extension.

Finally, *embrace strategic agility and adaptability*, two common business terms observed in every industry today, are both captured in the "Emerging Trends" chapter highlighting the need to embrace, adapt, and stay flexible with new opportunities and drastic revenue shifts.

The above concepts lead to a summary where you, the reader, must think about your career, your current job, and your current bosses. In the end, many business opportunities require a sense of creative destruction. The adage "things always change" is very important here and is one that we have both often discussed with our students and colleagues to emphasize that a career is a path, requiring many stages, successes and failures, and dedicated effort with coaching to prepare for where the future might or might not lead.

Said another way, and once again paraphrasing the Great One, having some of the answers in 2022 can't prepare you completely for where the puck will show up in 2025. But we hope you will take what we have humbly provided and start skating toward the future you want. The one where you win a scoring title, and your firm hoists the Cup!

Overtime

Throughout this labor of love, we constantly called on past moments where every reader might connect or possibly enjoy the distraction. Thus, for our last give-and-go, we offer two short stories – one from each of us – that characterize great hockey memories. We loved writing them and hope they provide valuable insight for taking hockey "from the ice to the office."

It's this simple: hockey and the NHL changed our lives and consistently cause us to believe an individual's business or career success can borrow a great deal from the NHL and the great game of hockey.

Rick's Recall

Most of us have a handful of "greatest" sport memories etched in our minds.

We know exactly where we were for a historic win when our favorite team overcame tremendous odds to win a game, series, or the Stanley Cup. It's the day or night when our heroes began living forever. When our favorite team became legendary.

Whether you are a Boomer or Millennial, that memorable outcome for older readers might still be the last time Toronto won the Stanley Cup. That was May 2, 1967, the swan song for the NHL's Original Six teams. It was a classic with the Leafs winning Game 6 at home, 3–1, largely because Leafs goalie Terry Sawchuk stopped 40 out of 41 shots and winger Jim Pappin, who took six shots on Gump Worsley that day, scored the game-winner with just 36 seconds left in the second period.

For later generations, Sidney Crosby's overtime goal for Team Canada (to beat the Americans in Vancouver on February 28, 2010) was the Olympic moment time stopped in Canada. Many have embellished that night to suggest the roar from Canada Hockey Place (now known as Rogers Arena) could be heard in Saint John and St. John's.

The game itself will always remain one of the most exciting ever played and like many sudden-death overtime moments (think Brett Hull and the Dallas Stars beating Buffalo in the 1999 NHL Stanley Cup Final), the 2010 gold medal game had it all. For Canadians trying to live down the disastrous 2006 campaign in Italy, a US goal by Zach Parise with just 24.4 seconds left in regulation was an ominous harbinger of doom. Surely, Team Canada would stuff things up for the second straight Games. But then future Hockey Hall of Fame forward Jarome Iginla found Crosby streaking in from the left side of the net, crossing the face-off circle, and suddenly the puck was bouncing behind the blue-shirted US goalie Ryan Miller.

Strangely enough, for an American born to Canadian parents (from Newfoundland before it was even a part of Canada), my singular "greatest hockey moment" involves a player from neither of those two fabled countries.

In February 1998, I was directing the University of Oregon's Warsaw Sports Marketing Center and consulting for various sports leagues around the world. That January the League asked me to accompany a group of executives to the Hawaiian island of Lanai where the NHL's marketing team would show League sponsors the 1998 Nagano Winter Olympics from a spectacular setting.

As a centerpiece of each day, the Olympic hockey competition was broadcast live from Japan to the NHL's guests. It meant I held a virtual front-row seat with the sounds of the Pacific Ocean booming just outside.

So, which "greatest game ever" do I remember? It's easy. The February night Czech Republic goalie Dominik Hašek seemed to single-handedly beat Team Canada in a momentous Olympics semi-final matchup. In the words of those around me, Hašek was "unconscious." Of the Czech's performance, there was unanimous consensus. Number 39, the NHL's MVP (Hart Memorial Trophy winner) in 1997 and 1998, was playing "out of his mind."

That night the Dominator, with his unorthodox flopping style, stymied Canada's best. He was so jaw-dropping good, he left the Great One, Wayne Gretzky (unused for the game-ending shootout), sitting alone, dejectedly, on an empty Team Canada bench.

I won't bore historians or Winter Olympics fans with details of the game itself or the tense overtime. Instead, I'll skip to the moments many hockey purists still discuss: Hašek's five consecutive stops on five of Canada's most accomplished scorers (in the first Olympics featuring NHL players).

The shootout on the Big Hat's rink began with Theo Fleury. Denied. The Flames right wing was followed by Ray Bourque (stopped), Joe Nieuwendyk (missed the net, right side), captain

Eric Lindros (deke, backhand, hits Hašek's catching glove and then the pipe), and ended with Brendan Shanahan. Stuffed.

On Lanai, there was disbelief. The Czechs had played conservatively the whole game, rarely taking offensive chances. Their apparent intent? Score a shootout goal and let Hašek win the game.

As was the case in 1980 when the Americans beat the Russians in the historic "Miracle on Ice" semi-finals (before beating Finland for the gold), the Czech gold medal win came two days later when Hašek recorded 20 more saves and shut out a Soviet team that included the Bure brothers (Pavel and Valery), Alexei Yashin, and Sergei Fedorov, 1–0.

As in the 1980s, no one talks about the gold medal game. In retrospect, it might be easy for an American author to select the 1980 US win over Russia as that "knew where you were" moment. The truth is "I'm not sure" where I was. My memory suggests I was working as a sportswriter and didn't see the game live.

But in 1998, with the NHL roaring back from the 1994–5 lockout that canceled the All-Star Game and shortened the season to 48 games, the 1998 Olympic semi-final, coming on the heels of an NHL marketing campaign called "Game On" (borrowed from the movie *Wayne's World*), was magical.

Norm's Nostalgia

If you're like either of us, you love sport. We are lifelong athletes and sharing these short stories allows us to share our experiences relevant to chapter topics and let you know a bit about each of us. In some cases, we may be telling you too much!

In my case, I played hockey as a kid up to my 16th birthday, with the highlight of my very ordinary and largely house-league career being a 55-goal season in my last year. The reason I point out my 55 is that I likely scored 55 total goals in total during the previous 10 years of my hockey life!

That single Mike Bossy–like season in Bantams had little to do with my hockey skills and much more to do with a terrific center named Darren Forget, who set up almost every one of my tallies, and with being fit. I had taken up the sport of triathlon a year earlier. Thanks to many hours running, biking, swimming, and weight-training (plus some cross-country skiing in the winter), I could outskate almost every other player in the third period, when I scored most of my goals.

After that 55-goal season, I retired from hockey and pursued my triathlon and skiing passions as career and family took over. It was not until my early 30s that I started playing hockey again in one of the many beer leagues of Toronto.

Let's fast forward nearly 30 years to the fall 2015 hockey season in the Bird Arena Hockey League (BAHL) at Ohio University, which is home to the Masters of Sports Administration (MSA) program that is the oldest and one of the highest-ranked sport management schools globally, with a storied history and very impressive students. In fact, in four of the five years that I was at Ohio, Sport Business International ranked us as the number one post-graduate sport business program in the world.[1]

That season was most certainly the most glorious on-ice experience of my playing career.

But, before delving into that season, we need to go back to January of 2014, when I arrived in Athens. Upon arriving, and with beer league having been a regular hobby for more than a decade, I sought out a place to play in Athens, quickly learning that the only arena in town was on the campus of Ohio University – Bird Arena – and that the only sign-up league (that worked for a dad with young kids at home) was the BAHL, a refereed league made up of student and community teams, which was known to be competitive, full of talented players, and – on some nights – some fiery tempers on the ice. My kind of game. So, I signed up and, in my early 40s, quickly became (by far) the oldest player in the league.

My first semester of playing was good from a hockey and fitness perspective but not ideal from a social one. You see, I had signed up (late) as an individual and was randomly placed on one of the clubs where I'm not sure if a group of 20-ish college students enjoyed having an anonymous old professor defenseman on their team. We were not good and lost most of our games but, fortunately, with my Canadian heritage and fitness from 30 years of doing triathlons, I helped on the ice and avoided embarrassing myself! But, from a fun/social perspective, it was not ideal. Rick jokes that I was the equivalent of Canadian comedians Bob and Doug McKenzie's famous "hoser."

Following that season, I thought that it was perhaps it was time to start a SportsAd hockey team. So, off I went to recruit faculty, staff, graduate students, and undergrad students.

Fortunately, I had an MSA student in my class, Brett Baur, who was keen to help set this up and also a former NCAA Division I hockey player at Wisconsin. He could play. With Brett on board, we went out to recruit all genders, levels, and skill sets. And, amazingly, enough interest was garnered from all of those groups, and in the fall of 2014, we launched our team.

In the first two semesters we played, we finished at the top in the regular season but were exited early (and painfully) in the playoffs.

But in the third schedule we played, the fall of 2015, we had a sole goal: to win.

In addition to Brett (who has gone on to work in the NHL for the Pittsburgh Penguins and Washington Capitals, and now with the Pittsburgh Pirates of MLB), our team was led by our stellar goaltender Tony Piccioni (currently working with the Chicago Bulls), Justin Stemler – a triple major undergrad (and now a fellow CPA working as a business consultant in Chicago), and a fellow Canadian Josh Staav (now managing the Calgary Tennis Club).

Here is a photo taken that night after the game. It is the class photo that any hockey player dreams of – holding the trophy!

From left to right, front row: Spencer Roth, Tony Piccioni, Norm O'Reilly, Josh Staav, Brett Baur, Jack Zanville; *back row*: Terry Burns, Kevin Yarcusko, Kirby Simeon, Conner Sunkle, Austin Moore.

A quick shout out to Brett. He was unquestionably the star of our team, and I was so fortunate to have been his defense partner for those two years.

Wow, did he make me look good and, yes, NCAA Division I skills are something else when you see them up close. At times, he carried our team and helped an old man win his only college (albeit recreational) championship!

Just as Canada's legendary rock group The Tragically Hip worked hockey into three of their songs, we hope you can integrate the NHL and "all the small things" (with apologies to Blink-182) into your professional lives. Keep squeezing the stick.

Afterword

When the authors of *Business the NHL Way: Lessons from the Fastest Game on Ice* asked me to provide an afterword for their wonderful manuscript, I couldn't help but think of my own book *Over the Boards: Lessons from the Ice*. It's clear both books strongly believe almost anyone can take traits, habits, and skills learned from playing the game of hockey and apply them to their personal or business lives.

That is an exciting premise but one I'm sure casual cynics might challenge. They might make the mistake of thinking someone who has played in the NHL or on an Olympic team was born gifted. That life consistently unfolded in the easiest possible ways. That success in a demanding team sport was translatable as advice for advancement in life.

As anyone who has ever played at an elite level will explain, achieving success in anything, but particularly hockey, is nowhere near that simple. Yes, I enjoyed the good fortune of representing Canada for more than 20 years (1994–2017), but I know that for myself and my teammates, nothing came easy. There were no gilded platters or silver spoons. We worked incredibly hard to earn every gold medal we captured.

What playing hockey has always provided, at least for me, is perspective.

Noted sports psychologist Harry Edwards has called this perspective the dominant sports creed and his research suggested there were (and are) seven values or themes that shape those who play sports. They include character building, discipline, competition, physical fitness, mental fitness, religiosity, and nationalism. Competition links these themes together to create individuals focused on achievement and success, which happen to be the very values we embrace in larger settings such as family life or the workplace.

Wanting to win games (or to make a team) requires I create trust with my teammates. That I earn their respect by showing that I am reliable, courageous, dependable, hungry, and committed to the team and not myself.

In my case, growing up in Shaunavon, Saskatchewan, hockey was more than a way of life; it was my chance to test myself and challenge my ambitions. My parents would probably say it was my North Star.

I played with and against boys until I was 15 and then professionally with the men. Early morning practices or playing hurt became elements of my life that I clearly understood and embraced. Having to outwork my teammates or, later, the world's best, was the fuel that always fed the wolf.

Like the authors of *Business the NHL Way*, Norm and Rick, I understand that not everyone is cut out for playing sport at an elite level. But I do believe everyone has the capacity to reach their own level of greatness. Aspirational dreams are what cause leadership books to get written every year. It's because all of us are looking for coaches or secret recipes that will push us to become our best selves.

I'm known for having played hockey, but I also wanted to achieve success in softball, as a university student, and in medical school. I may never have been the fastest on the ice or the most knowledgeable in the classroom, but there was never any question about my intent and my willingness to sacrifice to achieve my goals.

This book you hold in your hands, or may have just finished reading, is a wonderful way to take the joy of hockey and look through its prism at the business world to see what is possible for your career or entrepreneurial enterprise.

You may never skate another shift on the ice but I encourage you to join in me getting over the boards each day and doing things the NHL way.

Hayley Wickenheiser
Assistant General Manager, Maple Leaf Sports & Entertainment
Order of Canada

Acknowledgments

The authors wish to acknowledge with respect all firekeepers and Indigenous peoples on whose ancestral lands Canadians and Americans have built their cities and homes, not to mention those special spots where we have strapped on our blades and skated on frozen lakes and ponds.

Given this material was largely written during the COVID-19 pandemic, including the Delta and Omicron variants, we want to pay further tribute to the many lives lost and impacted, including readers, fans, administrators, and anyone involved in hockey and its business. The virus has forever changed society as we know it, and live events – including the NHL – profoundly.

No book is ever written without the often-unseen contributions of hundreds of supporters who provide a wide range of benefits. The names of the writers may appear on the front cover, but it is the work of countless others who make the book possible. With that in mind, Norm and Rick wish to acknowledge their wives (Nadège and Barb respectively) and families (Emma, Kian, Thomas, Leland) for consistently making it possible for us to write, re-write, edit, convene, Zoom, and manage this hockey-infused text.

In addition, we would like to thank NHL Commissioner Gary Bettman (for providing our foreword), Hayley Wickenheiser (afterword), Madison Horton (Gabriel Polsky Productions), Margie Chetney (tireless Syracuse University facilitator), Steven Warshaw, Taylor Boucher, Connor Blake, and Melanie Brooks (University of Maine Graduate School of Business), Julian Santiago (Syracuse University Graduate Assistant), NHL 21 gamer (and former SU grad assistant) Josh Hagwell, Gary, Peter and Matthew Burton, Alexa Potack, Myles Schrag, our *Sport Business Journal* editor Jake Kyler, plus John Dellapina, Brian Jennings, Jessica Johnson, and Susan Cohig of the NHL.

We would also like to express a sincere thank you to the entire team at the University of Toronto Press who holistically supported us, including Jennifer DiDomenico, Anna Del Col, Stephanie Mazza, Susan Bindernagel, Chris Reed, Leah Connor, Ani Deyirmenjian, Nikki Bell-Morrison, Jenn Harris, Jane Kelly, Sebastian Frye, Kayla Kiteley, Grusha Singh, Jodi Litvin, and Joanna Kincaide Moore.

Notes

Chapter 1

1 J. Piercy, "Gary Bettman's Language of NHL Labour Talks, Then & Now," *CBC Sports*, August 17, 2012, https://www.cbc.ca/sports/hockey/nhl/gary-bettman-s-language-of-nhl-labour-talks-then-now-1.1264736.

2 M. Ozanian and K. Badenhausen, "NHL Team Values 2020: Hockey's First Decline in Two Decades," *Forbes*, December 9, 2020, https://www.forbes.com/sites/mikeozanian/2020/12/09/nhl-team-values-2020-hockeys-first-decline-in-two-decades/?sh=71716aa770dd.

3 J. Andrew Ross, *Joining the Clubs: The Business of the National Hockey League to 1945* (Syracuse, NY: Syracuse University Press, 2015).

4 B. Adgate, "Hockey's Big Pay Day Is Coming," *Forbes*, January 15, 2019, https://www.forbes.com/sites/bradadgate/2019/01/15/hockeys-big-pay-day-is-coming/#4afaa874e445.

5 D. Rosen, "NHL, Rogers Announce Landmark 12-Year Deal," *NHL.com*, November 26, 2013, https://www.nhl.com/news/nhl-rogers-announce-landmark-12-year-deal/c-693152.

6 J. Mirtle, "NHL Players Cheer for Loonie's Recovery as Reduced Revenues Sink Salaries," *Globe and Mail*, January 18, 2016, https://www.theglobeandmail.com/sports/hockey/nhl-players-cheer-for-loonies-recovery-as-reduced-revenues-sink-salaries/article28253008.

Chapter 2

1 Gentry Estes, "Here's Why, Even on Hiatus, Sports Will Be More Important than Ever," *Nashville Tennessean*, May 19, 2020, https://www.tennessean.com/story/sports/2020/03/19/coronavirus-crisis-sports-more-important-us-than-ever/2869379001/.

Chapter 3

1   G. Foster, N. O'Reilly, and A. Davila, *Sports Business Management: Decision-Making around the Globe*, 2nd ed. (Routledge, 2020).
2   Foster, O'Reilly, and Davila, *Sports Business Management*.
3   B. Pine and J. Gilmore, "Welcome to the Experience Economy," *Harvard Business Review* 76 (1998): 97–105.
4   E. Rogers, *Diffusion of Innovations* (Simon and Schuster, 2010).
5   S. Nambisan, K. Lyytinen, A. Majchrzak, and M. Song, "Digital Innovation Management: Reinventing Innovation Management Research in a Digital World," *MIS Quarterly* 41, no. 1 (2017): 223–38.
6   J. Anderson and J. Narus, "Business Marketing: Understand What Customers Value," *Harvard Business Review* 76, no. 6 (1998): 53–5, 65.
7   Pine and Gilmour, "Welcome to the Experience Economy."
8   R. Morgan and S. Hunt, "The Commitment-Trust Theory of Relationship Marketing," *Journal of Marketing* 58 (July 1994): 20–38.
9   K. Kleps, "Cavs' 2018–2019 Ratings on Fox Sports Ohio Fall 58%, Still Rank 6th in the NBA," *Sport Business*, Crain's Cleveland Business, https://www.crainscleveland.com/kevin-kleps-blog/cavs-2018-19-ratings-fox-sports-ohio-fall-58-still-rank-sixth-nba.
10 D. Godes and D. Mayzlin, "Using Online Conversations to Study Word-of-Mouth Communication," *Marketing Science* 23, no. 4 (2004): 545–60. https://doi.org/10.1287/mksc.1040.0071.
11 R. Palmatier, R. Dant, D. Grewal, and K. Evans, "Factors Influencing the Effectiveness of Relationship Marketing: A Meta-Analysis," *Journal of Marketing* 70 (October 2006): 136–53.
12 P. Tallon, M. Queiroz, T. Coltman, and R. Sharma, "Information Technology and the Search for Organizational Agility: A Systematic Review with Future Research Possibilities," *Journal of Strategic Information Systems* 28, no. 2 (2019): 218–37.
13 B. Daly and R. Anderson, "SBJ Unpacks: League Leaders Talk Strategy during Turbulent Times," *Street and Smith's Sports Business Journal*, August 19, 2020, https://www.sportsbusinessdaily.com/SB-Blogs/SBJ-Unpacks/2020/08/19.aspx.

Chapter 4

1   A. Bell, "Record Television Audience for 2020 IIHF World Junior Championship Final," Inside the Games, January 21, 2020, https://www.insidethegames.biz/articles/1089429/russia-canada-ice-hockey.
2   "11 Million Canadians Watch the Instant Classic World Juniors Gold Medal Game on TNS and RDS," *The Lede*, January 6, 2017, https://www.bellmedia.ca/the-lede/press/11-million-canadians-watch-the-instant-classic-world-juniors-gold-medal-game-on-tsn-and-rds.
3   J. Grix and F. Carmichael, "Why Do Governments Invest in Elite Sport? A Polemic," *International Journal of Sport Policy and Politics* 4, no. 1 (2012): 73–90. https://doi.org/10.1080/19406940.2011.627358.
4   Foster, O'Reilly, and Davila, *Sports Business Management*.
5   IMI International, *Special Report – Support and Passion for Live Events*, April 20, 2020.

6 IMI International, *Wave 6 Global Recovery Update – Key Trends, Sentiment/ Expectation, Start of a Playbook,* May 19, 2020.

7 Gabe Polsky, dir., *Red Penguins,* 2019; Studio Hamburg Enterprises and Norddeutscher Rundfunk.

8 "Coronavirus Disease (COVID-19) Pandemic," World Health Organization, https://www.who.int/emergencies/diseases/novel-coronavirus-2019.

9 "Wimbledon Shows How Pandemic Insurance Could Become Vital for Sports, Other Events," *Insurance Journal,* April 13, 2020, https://www.insurancejournal .com/news/international/2020/04/13/564598.htm.

10 "NHL to Pause Season due to Coronavirus," *NHL.com,* March 12, 2020, https:// www.nhl.com/news/nhl-coronavirus-to-provide-update -on-concerns/c-316131734.

Chapter 5

1 K. Kuchefski, "The NHL Continues to Expand Brand Sponsorships," Instant Sponsor, March 15, 2019, https://medium.com/instant-sponsor /the-nhl-continues-to-expand-brand-sponsorships-7caba235f331

2 Mike Ozanian, "NHL Team Values 2021: New York Rangers Become Hockey's First $2 Billion Team," *Forbes,* December 8, 2021, https://www.forbes.com/sites /mikeozanian/2021/12/08/nhl-team-values-2021-22-new-york-rangers-become -hockeys-first-2-billion-team/?sh=97e3c94360cb.

3 D. Rosen, "NHL, Rogers Announce Landmark 12-Year Deal," *NHL.com,* November 26, 2013, https://www.nhl.com/news/nhl-rogers-announce -landmark-12-year-deal/c-693152

4 *Collective Bargaining Agreement,* NHLPA, https://www.nhlpa.com/the-pa/cba

5 A. Gretz, "NHL Salary Cap Ceiling Set at $81.5 Million for 2019–20 Season," Pro Hockey Talk, *NBC Sports,* June 22, 2019, https://nhl.nbcsports.com/2019/06/22 /nhl-salary-cap-ceiling-set-at-81-5-million-for-2019-20-season.

6 *Collective Bargaining Agreement,* NHLPA, https://www.nhlpa.com/the-pa/cba

7 Foster, O'Reilly, and Davila, *Sports Business Management.*

Chapter 6

1 M. Donovan, *The Name Game: Football, Baseball, Hockey & Basketball How Your Favorite Sports Teams Were Named* (Toronto: Warwick Publishing, 1997).

2 E. Duhatschek, "The San Jose Sharks Have Come a Long Way since Their First Season in 1991," *The Globe and Mail,* May 27, 2016, https://www.theglobeandmail .com/sports/hockey/the-san-jose-sharks-have-come-a-long-way-since-their -first-season-in-1991/article30196471/.

3 C. Sims, "In Disney's Hockey Venture, The Real Action Is off the Ice," *New York Times,* December 14, 1992, https://www.nytimes.com/1992/12/14/business /in-disney-s-hockey-venture-the-real-action-is-off-the-ice.html.

4 S. Boas, "Is Florida Really the Lightning Capital of the World?" *Orlando Sentinel,* June 11, 2006, https://www.orlandosentinel.com/news/os-xpm-2006-06-11 -swnewcomer11-story.html.

5 R. MacNeil, "History of How NHL Teams Got Their Names," *Sportsnet.ca,* September 17, 2010, https://www.sportsnet.ca/hockey/nhl/nhl-team-names/.

6 "Naming a Team: The Story Behind the Blue Jackets Name," *NHL.com*, November 11, 2005, https://www.nhl.com/bluejackets/news/naming-a-team-the-story-behind-the-blue-jackets-name/c-479316.

7 S. Thompson, "The History of NHL Expansion to Canada Part 3: Lost Franchises and a Bungled Bid," *Bleacher Report*, January 17, 2009, https://bleacherreport.com/articles/112071-the-history-of-nhl-expansion-to-canada-part-3-lost-franchises-and-a-bungled-bid.

8 "Minnesota Wild Primary Logo," Sports Logo History, https://sportslogohistory.com/minnesota-wild-primary-logo.

9 B. Davis, "Las Vegas Ranked as One of the Top Cities in the Country," *Vegas*, February 3, 2020, https://vegasmagazine.com/las-vegas-ranked-as-one-of-the-top-cities-in-the-country.

10 C. Ledra and P. Pickens, "NHL Team Nicknames Explained," *NHL Insider*, November 22, 2016, https://www.nhl.com/news/nhl-team-nickname-origins-explained/c-283976168?tid=277548856.

11 L. Steinberg, "Three Reasons the NHL's Golden Knights Had the Best First Year of Any Expansion Team," *Forbes*, June 9, 2018, https://www.forbes.com/sites/leighsteinberg/2018/06/09/three-reasons-why-nhl-golden-knights-had-the-best-first-year-of-any-expansion-team.

12 *Valiant* was produced by Sterling Productions in association with Osmosis Films and NHL Original Productions.

13 "NHL's Seattle Team Unveils 'Kraken' Name along with Logo, Jersey Design," *Sportsnet.ca*, July 23, 2020, https://www.sportsnet.ca/hockey/nhl/nhls-seattle-team-called-kraken.

14 M. Weinreb, "When the Stanley Cup Final Was Canceled because of a Pandemic," *Smithsonian Magazine*, March 18, 2020, https://www.smithsonianmag.com/history/when-stanley-cup-finals-was-cancelled-because-pandemic-180974439/.

Chapter 7

1 Associated Press, "Broken Sticks Nothing New in NHL," *Northwest Arkansas Democrat Gazette*, June 10, 2017, https://www.nwaonline.com/news/2017/jun/10/broken-sticks-nothing-new-in-nhl-201706/.

Chapter 8

1 B. Lippert, "Bo Regard," *Chicago Tribune*, August 4, 1989, https://www.chicagotribune.com/news/ct-xpm-1989-08-04-8901020025-story.html

2 The Canadian Press, "Wayne Gretzky's Brand Remains Strong More than a Decade after Retiring," *The Hockey News*, January 24, 2011, https://thehockeynews.com/news/article/wayne-gretzkys-brand-remains-strong-more-than-a-decade-after-retiring.

3 "Gretzky to Endorse Skechers Shape-Ups," *L.A. Business First*, January 11, 2011, https://www.bizjournals.com/losangeles/news/2011/01/11/gretzky-to-endorse-skechers-shape-ups.html.

4 P. Del Nibletto, "Four Reasons Samsung Chose Wayne Gretzky," *ITWC Blogs*, ITWorld Canada, July 9, 2009, https://www.itworldcanada.com/blog/four-reasons-samsung-chose-wayne-gretzky/56382.

5 "Hockey Night in Canada in Radio," History of Canadian Broadcasting, updated March 2014, https://www.broadcasting-history.ca/in-depth/hockey-night -canada-radio.

6 True North Wire, "Hockey Night in Canada Ratings Down after Cherry Firing," True North, January 1, 2020, https://tnc.news/2020/01/01/hockey-night-in -canada-ratings-down-after-cherry-firing/.

7 D. Zarum, "La Soirée du hockey," *L'encyclopédie Canadienne*, August 7, 2019, https://www.thecanadianencyclopedia.ca/fr/article/la-soiree-du -hockey.

8 Schedule, NHL International Broadcast Partners, *NHL.com*, http://www.nhl .com/ice/page.htm?id=74583.

9 L. Wells, "How Much Is Sidney Crosby Worth?" *Sportscasting*, March 9, 2020, https://www.sportscasting.com/how-much-is-sidney-crosby-worth/.

10 Sponsorship X, *Wave 4: SponsorshipX COVID-19 Impact Study*, September 10, 2020, https://sponsorshipx.com/covid-19-impact-study.

11 Sponsorship X, *Wave 4: SponsorshipX COVID-19 Impact Study*, September 10, 2020, https://sponsorshipx.com/covid-19-impact-study.

Chapter 9

1 "U.S.–Canada Women's Hockey Game Breaks Detroit Attendance Record," *Detroit News*, February 8, 2020, https://www.detroitnews.com/story/sports/nhl /red-wings/2020/02/08/womens-hockey-game-expected-break-detroit -attendance-record/4702884002/.

2 "Canada's National Women's Team Draws Record-Breaking Crowd to Ottawa in Last Game against United States before 2010 Olympics," *Hockey Canada*, January 1, 2010, https://www.hockeycanada.ca/en-ca/news /2010-nr-001-en.

3 S. Lane, *Roar: The Stories behind AFLW – A Movement Bigger than Sport* (Penguin, January 28, 2018), https://www.amazon.com.au/Roar-stories-behind-movement -bigger-ebook/dp/B076Z79G97.

4 "Players, AFL Reach Historic FLW CBA Agreement," AFL Players, November 15, 2018, http://www.aflplayers.com.au/article/players-afl-reach-historic-aflw -cba-agreement/.

5 Male Champions of Change, "Pathway to Pay Equality 2019," https:// malechampionsofchange.com/wp-content/uploads/2019/02/MCC-Sport -Pathway-to-Pay-Equality-Report-2019.pdf.

6 A. Schetzer, "AFLW Player Wage Rise Illustrates Tough Battle Women Face," *The Guardian*, November 16, 2018, https://www.theguardian.com/sport/2018 /nov/16/aflw-player-wage-rise-illustrates-tough-battle-women-face.

7 Quote drawn from Damon A. Williams, *Strategic Diversity Leadership: Activating Change and Transformation in Higher Education* (Stylus Publishing, 2013).

Chapter 10

1 Note that a few other leagues around the world, such as the Australian Football League (AFL), tolerate fighting without expulsion from the game.

Chapter 12

1 "Tommy Douglas Crowned 'Greatest Canadian,'" *CBC News*, November 29, 2004, https://www.cbc.ca/news/entertainment/tommy-douglas-crowned-greatest-canadian-1.510403.
2 B. Garrioch, "Top 5 Unforgettable Ottawa Senators to Leave," *Ottawa Sun*, July 5, 2014, https://ottawasun.com/2014/07/05/top-5-unforgettable-ottawa-senators-players-to-leave/wcm/83a99595-73a8-4e84-b6ac-9bef90b2a712.
3 J. Nadeau and N. O'Reilly, "Developing a Profitability Model for Professional Sport Leagues: The Case of the National Hockey League," *International Journal of Sport Finance* 1, no. 1 (2006): 46–52.
4 The Canadian Press, "'You People': Don Cherry under Fire for Claiming New Immigrants Don't Wear Remembrance Day Poppies," *National Post*, November 11, 2019, https://nationalpost.com/news/canada/online-backlash-against-don-cherry-for-comments-on-immigrants-and-remembrance-day.
5 R. Flanagan and J. Forani, "'I Don't Regret a Thing': Don Cherry Speaks Out on His Firing and Ron MacLean," *CTV News*, November 11, 2019, https://www.ctvnews.ca/sports/i-don-t-regret-a-thing-don-cherry-speaks-out-on-his-firing-and-ron-maclean-1.4680203.
6 B. Lilley, "Lilley: Dumping Don Cherry Hurting HNIC Ratings," *Toronto Sun*, December 25, 2019, https://torontosun.com/opinion/columnists/lilley-dumping-don-cherry-hurting-hnic-ratings.
7 D. Kahneman and S. Frederick, "Representativeness Revisited: Attribute Substitution in Intuitive Judgment," in *Heuristic and Biases: The Psychology of Intuitive Judgment*, ed. T. Gilovich, D. Griffin, and D. Kahneman (New York: Cambridge University Press, 2002), 49–81.
8 R. Solnit, *A Field Guide to Getting Lost* (New York: Penguin, 2006), 34.

Chapter 13

1 "18 Years Later, Manon Rhéaume Remembered for What She Was – an Inspiration!" Big Mouth Sports, September 23, 2010, http://bigmouthsports.com/2010/09/23/18-years-later-manon-rheaume-remembered-for-what-she-was-an-inspiration/.
2 S. Cannella, ed., *Greatest Athletes by Number* (New York: Sports Illustrated Books, 2014).
3 S. Hackel, "Wayne Gretzkey Talks Greatest NHL Teams," *NHL.com*, June 6, 2017, https://www.nhl.com/news/nhl-greatest-teams-qa-with-wayne-gretzky/c-289795490.
4 S. Whyno, "NHL Post-Quarantine: Recapturing Team Chemistry a Challenge," The Spokesman, June 2, 2020, https://www.spokesman.com/stories/2020/jun/02/nhl-post-quarantine-recapturing-team-chemistry-a-c/.
5 J. Ryan, *Intangibles: Unlocking the Science and Soul of Team Chemistry* (New York: Little Brown & Company, 2020), 11.

Chapter 15

1 M. Brehm, "NHL's Dumba Pledges to Fight Racism," *USA Today*, August 3, 2020, 6C.
2 C. Bumbaca, "Duo: NHL Playing Is 'Disheartening,'" *USA Today*, August 28, 2020, 5C.

3 S.R. Covey, *The 7 Habits of Highly Effective People: Restoring the Character Ethic* (New York: Simon and Schuster, 1989), 48.
4 "Eighth Annual Willie O'Ree Weekend Hosted by Wild," *NHL Enterprises*, Fall 2002.
5 "NHL's First Black Hockey Player Visits Newark School," *NJ Spotlight News*, February 1, 2018, https://www.njspotlightnews.org/2018/02/nhls-first-black-hockey-player-visits-newark-school.
6 C.J. Phillips, "Don't Congratulate the San Jose Sharks and the NHL for Being Last to Hire a Black General Manager," *Deadspin*, July 5, 2022, https://deadspin.com/don-t-congratulate-the-san-jose-sharks-and-the-nhl-for-1849142733.

Chapter 16

1 J. Stillman, "Got a Hard Decision to Make? Borrow Obama's Simple 3-Part Strategy for the Toughest Calls," *Inc.com*, accessed March 13, 2022, https://www.inc.com/jessica-stillman/president-obama-just-shared-his-simple-3-part-framework-for-making-even-toughest-decisions.html.
2 K. Baxter, "Five Nashville Players Test Positive for Coronavirus, Forcing MLS to Postpone Match," *Los Angeles Times*, July 7, 2020, https://www.latimes.com/sports/soccer/story/2020-07-07/nashville-players-test-positive-coronavirus-mls-tournament-game-postponed.
3 D. Feschuk, "How Did Toronto and Edmonton Beat Out Las Vegas as NHL Hub Cities? It's All about the Odds," *The Star*, July 1, 2020, https://www.thestar.com/sports/hockey/opinion/2020/07/01/how-did-toronto-and-edmonton-beat-out-las-vegas-as-nhl-hub-cities-its-all-about-the-odds.html.
4 "NHLPA, NHL Ratify Four-Year CBA Extension and Return to Play Plan," *NHLPA.com*, July 10, 2020, https://www.nhlpa.com/news/1-21889/nhlpa-nhl-ratify-four-year-cba-extension-and-return-to-play-plan.

Overtime

1 A. Nelson, "SportBusiness Postgraduate Course Rankings 2018," *SportBusiness*, June 8, 2018, https://www.sportbusiness.com/2018/06/sportbusiness-postgraduate-course-rankings-2018/.

Further Reading

J. Blake, *Canadian Hockey Literature* (Toronto: University of Toronto Press, 2010).
Sports Illustrated, *Sports Illustrated Hockey's Greatest* (Sports Illustrated, 2015).

Index

Author Biographies

NORM O'REILLY, MBA, PhD, CPA, is dean and professor of sport business at the Graduate School of Business at the University of Maine. He has authored or co-authored 16 books and more than 150 management journal articles. He has been involved extensively with the sport and hockey industries as a consultant, expert witness, volunteer, and player.

He was awarded the Career Achievement Award by the American Marketing Association's Sport Marketing Special Interest Group (2015) and is a Fellow of the North American Society for Sport Management. Dr. O'Reilly was assistant chef de mission for the Canadian team at the 2016 Paralympic Games in Rio, Brazil, and has been to five Olympic and Paralympic Games with Team Canada. He was inducted into the Lindsay Sports Hall of Fame in 2015.

RICK BURTON is the David B. Falk Professor of Sport Management at Syracuse University and served as the school's faculty athletic representative to the National Collegiate Athletic Association and the Atlantic Coast Conference from 2014–22. He is the former national advertising manager for Miller Lite, chief marketing officer of the US Olympic Committee (for the Beijing 2008 Summer Olympics) and commissioner of Australia's National Basketball League (2003–7). He currently serves as the chief operating officer, North America, for Playbk Sports and serves as an advisor to Point3 and XV Capital.

Burton has also been a regular contributor to Sportico.com and *Sports Business Journal* (with O'Reilly) and co-authored numerous books including *Sports Business Unplugged, 20 Secrets to Success for NCAA Student Athletes*, and a colorful 150-year history of Syracuse University entitled *Forever Orange*. He has three married children, two granddaughters, and lives with his wife of 41 years in the Finger Lakes region of Upstate New York.